THE SEA DEVILS

THE SEA DEVILS

OPERATION STRUGGLE
AND THE LAST GREAT RAID
OF WORLD WAR TWO

MARK FELTON

ICON

First published in the UK in 2015 by
Icon Books Ltd, Omnibus Business Centre,
39–41 North Road, London N7 9DP
info@iconbooks.com
www.iconbooks.com

This edition published in the UK in 2016 by Icon Books Ltd

Sold in the UK, Europe and Asia
by Faber & Faber Ltd, Bloomsbury House,
74–77 Great Russell Street,
London WC1B 3DA or their agents

Distributed in the UK, Europe and Asia
by Grantham Book Services,
Trent Road, Grantham NG31 7XQ

Distributed in Australia and New Zealand
by Allen & Unwin Pty Ltd,
PO Box 8500, 83 Alexander Street,
Crows Nest, NSW 2065

Distributed in South Africa by
Jonathan Ball, Office B4, The District,
41 Sir Lowry Road, Woodstock 7925

Distributed in India by Penguin Books India,
7th Floor, Infinity Tower – C, DLF Cyber City,
Gurgaon 122002, Haryana

ISBN: 978-178578-049-3

Typeset in Adobe Text by Marie Doherty
Printed and bound in the UK by Clays Ltd, St Ives plc

To Fang Fang,
with love

About the author

Mark Felton has written over a dozen books on World War Two, including most recently *Zero Night*, an account of a mass POW escape, described as 'a thundering good read' by *History of War* magazine. His *Japan's Gestapo* was named 'Best Book of 2009' by the *Japan Times*. He also writes regularly for publications including *Military History Monthly* and *World War II*. After a decade spent working in Shanghai, he now lives in Norwich.

His next book is *Castle of the Eagles: Escape from Mussolini's Colditz* (published November 2016).

Contents

Acknowledgements

I should like to extend my thanks to the following people, institutions and organisations for their superb and generous help during the researching of this book.

My very great thanks to former Sub-Lieutenant Adam Bergius, DSC, who, in 1945, was one of HMS *XE-4*'s brave and daring divers during Operation Sabre off Saigon. He very generously and patiently answered all of my questions.

Many thanks to William Fell, CMG, grandson of Captain W.R. 'Tiny' Fell, CMG, CBE, DSC, RN, Commanding Officer of 14th Submarine Flotilla, for his fascinating insights into his grandfather's life and access to family documents and photographs.

Thanks are due to Jane Gilbert and her family for sharing documents and photographs relating to her father, Vernon 'Ginger' Coles, DSM, who sadly passed away during the writing of this book.

A great many thanks to Donald Fullarton, Helensburgh Heritage Trust; Ron Rietveld, The Submariners Association, West of Scotland Branch; Emily Morris, Churchill Archives Centre, Churchill College, Cambridge; David Barnes, Old Worcester, New Zealand; Paul Johnson, The National Archives (Public Record Office), Kew; Shehara Begum, Imperial War Museum, London; Ellis Barker, *Newbury Weekly News*; Shirley Felton for assistance with research material; The National Maritime Museum, London; Chatham Historic Dockyard; Alison Firth and Stephen Courtney of The National Museum of the Royal Navy; and the kind contributors to the World Naval Ships Forum.

Many thanks to my splendid agent Andrew Lownie, whose encouragement and advice are always very much appreciated.

The team at Icon Books have been fabulous, and my thanks to my editors Duncan Heath and Robert Sharman.

Once again my accomplished wife Fang Fang proved to be a willing sounding board and unpaid research assistant, and most importantly lent me her critical eye during the gestation of this book. Her love, wise suggestions and generous support continue to be invaluable to me and I can't thank her enough.

A note on the text

Most of the dialogue sequences in this book come from the veterans themselves, from written sources, diaries or spoken interviews. I have at times changed the tense to make it more immediate. Occasionally, where only basic descriptions of what happened exist, I have created small sections of dialogue, attempting to remain true to the characters and their manners of speech.

List of abbreviations used in the text

CBE	Commander of the Order of the British Empire
CO	Commanding Officer
DSEA	Davis Submarine Escape Apparatus
DSC	Distinguished Service Cross
DSO	Distinguished Service Order
ERA	Engine Room Artificer
HMNZS	His Majesty's New Zealand Ship
HMS	His Majesty's Ship
HT	Handie-Talkie, Motorola SCR-536
IJN	Imperial Japanese Navy
LST	Landing Ship Tank
MBE	Member of the Order of the British Empire
PO	Petty Officer
RAF	Royal Air Force
RNR	Royal Naval Reserve
RNVR	Royal Naval Volunteer Reserve
SEAC	South East Asia Command
USAAF	United States Army Air Force
USS	United States Ship
VC	Victoria Cross
W&D	Wet and Dry Compartment
XO	Executive Officer, second-in-command of a vessel

List of Illustrations

The crew of the original X-craft submarine *X-24*: Sub-Lieutenant Joe Brooks, Lieutenant Max Shean, Engine Room Artificer 4th Class Vernon 'Ginger' Coles and Sub-Lieutenant Frank Ogden.

Some of the officers and men of 14th Submarine Flotilla photographed aboard the depot ship HMS *Bonaventure* in Scotland, late 1944.

HMS *XE-1* surfaced during training in Scotland.

An XE-craft approaches the practice anti-submarine boom in north-west Scotland.

Lieutenant Max Shean, the Australian commanding officer of HMS *XE-4*.

Captain William Fell, commanding officer of 14th Submarine Flotilla, with his second-in-command, Lieutenant-Commander Derek Brown, HMS *Bonaventure*, 1945.

Acting Leading Seaman James 'Mick' Magennis with his commanding officer Lieutenant Ian 'Tich' Fraser. *(Photo: Imperial War Museum)*

The crew of HMS *XE-5* photographed in Scotland before departure for the Far East: Sub-Lieutenant Beadon Dening, Lieutenant Herbert 'Pat' Westmacott, Sub-Lieutenant Dennis Jarvis and Engine Room Artificer 4th Class Clifford Greenwood. *(Photo: Imperial War Museum)*

HMS *Bonaventure* passing beneath Sydney Harbour Bridge in Australia.

The Davis Submarine Escape Apparatus (DSEA), an early rebreather modified for use by commando divers.

The commanding officers of the four XE-craft submarines used in Operations Struggle, Foil and Sabre: Lieutenant Jack Smart, Lieutenant Tich Fraser, Lieutenant Pat Westmacott, and Lieutenant Max Shean. *(Photo: Imperial War Museum)*

Rear-Admiral James Fife, commander of submarines, US 7th Fleet, with Captain Fell on the bridge of HMS *Bonaventure*, Brunei Bay, July 1945.

The attack and passage crews of *XE-1* and *XE-3* being addressed by Rear-Admiral Fife on the quarterdeck of HMS *Bonaventure* shortly before departing Brunei Bay for Singapore, 26 July 1945.

Rear-Admiral Fife and Captain Fell bidding a final farewell to the attack and passage crew of one of the XE-craft involved in Operation Struggle.

Tich Fraser's *XE-3* departs for Singapore under tow from HMS *Stygian*, 26 July 1945.

XE-craft interior showing the steering position in the foreground.

XE-craft interior: planesman's position.

The Japanese heavy cruiser *Myoko. (Photo: Japanese Navy via Wikimedia Commons)*

Captain Fell and Lieutenant-Commander Brown on HMS *Bonaventure*.

VJ Day party aboard HMS *Bonaventure*, Brunei Bay, 2 September 1945.

The VJ Day party one hour later.

Jimmy Fife salutes the quarterdeck as he departs HMS *Bonaventure* for the final time in early August 1945.

An XE-craft surfaced in Brunei Bay shortly after the end of the war.

Captain William Fell, commander of 14th Submarine Flotilla, and Captain William Banks, commander of 12th Submarine Flotilla, photographed at Buckingham Palace just after the war.

Prologue

'You are all sentenced to death by beheading,'[1] stated Colonel Masayoshi Towatari, the president of the court. His face betrayed no emotion, his dark eyes flicking across the faces of the ten 'defendants' who stood before him. There was a sharp intake of breath among the British and Australian servicemen, who looked lean and hollow-cheeked from months of brutal imprisonment.

'But, sir, we are prisoners of war,' exclaimed Major Reginald Ingleton, the 25-year-old senior surviving officer of Operation Rimau. Ingleton's face was badly bruised on one side from the beatings that he had suffered, his uniform dirty and torn, but he still had the air of a leader about him and the others looked to him in this, their moment of greatest despair. Ingleton, a Royal Marine, stood ramrod straight, his eyes burning with intense anger and his voice cracking as he spoke. 'We were captured in British uniform attacking legitimate military targets. We have rights under the Geneva ...' Before Ingleton could finish his sentence a small and wiry Japanese major, his white armband emblazoned with red characters indicating membership of the dreaded *Kempeitai* military police, jumped up from his chair near the prisoners, the hilt of his sheathed samurai sword banging loudly on the table in front of him. Red faced, he bellowed out a long stream of guttural Japanese at them. Although Ingleton and his men understood little, the tone was unmistakable.

Colonel Towatari muttered something in Japanese to the major, who abruptly stopped shouting, bowed stiffly and then resumed his seat, a malevolent look on his face. Turning to Ingleton, Towatari continued in heavily accented English, 'The verdict of the court has been reached.' With that Towatari issued orders to clear the court and the prisoners were unceremoniously bundled out of the room by *Kempeitai* guards and marched back to their cell. It was 3 July 1945. During the course of their 'trial' the defendants had received no legal representation, nor had they been given the opportunity to defend themselves. Their guilt had already been decided long before their appearance before Towatari.[2]

The crime that Major Ingleton and his nine fellow defendants had committed was to have been part of one of the most daring raids on Singapore yet mounted by the Allied forces. The previous October, Lieutenant-Colonel Ivan Lyon and 23 British and Australians, drawn from the top-secret Force Z based in Australia, had infiltrated the seaway around Singapore intending to penetrate the harbour using a group of ingenious one-man submarines called 'Sleeping Beauties' and mine as many ships as they could find. Rimau appeared set to emulate the earlier success of Operation Jaywick in September 1943, when 29-year-old Lyon had led thirteen army commandos and sailors in folboats, a kind of collapsible kayak, and blown up seven Japanese merchant ships with limpet mines inside Singapore Harbour for no loss to the raiding party.[3]

But the Rimau mission had been blown among the jungle-covered islands south of Singapore. Due to bureaucratic fumbling and incompetence, the Royal Navy submarine detailed to pick up Lyon's men did not arrive, making their escape unlikely. Abandoned to his fate, Lyon had refused to give up and with a small party of men had gone north in black kayaks and, like the Cockleshell Heroes, paddled into Singapore Harbour and managed to mine three ships. He and his men had then fought a terrible running battle through a string of tiny islands as they tried to escape south to Australia. Thirteen had been killed in action, including Lyon, or had committed suicide to avoid capture, while Major Ingleton and nine others were eventually rounded up.

The Japanese had horribly tortured Ingleton and his men. They all knew that only one fate awaited them – death. They were placed on trial for 'perfidy and espionage'[4] but the fact that the Japanese had resorted to a show trial was, in their opinion, just one more indignity at the hands of a dishonourable foe before they finally met their maker.

That day came on Saturday 7 July 1945 on a scrappy piece of waste ground on the Bukit Timah Road in Singapore. Ingleton and his men had been driven to the execution ground in a Japanese army truck; during the journey they had said little to each other. Each man was resigned to his own thoughts. A group of senior Japanese army officers stood off to one side watching the proceedings with grim expressions. The judge Colonel Towatari stood chatting with Major General Otsuka, the local *Kempeitai* commander as well as the commandant of Outram Road Jail, where Ingleton and his men had been held and abused.[5] *Kempeitai* officer Major Hisada commanded the execution. Ingleton and his men had had their hands tied painfully behind their backs and ragged blindfolds wrapped around their heads. Hisada hissed an order and the first prisoner was dragged forward by a group of five Japanese sergeants who would take it in turn executing the Allied servicemen. Three rough burial pits had been dug, and each man was forced to kneel on the edge of one, his head forced down to expose his grimy neck.[6] A Japanese sergeant unsheathed his katana sword, took careful aim and with a cry brought the razor-sharp blade down in a terminal arc. The head fell into the pit while dark arterial blood pumped from the prisoner's still-quivering corpse. Laughing and clapping, the other Japanese quickly kicked the body into the pit and then snatched up another victim.[7] Hardly expert swordsmen, the Japanese soldiers slashed at their victims, often taking two or three strikes to remove the heads.[8] Each British or Australian prisoner could only sit in darkness, listening to his comrades being horribly butchered, and wait for his own terrible moment to come. Some prayed aloud, others stoically said their goodbyes to their mates or to their wives, sweethearts or children back home.

Such was the price for failing on a mission against the Japanese.

*

Unbeknown to Ingleton and his doomed men, a thousand miles away in Australia a new plan was taking shape to attack Singapore. A band of highly experienced submariners, among them some of the men who had audaciously crippled the giant German battleship *Tirpitz* in Norway in 1943, were preparing to mount the most audacious raid yet against Japan's most important Asian conquest. The men involved knew that the stakes were very high. If they succeeded, the way would be open for a British liberation of Singapore. If they failed they could expect to join the Rimau commandos in ragged graves in the colony's lush tropical soil. Eighteen men, all under 30 years old, prepared for missions aboard vessels that the Americans had derisively christened 'suicide craft'. If the Japanese thought that by murdering Ingleton and his men they would frighten the British off from mounting any further raids on Singapore they were sorely mistaken. The Japanese were about to come face-to-face with some of the bravest and most determined special operations personnel the British possessed, men for whom the word 'danger' was a matter of mundane routine.

The Japanese were about to face the 'Sea Devils'.

CHAPTER ONE

The Expendables

'Keep your mouth shut, your bowels
open, and never volunteer.'

—Old Navy maxim

'Thirty feet, sir,' called out Acting Leading Seaman James 'Mick' Magennis, watching the depth gauge like a hawk watches a mouse. Lieutenant Ian 'Tich' Fraser, the 5ft 4in commander of midget submarine HMS *XE-3*, did not move from the attack periscope, his eyes glued to the huge target that filled its tiny lens. His submarine was slowly creeping west down the shallow Johor Strait, the long, thin channel that separates Singapore Island from the Malayan mainland. Before him, off the old British naval base, was moored the 15,500-ton Japanese heavy cruiser IJN *Takao*, her fearsome 8-inch gun turrets pointing north up the Malay Peninsula towards where an Allied invasion was expected any day.

The *Takao*'s superstructure was heavily camouflaged in a crazy green and brown disruptive paint pattern that made her blend in well with the thick jungle ashore. To Fraser, the ship appeared immense, her great pagoda-like superstructure bristling with anti-aircraft guns, fierce tropical sunshine glinting off her bridge windows and upper works. Her five turrets with their ten 8-inch guns looked both menacing and potent. She was moored with her stern facing Singapore Island so that her 630ft-long hull stuck out into the mile-wide Strait like an armoured finger, an immense static gun battery that dominated all approaches for fifteen miles in every direction. Fraser knew that just over a mile downstream the equally huge heavy cruiser IJN *Myoko* occupied a similar position, the two ships very sharp thorns in the side of Britain's invasion plan.

The atmosphere inside the black-painted British submarine was electrifying. Its four crewmen sweated profusely in the clammy heat, the air as fetid as a tomb. Each man sat at his assigned station, his face a rictus of tight concentration. The main hatch had been shut many hours before as the submarine had crept into the Strait from the open sea to the east of Singapore.

In comparison to its huge target, the *XE-3* was a minnow approaching a whale. But it was a minnow that packed a potentially devastating punch. On one side of the 53ft-long boat was a two-ton Amatol high explosive Mark XX saddle charge, on the other a special rack loaded with six 200lb magnetic limpet mines that would be placed into position by Magennis, the submarine's main diver.[1]

Fraser, dark haired, short and at only 24 years old already a veteran wartime submariner with a Distinguished Service Cross to his name, smiled slightly as he watched the distance to his target drop. 'All right, Magennis, the range is 200 yards,' he said, 'we should touch bottom in a moment.'

Magennis, a dark-haired and slightly built 25-year-old Ulsterman from the tough Falls Road area of Belfast, nodded and smiled grimly.

So far, Operation Struggle had gone mostly according to plan, though the *XE-3* was running behind schedule by a couple of hours. The submarine had motored for almost 40 miles behind Japanese lines without being detected, passing through a minefield and several sets of underwater listening posts. Now she was only a stone's throw away from her target. But the most difficult part of the mission had arrived. Fraser had to manoeuvre his submarine directly underneath the keel of the great behemoth before he dropped his main charge, otherwise the damage he would inflict would not be sufficient to sink the steel monster.[2]

'Keep her as slow as you can,' he said to Engine Room Artificer Third Class Charlie Reed who was at the helm steering and controlling the engine. 'Aye aye, sir,' he replied.

Sub-Lieutenant William 'Kiwi' Smith, the sub's second-in-command, worked the hydroplanes to control the submarine's depth and direction. Ordinarily he was a cheerful New Zealander but his face was now a mask of deep concentration as he stared fixedly at the dials and gauges in front of his seat.

The run in was almost silent, with only the gentle hum of the propeller and the electric motor that was driving it breaking the quiet. Suddenly there was a bang as the *XE-3*'s bow struck the bottom of the channel, the crew lurching forward and grabbing pipework and fittings to steady themselves, followed by loud scraping noises as the submarine's keel bumped through the mud and debris. Smith had a difficult time keeping the little submarine on course as she crashed, dragged and scraped along just thirteen feet below the surface of the crystal-clear Johor Strait.

Fraser, using the night periscope that was designed for underwater work, could see the water's surface from below moving like a wrinkled and winking pane of glass, growing gradually darker as the submarine came into the *Takao*'s great shadow. Suddenly, something scraped noisily down the *XE-3*'s starboard side, a sound alarmingly like giant fingernails being drawn down a huge blackboard, followed seconds afterwards by a violent crash as the submarine struck the *Takao*'s hull with a reverberating thud.

'Stop the motor!' yelled Fraser, wincing at the noise. Reed immediately shut off the engine. Inside the *XE-3* the collision had sounded loud enough to wake the dead. But the *Takao*'s main belt of armour around her waist, designed to absorb the impact of torpedoes, was up to five inches thick. The collision had probably gone unnoticed aboard the warship.

'I wonder where the hell we are,'[3] muttered Fraser, almost to himself. The submarine's position didn't feel right. He could see nothing through the underwater periscope. It felt as though the boat was too far towards the *Takao*'s bow and Fraser suspected that the heavy scraping noise that they had heard had come from one of the cruiser's thick anchor cables. Fraser decided to back away and line up for another run-in.

'Port 30,' he ordered, 'half ahead group down.' The electric motor whirred and the propeller turned faster, the submarine beginning to vibrate as the revolutions increased. But the *XE-3* did not move. 'Half ahead group down!' repeated Fraser, his face sheened with sweat. He began issuing a stream of orders as he vainly tried to move the submarine from under the *Takao*. But the *XE-3* stubbornly refused to budge. Fraser, panic starting to rise almost uncontrollably inside of him, realised that his submarine was trapped. Four men inside a tiny XE-craft, made of only quarter-inch-thick steel and loaded down with enough explosives to sink a battleship, were trapped beneath 15,500 tons of enemy warship deep inside Japan's most prized harbour. Because the submarine had arrived later than planned, with each passing minute the tide was ebbing away and the *Takao* was settling lower and lower into the channel, its vast keel pushing down upon the *XE-3*.

Fraser, hardly pausing for breath, continued to give orders to the helm and engine. 'Group down, half ahead,' he called for what seemed like the thousandth time. But his orders were met only by the sound of the propeller spinning impotently and the whine of the motor as it sucked more juice from its two big batteries.

'Christ, she's not budging, Tich,' exclaimed Kiwi Smith, his voice betraying his fear.

'Full astern!' said Fraser. The air inside the submarine was almost unbearable, and the pressure of the situation made that air feel even thicker and more noxious than a few minutes before. Still the *XE-3* refused to move. Fraser's eyes darted about the submarine's narrow interior blankly as his mind raced through options and drills. As he listened to the propeller, his wife Melba's face suddenly came to him, his pregnant wife back home in England. *How in the hell did I get myself into this?* he thought angrily. He slapped his hand hard against the periscope shaft and ordered again, 'Half ahead group down', already feeling horribly like a drowning man as he spoke.

*

About a year and a half before, early in 1944, Tich Fraser had been drinking tea in the wardroom of the submarine HMS *H.44* with his best friend, David Carey. The boat, an old H-Class built in 1919, the year before Fraser was born, was docked in Londonderry after yet another sonar sweeping exercise and both men were bored.[4] The boat was quiet, the crew going about routine matters or ashore. Rainy and grey Northern Ireland was a long way from the shooting war in the Mediterranean, where both men had served with distinction aboard more modern fighting submarines.

Fraser's father had been a marine engineer, so it had come as little surprise to his family that he himself had chosen to go to sea shortly after leaving High Wycombe's Royal Grammar School. He joined HMS *Conway*, a 19th-century battleship that had been converted into a training vessel, before serving in the Merchant Navy for two years, which included visiting Australia. In 1939 Fraser had been commissioned into the 'Wavy Navy', the Royal Naval Reserve, so named because the officer's rank rings on their cuffs were styled in a wave pattern.

Fraser had ended up kicking his heels aboard the *H.44* all because of an errant ashtray. He had been a junior officer aboard the S-Class submarine HMS *Sahib* in the Mediterranean. During a spectacularly successful patrol the *Sahib* had sunk seven Italian ships and a German U-boat. Fraser was one of several officers awarded the DSC. During a raucous celebratory party in the wardroom of the flotilla depot ship at Algiers the drunken officers had attempted to recreate Twickenham and Lord's with any objects that were not nailed down. Someone had picked up a large, heavy brass ashtray, called out 'Catch, Tich' and slung it at Fraser. He ended up with a broken big toe, a long stay in hospital and a transfer to the UK after the *Sahib* sailed without him.[5]

The two positive things to emerge from Fraser's transfer were the opportunity to marry his sweetheart, Melba, who was serving in the Wrens, and his promotion to first lieutenant aboard the *H.44*.

A young rating entered the wardroom with the signals log tucked under his arm. 'Thanks, Davis,' said Fraser as the rating placed the log on the scuffed wooden table between the two officers and withdrew quietly. Fraser leaned forward and cast his bored eye over the pad, expecting to see the usual mundane orders and requests neatly typed out for his review. But today a single word, printed in bold capitals, jumped off the page. That word was 'SECRET' and Fraser saw that the signal was from the Flag Officer Submarines to all of His Majesty's underwater boats. Fraser read on.

> Two Lieutenants and two Sub-Lieutenants R.N. or R.N.R. are requested for Special and Hazardous Service in submarines stop Names of Volunteers should be signalled to Flag Officer Submarines immediately.[6]

Fraser said nothing but slid the pad across the table to Carey, a slightly mischievous smile on his lips. While Carey read, Fraser thought to himself, *Well, it's made to measure. Here am I, a Lieutenant R.N.R. There's David, a Sub-Lieutenant R.N. That's two for the price of one for the F.O.S.*[7]

Fraser watched as Carey read the signal through again. He looked up slowly, his inquisitive blue eyes meeting Fraser's. 'Shall we?' Carey whispered conspiratorially. Fraser replied, a large grin forming across his impish face, 'Why not?'

*

Fraser and Carey joined other volunteers who had responded from across the fleet. The navy had also recruited several dozen midshipmen, petty officers and ratings for the secret programme. They were joining probably the most secret section of the British armed forces, yet they had very little idea of what they were actually getting themselves into.

'Special and Hazardous Service' began with a train ride down to Portsmouth, the home of the Royal Navy. A short ferry ride took Fraser, Carey and the others across the harbour to Gosport and HMS *Dolphin*. The *Dolphin* wasn't a ship but a 'stone frigate', a commissioned shore establishment.

The navy began by trying to weed out those who were completely unsuited for the kind of work that they would be undertaking.

'What are your hobbies?' asked a pleasant naval psychiatrist after the medical tests were completed. Carey thought it a reasonable question, though the next one was a bit odd. 'What time do you get up at home on Sunday?' At each response, the psychiatrist made careful notes. 'Do you like cats?'[8] was the next question, and Carey stifled bewildered laughter.

In the subsequent interview the commanding officer was evasive, to say the least. 'The "Special Service" is most terribly secret,' he said to Fraser. 'I cannot tell you what manner of vessel you will serve in except that it is quite small, and navigates with the use of a periscope.'[9] When Fraser and Carey met up later in the day to compare notes, Fraser joked about the CO's description. 'He might as well have drawn me a picture of it.'

After a few of the candidates had been rejected on medical grounds or for failing their psychological profiling, the survivors were asked back to *Dolphin* to begin their training. It was at this point that the trainees had the first inkling of what they had let themselves in for.

The commanding officer gathered them all together in a small room with all the windows shut and the door firmly locked. 'What

I am about to tell you is absolutely top secret,' he said. 'You are not to tell anybody – don't tell your wife, your girlfriend, don't tell your mother, sisters, anybody. Nobody at all.' Fraser and Carey looked at each other, more intrigued than ever. An expectant air seemed to raise the room temperature as the young officers and ratings listened to the briefing, keyed up, excited and a little apprehensive.

'You have been recruited to man a 30-ton submarine which has been designed to enter enemy harbours and attack enemy ships,' said the CO. 'The submarines are fitted with equipment to enhance their chances of entering and leaving enemy harbours undetected and providing you aren't detected you have a good chance of a successful attack and retreat.'[10] The CO talked for a while longer before abruptly changing the subject.

'However, before we begin to train you in submarine handling, you must achieve a level of proficiency underwater using the Davis Submarine Escape Apparatus. You have ten days, gentlemen, to master submarine escapes. Those of you who pass this section of the course will progress to submarine training. Good luck.'[11]

*

For men like Fraser and Carey who transferred from the regular submarine branch, this part of the course was simply a refresher. For men from the surface fleet, it represented much more of a challenge.

Day one began in *Dolphin*'s large heated water tank, a sort of swimming pool that measured 40 feet wide and 30 feet deep.[12] The trainees, in swimming trunks, gathered around the edge in front of the training staff.

'Right, gentlemen, this 'ere is the Davis Submarine Escape Apparatus or "DSEA",' announced Warrant Officer Chadwick, the chief instructor. He held the rig up so that the class of trainees could all see it. Invented by Sir Robert Davis of the diving equipment firm Siebe Gorman,[13] it had dramatically increased the chances of surviving a submarine sinking. 'Now, pay attention, as your life may depend on it one day,' said Chadwick. 'This is the breathing bag,' he continued, pointing at a square canvas and rubber bag. 'It's worn on the chest.' Another instructor demonstrated by placing the set over his head and securing the waist straps. 'Inside the bag is a Protosorb canister that scrubs your exhaled breath,' explained Chadwick. He then pointed to a pocket on the end of the breathing bag. 'This holds a steel oxygen cylinder. There is a control valve connecting it to the breathing bag here,' he said, pointing. 'When you open the cylinder's valve it lets oxygen into the bag and charges it to the pressure of the surrounding water. Everyone keeping up so far?'

The group, eagerly concentrating, muttered agreement in unison and Chadwick continued.

'Now, the canister that I mentioned inside the breathing bag, that's connected to a mouthpiece by this 'ere flexible corrugated tube,' he said, pointing to a long brown pipe that looked like something pulled off an army gas respirator. 'Not surprisingly, you stick this bit in your mouth. Right ho, Jim,' said Chadwick, and his partner popped the mouthpiece in. 'You can only breathe through your mouth, so you wear this on your nose,' said Chadwick, holding up a flexible rubber nose clip. 'Lastly, you 'ave yer goggles,' and his partner slid on a pair of rubber and glass goggles.

'Right, Bob's yer uncle, now you're ready to dive,' Chadwick said, grinning. 'Now, before we try the set out, one more thing. The breathing bag is also fitted with a non-return release valve,' he said, pointing to the toggle. 'This allows air to escape from the bag as you ascend towards the surface and the water pressure decreases. Once you are at the surface, you can close this valve and the air in the bag will then act like a lifejacket. If it deflates, you refill it by opening the non-return valve and blowing into the mouthpiece.' Chadwick paused and smiled. 'Right, gentlemen, I hope I haven't blinded you all with science this morning. By the end of today you are all going to be very, very familiar with these sets.' A few of the trainees choked back nervous snorts of laughter.

'Now for the bit you've all been waiting for. PO Stevens has a DSEA for each of you. Once you've got your sets on we'll try them out in the tank.'

The DSEA was basically a primitive rebreather and was readily adaptable for use by frogmen operating from submarines because the set did not emit any telltale bubbles like a regular aqualung.[14] This meant that enemy sailors looking over the sides of their ships should not see anything untoward on the surface of the water. The downside was that after a certain amount of time the Protosorb filter would be used up and the air would turn poisonous. The amount of time spent in the water was therefore critical.[15] Breathing pure oxygen over an extended period of time resulted in narcosis. The divers created a mythical monster named 'Oxygen Pete' that lurked in the depths ready to snare the unwary. Only death awaited those who fell into his clutches.[16]

The trainees pulled on the bulky equipment, set their nose clips and settled their goggles over their eyes. Chadwick told them to put their faces into the water while continuing to breathe normally. Several panicked or held their breath. Overcoming this natural urge was hard for many in the class. 'As you go under, you breathe out one long breath,' said Chadwick. A few more attempts and they soon realised that they wouldn't drown.

After several days of getting familiar with the DSEA in the tank the make-or-break test was a simulated escape from a flooded submarine. A steel chamber had been set into the bottom of the tank about 25 feet below the surface, accessible through a separate steel door. One instructor and three trainees would be sealed into the chamber with hardly any space to move.

Lieutenant Max Shean, a 26-year-old softly spoken Australian from Perth, had been one of the original recruits to the secret programme back in 1942. Shean had learned all about the sea from his father, and together they had built and sailed boats. Mechanically minded, Shean had been halfway through an engineering degree at the University of Western Australia when war broke out. While ashore on leave from the corvette HMS *Bluebell* in mid-1942 Shean had seen an Admiralty Fleet Order calling for volunteer officers and ratings for 'Special and Hazardous Service'. The ad had also rather ominously stated that the volunteers should be good swimmers, under 25 years of age and unmarried.[17]

Shean had signed up before he realised what he had let himself in for. The *Dolphin* course was a shock. Shean never forgot the reaction of several of the trainees when confronted by the submarine escape test.[18] The ones who'd had the most to say during DSEA training were the first to crack up once inside the chamber. 'That was when the noisy peckers went quiet, except for one who screamed, "Let me out. Let me out. Let ..." This the instructor did, and that was the last we saw of that volunteer.'[19] In Shean's class of twelve, three washed out at this point.

'Right, sets on,' said the instructor to Fraser's new group almost two years later, as the steel door was banged shut with grim finality. Fraser had done this test before when he had first joined the submarine service, but everyone hated it. It was so unnatural and so claustrophobic. The three trainees squeezed inside the chamber inserted their mouthpieces, opened their oxygen tank valves, put on their nose clips and then pulled down their goggles. 'Right, I'm equalising now,' said the instructor, before he also put in his mouthpiece. Inside the dim metal chamber the feeling was oppressive. The instructor opened a valve and water started to rush into the small space, incredibly loud and violent. The pressure in their ears soon started to become painful. The trainees looked at each other, their round eyes behind their goggles clearly alarmed. The first-timers looked terrified. Soon the water was up to their waists, then their chins. The recruits fought down the urge to panic as the rushing water rose inexorably, bringing with it the primeval terror of drowning. They breathed rapidly, then suddenly their heads were fully submerged, four men entombed inside a metal coffin. The instructor, now that the pressure was equalised, stretched up and opened the hatch in the roof of the tank, the metallic bumps as the door swung open muted and dull beneath the water.

The chamber at *Dolphin* replicated the one-man Wet and Dry (W&D) compartment found aboard an X- and XE-craft submarine. In the W&D, the diver would flood the chamber while the submarine was submerged, open the hatch in the roof and swim out to complete net cutting or limpet mining. By the same method the diver could re-enter the submerged submarine, all without upsetting the submarine's delicate buoyancy or trim.[20] It was an important underwater innovation and unique to the Royal Navy.

Once out of the chamber in the tank at *Dolphin* the trainees swam into a canvas-type trunk, which was rolled down from the top of the tank and fitted around the escape hatch.[21] Breathing from the DSEA, the trainees ducked down into the trunk and floated up to the surface. Exits were also practised into open water, until the trainees had become very comfortable with the process.

There followed a physical reaction test, where the trainees were placed 60 feet down beneath the murky water of Portsmouth Harbour – twice the safe depth for DSEA diving.[22] But it was necessary so that the divers could identify the onset of oxygen narcosis and guard against it.

Able Seaman Mick Magennis, who volunteered to train as a diver after being a spare crewman during an earlier operation, judged this to be the worst part of the training at *Dolphin*. Once he had been down on the bottom for a few minutes Magennis felt his lips begin to twitch until he could scarcely keep the DSEA mouthpiece in. His arms and legs began to go numb with pins and needles. He knew that in a few minutes they would start to twitch involuntarily as oxygen poisoning began to invisibly take over his body. A pounding headache, like a sledgehammer inside of his skull, had started. Magennis knew that soon he would start having convulsions, black out and drown. He fought these symptoms as long as he could, but his body was shutting down as the narcosis slowly killed him. But just when he was about to give in he was hauled back to the surface, half-conscious, dazed and confused, by two strong instructors. 'You've passed, lad,'[23] bellowed a chief petty officer, clapping Magennis hard on the back. Magennis could hardly speak, his lips numb and his body shivering with cold. The instructors quickly stripped off his DSEA and laid him down on the floor until his circulation began to return to normal. 'Jesus, Joseph and Mary,' gasped Magennis, before he managed to sit up groggily, 'what a hell of a way to fight a war.' Now he knew why the *Dolphin* course had been christened the 'Perisher'.

CHAPTER TWO

Cloak and Dagger

'I think they must have been, without exception,
the most uncomfortable little ships ever built.'

—Lieutenant-Commander John Beaufoy-Brown, HMS *Varbel II*

Tich Fraser, David Carey and ten other officers and men all crowded aboard the night train to Glasgow at London's King's Cross Station. Though they had first-class tickets, the train was so overcrowded with servicemen and women that most of the group had to stand in the corridor. All except one young sub-lieutenant, who was so tall that he stretched out across the laps of seven accommodating Wrens. It was a long journey north during wartime, but among the new recruits, who had faced the terrors of the 'Perisher' and passed the test, a certain élan had already surfaced – they thought of themselves as an elite.

At Glasgow the group changed trains to Wemyss, then took a ferry to Rothesay Bay on the Isle of Bute. They appeared to be heading to the far end of the British Isles, to a rural Scottish backwater about as far away from the shooting war as it was possible to get. It was idyllic after bomb-scarred Portsmouth and London, with green rolling hills, low mountains, flocks of sheep, and picturesque lochs. The air was fresh and lightly scented with the smell of the sea.

Gulls shrieked and cawed overhead as the small passenger ferry arrived at its destination. The recruits piled off the ferry onto the stone jetty, their kit bags slung over their shoulders, and looked around.

'Over here, chaps,' announced a well-spoken female voice. They turned and saw a blue-painted Royal Navy truck pulling in beside a row of tiny fishermen's cottages. Leaning out of the driver's window was an attractive blonde Wren in her early 20s. 'Jump aboard,' she said, flashing them a winning smile.

'This job is getting better by the minute,' quipped David Carey, as they all piled into the back of the truck. A mile down the road, which was really only a country track, the truck was stopped at a checkpoint. Two sailors in landing rig armed with Lee Enfield rifles spoke to the Wren before peering into the back of the truck. One ticked off the party on a clipboard. The white-painted wooden barrier was raised and the truck rumbled on down the road for another mile before jerking to a halt on the shores of a stunning loch.

'This is it, chaps. The end of the line,' said the Wren, banging her hand on the side of the truck as she leaned out of the cab. The trainees, gathering their kit, jumped down from the tailboard and looked around. 'Where on earth are we now?' murmured Fraser. A tall and imposing grey stone building stood before them. Unknown to Fraser and his comrades, they, along with several other fresh intakes, had arrived at one of Britain's most secret bases – HMS *Varbel*.

*

British secret underwater warfare had come about in reaction to the successful deployment of frogmen and human torpedoes by the Royal Italian Navy early in the war. The British decided to copy the Italian method and create their own human torpedoes, christened 'chariots', with the two-man crews of these sit-on contraptions wearing early diving suits and modified DSEAs. In June 1942 the unit had moved to Loch Erisort in Scotland to begin training for missions against the enemy. Chariots were used against the 'pride of Hitler's navy', the battleship *Tirpitz*, in Norway in October 1942, and extensively in the Mediterranean, though with only limited success. Concurrently, the British had also started development of an extraordinary new type of small submarine codenamed the X-craft. The Flag Officer Submarines, Vice-Admiral Sir Max Horton, was particularly keen on midget subs. A successful First World War sub skipper, Horton realised that the chances of standard-sized submarines penetrating enemy harbours to attack capital ships had been virtually neutralised by booms, anti-submarine and anti-torpedo nets. Small submarines equipped with divers who could cut through the defences were the obvious solution. Midget submarines also had distinct advantages over chariots – they could travel much further and stay on a mission for much longer. By January 1943 six new X-craft were operational. Most famously these six subs attacked the *Tirpitz* on 22 September 1943 in what was codenamed Operation Source. They inflicted serious damage, though at heavy cost to Britain's most secret new naval arm.

*

The Kyles of Bute Hydropathic Hotel was a grand old Victorian pile outside the town of Rothesay on Loch Striven in northwest Scotland. It was a long, three-storied building, with only an entrance porch to break its straight line. Of a rough-faced grey local rock, the basements contained a fascinating collection of baths from the time when the hotel had been a relaxation spa for the wealthy.[1] It was positioned high on the side of a hill overlooking the quaint fishing village of Port Bannatyne.

Loch Striven sticks up like a crooked forefinger adjoining the west side of the Firth of Clyde north of the Isle of Bute, penetrating about eight miles into the Cowal District of Argyll. The navy had reserved the hotel and the loch as a submarine exercise area, and the waters were closed to civilian traffic. An early bend hid most of the loch from view, but once this was rounded a long, narrow fjord-like waterway stretched off into the distance. It had steep rock walls that were almost devoid of vegetation, those high walls casting dark shadows over the loch at all hours, giving the place an air of mystery, and for some of the recruits an impression of menace and evil.[2]

Fraser, Carey and the new recruits arrived at HMS *Varbel* only a few months before D-Day in 1944. The once-luxurious health resort had been largely stripped of its furnishings and paintings but it was bustling with Wrens in their attractive blue uniforms.[3] Outside, the White Ensign snapped out in the breeze from a flagpole as naval personnel of all ranks and trades bustled in and out of the hotel's grand entrance.

The rather curious name 'Varbel' had been derived from the names of the two officers most closely associated with the creation of X-craft, Commanders Varley and Bell.[4] They were extraordinary men.

Cromwell Varley, DSC, had been a successful submarine skipper during the First World War. In developing the original X-craft concept at his engineering works on the River Hamble, Varley had drawn on his experience of chasing a German cruiser across the North Sea and up the Elbe River before torpedoing her in sight of the crew's welcoming families. Varley's original idea was for a small submarine that could be sent up the Rhine into Germany to place charges under the bridges during the transition to war. The Admiralty turned the idea down as both impractical, which future operations would prove it was not, and unethical.[5]

Fraser, Carey and the other young officers were shown into the wardroom at *Varbel* where they discovered several highly decorated midget submarine veterans already in residence. These men were the survivors of Operation Source. Though controversial at the time, the explosive charges from two X-craft had caused extensive damage to the 42,000-ton *Tirpitz*. Two X-craft skippers had been awarded the Victoria Cross. However, of six hard-to-replace X-craft sent on the raid, five had been lost with eight highly trained 'X-men' killed and a further eight taken prisoner by the Germans.

Small wonder that X-craft soon earned the name 'suicide boats' from those not directly connected with the programme.

A few of those who had survived Operation Source had gone on to take part in two more operations in Norway. Both had been attempts to sink the Laksevåg floating dock in Bergen. *X-24*, commanded by Max Shean, had, in error, mined a German merchant ship tied up at the dock on 15 April 1944, but under a different skipper and crew the boat had returned and finally destroyed the dock on 11 September.[6]

When Fraser, Carey and the wide-eyed new officers arrived, the veterans, a mixture of skippers, first lieutenants and divers, were lounging in leather club chairs before the wardroom's large unlit fireplace.

'Hello, Ian Fraser.' Fraser extended his hand to a tall Royal Navy lieutenant who rose from his seat to return his greeting. 'Everyone calls me "Tich",' Fraser added.

'Hello Tich, I'm Pat Westmacott,' the officer replied, shaking Fraser's hand warmly. At six feet tall, Herbert 'Pat' Westmacott towered over Fraser and was a tight fit inside an X-craft.

'And this is David Carey,' said Fraser. The two men shook hands.

'Pleasure to meet you, David,' replied Westmacott.

'Your accent, sir, Australian?' asked Carey.

'No,' smiled Westmacott, 'I'm from New Zealand. And you can ditch the 'sir', we don't tolerate any of that quarterdeck bullshit here.' Carey was a little shocked at Westmacott's bluntness, but the change was refreshing. Westmacott, who was 24, had been awarded both the Distinguished Service Order (DSO) and the DSC, and had been the commander who had taken the *X-24* in to finally sink the German floating dock at Bergen.

'If it's an Aussie you're after, you'd better meet Max,' said Westmacott, indicating Shean. He rose from his seat by the window, a crooked grin spread across his friendly face.

'Max Shean. G'day,' said the Australian lieutenant, shaking hands with Fraser and Carey. The other new officers followed suit, introducing themselves around. Soon the air was filled with good-natured laughter and the burble of conversation.

Blond-haired and fork-bearded Lieutenant Jack Smart, a handsome 27-year-old, looked more like a 17th-century buccaneer than a Volunteer Reserve officer. He strode over to greet the newcomers. 'Welcome to the asylum, chaps,' he said. Smart, born in Northumberland in 1916, had joined the Royal Naval Volunteer Reserve in 1938. After service on a minesweeper in the Mediterranean he had volunteered for X-craft. On the *Tirpitz* operation Smart had commanded HMS *X-8*, and was ordered to attack a secondary target, the German battlecruiser *Lützow*. Smart and his crew had barely made it back alive from the mission. Before they had got anywhere near the *Lützow* the *X-8*'s towing line to the 'mother' submarine HMS *Sea Nymph* had parted. When Smart had surfaced his boat the *Sea Nymph* was nowhere to be found. Smart had decided to go on with the mission regardless but the X-craft had sprung serious leaks. Jettisoning his two side charges, four tons of Amatol high explosive, these had blown up, one close enough to have damaged the submarine, to such an extent that the crew, after drifting for 37 exhausting hours, had finally abandoned it.[7] Smart had been awarded the MBE and had bravely volunteered to stay on with the programme.

Several of the younger sub-lieutenants, mostly employed as divers, introduced themselves. They were a friendly bunch and soon put Fraser, Carey and the newcomers at ease. After dumping their kit in their accommodation and having a quick look around, Fraser's group joined the other recruits, officers and ratings for their first official meeting.

*

'Good morning, gentlemen,' said the Royal Navy captain to the assembled recruits in the hotel's former dining room. The view through the large picture windows was stunning, the flat expanse of the loch stretching away to distant mountains. But no one looked out of the window – all eyes were on the older officer standing on a small wooden stage before them.

'My name is Banks and I'd like to take this opportunity of welcoming you all to the 12th Submarine Flotilla,' he announced in an authoritative voice. William Banks was 44 years old, ancient in the eyes of the many young officers and ratings in the room, most of whom were barely out of their teens. Banks exuded experience. Of medium height, with a large forehead and receding swept back brown hair, he was a pre-war professional. The rows of medal ribbons on his left shoulder were testimony to that. He'd joined the navy in 1918 and been in submarines since 1923. He'd won a DSC in 1940, been mentioned in despatches in 1942 and taken command of the X-craft project in April 1943 as commander of both HMS *Varbel* and 12th Submarine Flotilla. Banks had personally planned the attack on the *Tirpitz*.[8] For putting the mighty battleship out of action for six months Captain Banks had received the CBE from a grateful King George VI. The recruits were to discover that Captain Banks was a charming man to talk to, and a man who got things done.[9]

'What we do here is very hush-hush, that much I'm sure you've already guessed,' said Banks. 'But before I begin, I have to insist that what I say is not merely confidential, but top secret. So I must ask you beforehand, every one of you, to undertake as officers and gentlemen, or as loyal servicemen, never to divulge anything of the details I'm about to give you until the operation is over.'[10]

They responded to a man, giving the time-honoured naval response of 'Aye aye, sir.'

'You already have some idea of what you've volunteered for, but not the details. Well, now I'm going to put you out of your misery.' Banks turned and walked over to a large board mounted on an easel that was covered with a dust cloth. A petty officer stood beside it. Banks nodded and the petty officer removed the cover, revealing a large diagram of an X-craft in profile. The trainees all craned forward in their seats and a ripple of excitement flashed around the room.

'Settle down,' said Banks in his schoolmasterly way. 'This, gentlemen, is the X-craft midget submarine. The "X" stands for secret. With this weapon we have been able to strike stealthy blows against the enemy on several occasions. It's my job to train you to use this ingenious machine. Well, let's have a look at her, shall we?'

Banks picked up a pointer from a side table and began to outline the diagram to his audience.

'The X-craft is a real submarine, only in miniature,' announced Banks. 'It has a crew of four – a commander, pilot, engineer and a diver. The range is just over a thousand miles under its own power and it can dive safely to 300 feet.' Banks pointed out the various ballast and trim tanks and briefly described their operation.

'So, gentlemen, the X-craft can do everything that a big submarine can do except fire torpedoes.' Banks pointed to the side of the craft. 'Here you'll notice this crescent-shaped object. This is called a "side cargo". It contains two tons of Amatol high explosive. One can be carried on each side. This is the X-craft's main weapon and it is dropped beneath an enemy warship. Naturally, you'll want to be very far away when they go up. She can carry limpet mines as well, and in this configuration the X-craft will carry one side cargo and one limpet carrier containing six 200lb mines in lieu of a second side cargo. Naturally, the diver's job will be to emplace the mines on enemy ships. However, the primary function of the diver is to cut holes in anti-submarine nets to allow the X-craft to get at protected enemy warships and the like.'[11]

The trainees were intrigued, and Fraser, like many listening to Banks, was slightly unsettled by what he had volunteered for.

'Now, the X-craft is about 50 feet long externally and about five-and-a-half feet across the beam. If you look around you might notice that many of the chaps who've been selected for this programme are, how shall I put it, jockey-sized. This is because the submarines are quite cramped inside. The only place where an average-sized chap can just about stand up is in the periscope chamber. So, the short-arses have the advantage.' The audience all laughed. It was certainly plain to see that a lot of the men present in the room were well below average height, including the appropriately named 'Tich' Fraser and the equally small Mick Magennis.

'Internally, the space is reduced to about 35 feet because of the propeller, diving rudders and so on,' continued Banks. He spoke for another ten minutes, roughing out for the men the subjects that they would shortly start to learn in great detail both in the classroom and in practice. It was clear to everyone in the room that this was a completely different kind of warfare, and both exciting and daunting in equal parts.

'We've plenty of targets but limited time. You will have to work your socks off but there will be missions aplenty for those who complete the programme.' Banks paused and folded his arms. 'I'm not going to soft-soap you, gentlemen. What we do here is damned dangerous work. But you chaps have been selected because you're the best we can find to do this sort of work. You'll be sailing in a very small boat, she's unarmed, and you're going to take her into some of the best-defended stretches of water that we know of.' Banks paused for a moment to let what he had said sink in.

'If you are successful, your actions *will* shorten the war,' said Banks. 'Work hard and pay attention to the training staff. The programme is challenging, but none of you would be here if we thought you couldn't complete it.' A ghost of a smile passed over Banks's lips. 'Well, chaps, that's my pep talk, for what it's worth,' he said, and rubbed his hands together gleefully.

'Right, let's get to work.'

*

For the first couple of weeks after arriving from London the trainees were lectured on the principles and operation of X-craft submersibles in the hotel's dining room. The lectures lasted from morning till night.[12] For men like Fraser, who was already a seasoned submariner, the work was not particularly challenging, but for those who had come from the surface fleet it was a steep learning curve. Nearly all of the officers were not submariners but reservists from either the RNR or RNVR, essentially civilians with limited sea experience. Most of the engine room artificers were already qualified submariners, along with some of the stokers and electrical artificers.[13] The need for secrecy was constantly drummed into them.

They were also given a course in hard-hat diving in Kames Bay. For nearly everyone, it was his first introduction to this Victorian form of underwater exploration. In practice, the X-craft divers would not use the equipment but Captain Banks had decided that it was an excellent method to get the trainees comfortable in open water.[14] The thick tan-coloured Siebe Gorman diving suits, with polished brass fittings and grey lead shoes, were cumbersome and extremely heavy. Once screwed into the brass helmet the trainees all had to fight off dreadful feelings of claustrophobia. It took a lot of self-control to calm down as they were winched 60 feet down into the dark peaty waters from a motor cutter.[15]

By the end of the first part of their course the recruits had digested the theory of X-craft operations and increased their confidence under the water. The recruits were then loaded aboard trucks and driven ten miles north up Loch Striven, to another top-secret training base. It was time to start practical training.

Nestled on the loch's steep mountainous sides were one or two crofters' cottages, and, at the loch head, a gently sloping alluvial plain. Here was located Ardtaraig House, the country shooting lodge of a 19th-century shipping magnate, built in traditional Scottish grey stone.[16] The cluster of buildings had been leased to the navy and commissioned as HMS *Varbel II*, the advanced diving training centre for 12th Submarine Flotilla.[17]

The commanding officer was 35-year-old Lieutenant-Commander John Beaufoy-Brown. Born in 1910, Beaufoy-Brown had joined the navy in 1927 and transferred to submarines in 1931. In 1940–41 he had commanded the T-class submarine HMS *Taku* during operations in the North Sea and Atlantic, winning a DSC. Before taking command of *Varbel II* in 1943, Beaufoy-Brown had been on the staff of Admiral Sir Max Horton, Flag Officer (Submarines).[18] He was an experienced sub skipper and a no-nonsense character held in high regard by both the trainees and the staff.

The programme's 'mother' ship, the 10,000-ton former Clan Line steamer HMS *Bonaventure* was moored on Loch Striven ready to take crews and training submarines to even more remote practice grounds further to the northwest. Built to handle heavy lifting, the grey-painted *Bonaventure* could carry four X-craft on her fore-deck, two on her after-deck, and two in her after-hold. Her crew contained specialists in every trade, and she had a well-equipped workshop capable of handling almost any type of repair as well as plenty of accommodation space for the over 50 men who would be required to provide crews for the twelve new top-secret XE-craft submarines that were under construction in England for operations in the Far East.[19] It was planned that the first six boats would comprise the senior division of a new flotilla to be based aboard the *Bonaventure*. They would sail to the Far East first.

The atmosphere aboard the *Bonaventure* was severe and purposeful, bristling with activity and tense with deadlines to be met.[20]

The area around *Varbel II* was stunningly beautiful, the surrounding steep hills covered with golden gorse; a swift flowing burn divided a thick forest where the trainees cut firewood for exercise and for the wardroom fire. HMS *Bonaventure* anchored just off the burn and pipes and cables for water and telephones were connected to her from the land. The base was accessible to the outside world by a single guarded road that ran up over the hills to the town of Dunoon many miles away.[21]

Apart from the old stone house and its outbuildings, *Varbel II* consisted of two Nissen huts that the navy had erected near the shore to serve as a store and workshop for diving gear. Anti-submarine and anti-torpedo nets, suspended on steel buoys, had been placed out in deep water to simulate the sorts of barriers that the men would encounter and probably have to cut their way through on operations against the enemy.

The trainee divers' first attempt at using the X-craft's Wet and Dry Compartment was always memorable, and often for the wrong reasons. *Varbel II* had a special training apparatus that had been built by Vickers-Armstrong at the same time that they had constructed the first generation of X-craft used to attack the *Tirpitz*. It was a replica section of an X-craft consisting of a fully functioning W&D with a short section of hull sealed with a blank bulkhead. The W&D had only one door internally, and a main hatch on the top. All the valves and pumps necessary for its proper operation were fitted and functional. The whole apparatus was suspended from wire ropes running from a winch fixed to a catamaran-type barge moored just offshore. The water was deep enough for the barge to lower the apparatus down to a depth of 20 feet. The trainee divers could then practise leaving and re-entering a 'submarine' until they perfected the technique and it became second nature.[22]

But first, the trainees had to contend with the diving suits, which soon earned a reputation for being both uncomfortable and slightly repellent.

'Urrgh,' exclaimed a young sub-lieutenant as he took his turn dressing in the diving suit, 'it's all cold and slimy!'

Several of the other trainees, including David Carey, who were watching, laughed.

'Don't worry, sir,' said the young able seaman who was helping him to dress. 'That's the ERA gob.'

'I beg your pardon?' replied the young officer, his nose wrinkling in disgust.

'That's what we call the lubricant used to disinfect the suits, sir. ERA gob. You know, like spit, sir.' 'ERA' stood for Engine Room Artificer. There were more peals of laughter from the audience. The original *Tirpitz* operation trainees had first coined the nickname and it had stuck.[23]

The Dunlop Rubber Company manufactured the black Underwater Swim Suit Mark III – what the divers had quickly christened the 'Clammy Death'. A diver needed help to dress himself. The suit, thinner and less bulky than that used for traditional hard-hat diving, was entered feet first, into the lower part through a pliable rubber trunk at the stomach. The upper part of the suit was then pulled over the head, which pushed up into the closely fitting head-and-mouth piece. Shoving the head through the tight rubber hood was painful; it hurt the scalp and the ears. The unpleasant job of thrusting hands and wrists through the very narrow and strong rubber cuffs of the suit was equally uncomfortable.[24] Once dressed, the entry trunk was then folded and sealed with a large Jubilee clip around the wearer's waist. The DSEA submarine escape rebreather was fastened to the wearer's chest and the breathing pipe connected.[25] Finally, in place of goggles, the diver wore his nose clip and a round diving mask with a Perspex faceplate.

Every recruit dreaded and grew to loathe the W&D compartment training apparatus. Though they had all been through the 'Perisher' at Gosport, the much smaller W&D was by turns frightening, peculiar and claustrophobic. 'It was the most unnatural set of circumstances. At that time you wish you'd never been born,'[26] recalled Max Shean.

The second generation of recruits found the experience unchanged from Shean's day. David Carey was amused to be told that on the real X-craft the boat's head, or toilet, was located underneath the floor of the W&D compartment.

'Today's test is just to get you familiar with the Wet and Dry,' said the lieutenant who was instructing Carey's group. 'You will get inside the chamber and pump the water in till it's full, then swing the arm, press the equalising cock here,' the lieutenant pointed to the various features, 'and lift the hatch. Get out and ascend to the surface. Later, we'll teach you how to re-enter the submarine and flood down.'

'Do we control the pump?' asked Carey.

'No, that's from inside the X-craft. You signal to the instructor who will be playing the role of skipper through this porthole covered with thick glass.'[27]

The trainees all craned forward.

'Your controls are only three, apart from the door clips fore and aft,' continued the lieutenant. 'There's the flooding lever here,' he said, turning to a large handle set into the wall of the W&D, 'the hatch clip above your head, and the equaliser cock.'

'Now, this rig is quite different from the dives you did in the tank at *Dolphin*,' said the lieutenant. 'It gets bloody dark in the W&D. Dark and tight because of the pressure. That is till the equaliser finally works. But follow the procedure that I will teach you, and you *will* be fine.'[28] The lieutenant smiled reassuringly.

David Carey's turn soon arrived. After clambering into the W&D, his diving gear bulky in the confined space, he switched onto oxygen, flushed two or three lungfuls from the DSEA bag into the craft, and then stayed on oxygen. Once all was well Carey gave the instructor inside the replica X-craft the thumbs-up through the W&D's tiny inspection window, opened the water and return air valves, and started the pump. Inside his control room next door the instructor had a duplicate set of controls, so he could make sure that the trainee was following the correct procedure.[29]

Inside the W&D, water started to flood in. Quickly, the water level rose, first covering Carey's ankles, then his knees, waist, chest and finally reaching visor level. The instructor was right, it was much worse than the chamber at HMS *Dolphin*. It was very small, dimly lit and in the open sea. As the cold water crept up his face Carey fought to control his rising panic. Nearly all of the men experienced a natural tendency to panic, no matter how many times they went through this process.[30] And all of them were put through this horror again and again before they finally mastered leaving and re-entering the W&D with confidence. The drills had to become second nature. The anxiety of midget submarine work never left any of the men, it was always in the back of their minds. Though it never fully subsided, the rigorously taught drills and procedures did help to control the fear as the training kicked in.[31] When the pressure was equalised and the hatch was pushed open, Carey felt a happy release, swimming into the light shining down through the water above, free of the tiny steel chamber. *I'm still alive!* was the first thing that popped into Carey's mind as he pulled himself out of the hatch for the first time. He kicked his fins and rose slowly to the surface, emerging from the brown water beside the barge like a seal coming up for air. Strong arms reached over the side and helped him climb unsteadily up the ladder. It was Fraser's turn next. As he waited the winch began to whine, its engine thumping noisily as the W&D apparatus was hauled back to the surface. Fraser finished dressing, a knot of apprehension coiled in the pit of his stomach. He picked up his swim fins and stepped forward.

CHAPTER THREE

'Softly, softly, catchee monkey'

*'I decided to stay on because I felt that I had something
to contribute, liked submarines, and our flotilla was to
be sent to the Pacific, which would satisfy any Australian
who had been restless since Japan had entered the war.'*

—Lieutenant Max Shean, HMS *XE-4*

HMS *X-20* lurked submerged off the entrance to the bay, waiting. Tich Fraser popped the attack periscope up several
times, scanning for the ferry that he knew would soon be arriving.
Suddenly, the red-and-white-painted steamer appeared around
the headland, its single stack puffing thick black smoke into the
clear air, seagulls wheeling and cawing noisily in her wake. 'Group
up, half ahead together,' ordered Fraser, giving a compass bearing as the little submarine surged forward towards the stern of the
steamer. Inside the *X-20* the crew could hear the steamer's screw
churning away in the water and the sound of her engine's rhythmical thumping echoing through the quarter-inch-thick steel hull of
the submarine. Changing to the night periscope used for seeing
when underwater, Fraser manoeuvred the *X-20* below and into the
steamer's wake, 'tagged on behind'[1] as he put it, and followed the
vessel between the steep headlands into the bay. The sound of the
X-20's small motor was completely smothered by the much larger
and noisier engine and propeller mounted on the ferry, and the
hydrophone posts on the headlands registered only the passage
of the big surface vessel. A Japanese midget submarine had used

exactly the same technique during the attack on Pearl Harbor on 7 December 1941.[2]

Once the ferry had passed the headlands and started for its landing jetty, Fraser changed course and headed for a large converted steamer that lay anchored on the quiet waters of the bay. Five minutes later he suddenly surfaced right beside the big navy ship, lookouts on deck shouting and pointing down as the tiny submarine's main hatch popped open and Tich Fraser clambered out on to the casing. But instead of being met by gunfire Fraser received only some half-hearted cheering and clapping from the big ship's crew, along with a few sarcastic comments. Fraser laughed, and holding on to the partly raised air induction trunk, gave a mock bow to his audience. Then a familiar face appeared over the bridge wing, a pair of binoculars hanging around his neck. 'Good show, Fraser,' shouted down Captain Willie Banks. 'Stand by to be lifted aboard!' HMS *Bonaventure*'s 50-ton crane swung immediately into action to retrieve the little submarine.

It was early August 1944 and for the fourth time in a week Fraser had managed to make a successful 'attack' on the *Bonaventure*. It was Fraser's final test before taking command of a brand-new XE-craft.[3] He couldn't afford to make a single mistake.

*

Five old X-craft, built before the *Tirpitz* operation and now deemed surplus to requirements, had been moved to HMS *Varbel II* to be used to train new crews in the basics of midget submarine operations. The improved design, codenamed 'XE-craft', was under hurried development in England. Because the boats were to be towed into action by larger submarines, each XE-craft, like the original X-craft, would require three crews – a three-man passage crew for the exhausting outbound journey, a four- or five-man attack crew for the actual operation against the enemy, and another three-man passage crew for the return tow to base.[4] This overmanning provided a large pool of volunteers for the skippers to choose the best men for the operational crews.

In spring 1944 the most experienced of the new recruits had been given command of the training boats. Ian Fraser's first command was to be the *X-20*. On arrival it lay very low in the lonely waters of the North Minch, its black steel casing looking like some prehistoric animal broaching the still surface. The *Bonaventure* had deposited the *X-20* off Cape Wrath, the most northwesterly point in Britain. It was make or break time for Fraser – he was to complete a series of four command exercises before being allowed to commission a brand new XE-craft. David Carey was appointed his 'XO', or executive officer, the boat's second-in-command.

There was no conning tower like that found on a traditional full-size submarine, just a metal deck, a couple of round hatches and a small dome housing the craft's two periscopes. The X-craft was designed to be low in the water, making it harder for radar or visual detection.

Fraser had stepped aboard from a tender, his seaboots clanging on the wet casing. He gripped the partially raised air induction trunk for balance, a long *schnorkel* that could be raised while the submarine was submerged, allowing the faster diesel engine to continue running instead of the electric motor. The diesel was a modified 42hp Gardner taken from a London double-decker bus.

Fraser had clambered down the hatch into the submarine's cramped white-painted interior, which to the untrained eye appeared to be a narrow confusion of brass wheels and switches, green instrument panels, dials and small bulkhead doors.

Damp was a constant problem in the old X-craft. This was overcome by the most unusual piece of kit ever carried aboard one of His Majesty's fighting submarines – a ladies' hairdryer. Nearly all of the important bits of machinery were electrical. Damp played havoc with them, so once an hour a crewman went around and blew hot air on them to dry them out. Headroom inside the boat was only 5ft 3in, a challenge even for very small men like Tich Fraser, and agony for a tall man like David Carey.

Each mock attack was a major undertaking and hazardous, testing not only the commander but also the entire four-man crew's ability to work together as a team. Each commander was expected to train three crews, selecting the very best men for his main attack crew, with the rest forming the two passage crews.

The essential factors required of an X-craft commander were daring and the ability to react quickly to changing circumstances. When on a real mission, once out of contact with superiors, the X-craft and its crew would be on their own, and everyone knew the old maxim about best-laid plans.

The X-craft was designed to do one thing very effectively, and that was to creep up on a larger surface warship, get beneath her and lay huge mines, before escaping unseen. The *Bonaventure* was the ideal practice target.

Fraser had demonstrated during his first 'attack' on the *Bonaventure* the élan that X-craft skippers had to possess. The *Bonaventure* had been moored in Loch Cairnbawn, way up north off the Minch, the sea area between the Scottish mainland and the Isle of Lewis. A second midget submarine training base had been established there codenamed 'Port HHZ'.

The advanced training base Port HHZ had headlands of ancient, menacing rock, quite different from *Varbel* and *Varbel II*. Patches of yellow, sparse grass were interspersed with outcrops of grey stone. It was an altogether unforgiving environment, a bleak place worn by wind and weather and savaged by the cold North Atlantic.[5]

Bonaventure's skipper, Captain Banks, had been told when roughly to expect Fraser's *X-20*, so lookouts were posted both aboard the vessel and ashore. This would be the most difficult type of attack to make, against an enemy who was already primed and ready. But Carey came up with a brilliant plan.

The *Bonaventure* was, like most navy ships, equipped with hydrophones, an underwater listening device that could pick up the noise of a submarine's propeller and diesel engine or electric motor. The problem was how to approach the *Bonaventure* without being seen or heard. Carey had realised that they could use the tide. The target vessel was in a bay, so, timing their attack perfectly, Fraser and Carey had simply drifted into the bay with the rising tide, engine off, using only the pump motors spasmodically to control the submarine's depth.[6] Engaging the almost silent electric motor, Fraser had used the smaller night periscope to see underwater, positioning the *X-20* right under the *Bonaventure*'s keel for a textbook attack that earned Fraser high marks from Captain Banks.

The second attack had been altogether different. The *Bonaventure* simply 'disappeared', so that Fraser and the other four X-craft skippers had to find her before launching dummy attacks. Fraser, again using his wits, managed to glean enough information from Banks before he departed to work out where she would most likely be found: Loch Erisort on the Isle of Lewis.

The next day Fraser, after a pleasant and untroubled night's sleep aboard a fishing trawler in Stornoway, had nosed his submarine into the loch, hugging the high cliffs only 20 feet from the shore. The submarine was running its diesel engine underwater, with the air induction trunk raised just above the surface.

'Periscope depth,' ordered Fraser, the *X-20* rising.

'Periscope depth, Tich,' reported Carey a few seconds later.

'Up periscope', ordered Fraser, and the 10ft-long attack periscope slid out from the small dome on the X-craft's hull, its small head no thicker than a finger poking just above the waves.[7] Inside the submarine Fraser pulled down the two brass handles at the base of the periscope and pressed his face to the rubber eyepiece. Such was the limited space that midget submarine commanders had to kneel when using the periscope. The drill was to make a fast 360-degree sweep of the surface to make sure that there was no immediate danger, before settling into a slower sweep to acquire the target. 'Down periscope. Thirty feet. Eight-five-oh revolutions,' ordered Fraser. The periscope was hastily retracted and Fraser called out a course as the *Bonaventure*, its grey sides speckled with rust, swung slowly around its anchor cables with the lazy movement of the calm green water. But this time Fraser had made a mistake, and in a real attack situation it could have cost him his life and the lives of his crew.

Atop the 40ft-high cliffs two lookouts had been posted with powerful navy-issue binoculars. Suddenly, one of the lookouts gave a cry and pointed below the cliffs. A tiny white wake was visible on the surface as the *X-20*'s small air induction trunk head cut through the water. As the lookouts watched, a second, almost imperceptible wake appeared close by as Fraser raised his attack periscope to take a quick bearing on the *Bonaventure*. It was unmistakable – the signature of a hunting submarine. One of the naval ratings quickly shrugged off his uniform and dressed only in his underwear gingerly clambered down the steep cliffs and stepped into the calm sea. A strong swimmer, the sailor struck out for the *X-20*, intending to grab hold of the submarine's periscope but, fortunately for Fraser, his vessel was too fast for the swimmer and he tired and gave up.[8] But if this had been for real, lookouts would have reported the submarine's position to gun crews atop the cliffs and fast patrol boats in the bay and Fraser would soon have found himself dodging shells and depth charges. As it was, Fraser had no idea that he had been spotted and continued with his mission, making another successful 'attack' on the *Bonaventure*. But his little mistake cost him many marks from the instructors.[9]

Attack number three had presented fresh challenges. Fraser and Carey were briefed that the *Bonaventure* would be in a loch 'somewhere'. But Fraser knew that Captain Banks was a keen trout fisherman. Sitting around moored offshore for days on end waiting for X-craft to make mock attacks was not the most thrilling of occupations, and Fraser decided to use his intelligence to narrow down where the captain would hide his ship. Fraser made some discreet local enquiries concerning fishing possibilities and had soon compiled a shortlist of likely locations.[10] Taking into consideration the size of the target vessel and other factors, Fraser selected Loch Eynort on the Isle of South Uist and set off. His hunch was bang on. *X-20* made another successful, and, this time undetected, attack on the *Bonaventure*, scoring maximum marks.

The fourth and final training attack had been by far the most daunting, and the closest yet to the conditions that the X-craft were likely to encounter on missions against the enemy. The *Bonaventure* was anchored in Gairloch, a bay with a narrow inlet that the navy had rigged with listening posts and hydrophones to pick up submarine engine noises. Though the X-craft's propulsion machinery and auxiliaries like pumps and the periscope hoist were designed to be as quiet as possible, they would be detected if they attempted to motor into the bay. Also, Carey's plan of floating in with the tide was impossible to repeat at Gairloch. But Fraser and his crew had been long enough in northwest Scotland to pick up local knowledge to aid their plans. The day nominated for the exercise was the same day a MacBrayne steamer would put into the bay to pick up passengers and parcels for the Western Isles. Fraser had used the steamer as camouflage, hiding in its wake to fool the hydrophones and soon getting beneath the *Bonaventure*. His motto was '*Softly, softly, catchee monkey*', and such patience brought results.

At the conclusion of the last exercise the *X-20* and the other submarines had been hoisted aboard the *Bonaventure*, which sailed back to Port HHZ.

*

While 12th Submarine Flotilla worked up in the Western Isles, in London, Prime Minister Winston Churchill's mind was far away from Europe, even though the ferocious battle for Normandy was still raging. Churchill had closeted himself inside 10 Downing Street with his senior advisors for three days in mid-August. His mental energies were devoted to attempting to evolve a strategy for the war in the Far East. The decisions taken would have a direct bearing on the midget submariners busily training far to the north. Two conflicting claims were on the table before the PM – the Pacific and the Bay of Bengal.[11] It was decision time.

The Far Eastern winds of war had finally started to blow in Britain's direction following the strategic defeat of Japan's invasion of India at the battles of Kohima and Imphal in July 1944. The Japanese army, broken, starving and diseased, was retreating from the Assam border back through Burma. Two strategies had immediately presented themselves to Churchill's newly appointed commander in southeast Asia, the King's elegant and urbane cousin Admiral Lord Louis Mountbatten.

The first was Operation Capital, a drive by General Sir William Slim's 14th Army to cross the Chindwin River in pursuit of the Japanese and capture the strategically vital town of Mandalay. The second, the plan that really excited Mountbatten, was an air- and seaborne invasion of Burma's capital, Rangoon. Designated Operation Dracula, it was well named for it was designed to cut the Japanese main line of communications to their troops in Burma, slicing through the enemy's exposed jugular and bleeding out his supplies.

On 9 August Churchill gave his approval to Dracula, but with an important proviso. It could be launched only if Hitler was defeated by October 1944. An early collapse of Nazi Germany might also offer the possibility of switching the main amphibious assault from Rangoon to Singapore.[12] This would mean Britain becoming an equal player with the United States in the defeat of Japan. With much of the Japanese fleet bottled up in ports throughout Asia, Captain Banks's declaration of targets aplenty when he had first briefed the new X-craft recruits at HMS *Varbel* didn't look like empty rhetoric.

*

Captain Banks selected six men from his pool of veteran and fresh X-craft skippers to take command of the first division of the new XE-class midget submarines. The boats were still under construction at Broadbent's of Huddersfield, Markham's of Chesterfield and Marshall's of Gainsborough, but the men had to be ready to take them over the moment that they were completed. The chosen skippers were gathered in *Bonaventure*'s wardroom to be told the good news.

'Jack,' said Banks to the bearded Lieutenant John Smart, 'you'll command *XE-1*.' Smart was elated to get the class leader. Banks knew that it took real guts to volunteer for another tour in X-craft after the harrowing experience Smart had had on the *Tirpitz* operation, and giving him the lead boat showed everyone how much faith Banks had in him. It would be his third midget submarine command.

'Pat,' said Banks, looking across the table at Lieutenant Pat Westmacott, the tall, handsome New Zealander. 'You'll have *XE-2*.' Westmacott smiled broadly. 'Yes, sir, thank you, sir,' he said, simply.

'Tich, you get *XE-3*,' said Banks to Fraser. His appointment was a testament to just how effective an X-craft skipper new boy Fraser had become in so short a time.

'Max, *XE-4*,' said Banks to Max Shean, the only Australian at the table. Like Smart, this would be his third tour in command of an X-craft. The ribbon of the Distinguished Service Order, second only to the VC, on his left shoulder was testament enough to his bravery and tenacity. He nodded solemnly.

'Terry, *XE-5*,' said Banks to Lieutenant J.V. Terry-Lloyd. A South African who had been awarded an MBE during the *Tirpitz* operation, Terry-Lloyd beamed. He had something of a mad streak in him and also a fine singing voice.[13] 'Thanks Boss,' replied Terry-Lloyd in his strong accent.

'And last, but by no means least, young Bruce,' said Banks. Lieutenant Bruce Enzer, another young Volunteer Reserve officer, looked up excitedly. '*XE-6*.'

The first division was fast shaping up into a real Commonwealth flotilla, with three Britons, a Kiwi, an Aussie and a South African as skippers.

*

Much was expected of the new XE-craft. The Admiral (Submarines), who commanded all the navy's submersibles, had wasted no time in writing to Admiral James Somerville, Commander-in-Chief, Eastern Fleet, Britain's largest naval force then in southeast Asia, pointing out the extraordinary improvements that had been made to the original X-craft design. The first generation of X-craft had shown during three operations in Norway 'their exceptional value for attacking enemy ships even in the most strongly defended harbours'.[14] The improvements in both design and crew training since then made the XEs much more potent weapons than before. The Admiral reported to Somerville that the first division of the new flotilla would be ready for action in the Far East by March 1945.[15]

*

Shortly after Captain Banks had assigned the new commanders to their boats, Fraser and some of the other officers were ordered to visit England to look over the six new XE-craft while they were still under construction, to 'stand by' their boats in naval parlance. The submarine assembly areas at Broadbent's, Markham's and Marshall's all rang to the sounds of hammers and pneumatic tools as a small army of civilian craftsmen laboured around the clock to finish the boats. Although outwardly almost exactly the same as the

40

older X-craft, the XEs had been slightly lengthened to 53¼ feet, an increase of eighteen inches, and been fitted with some improved equipment, including most vitally air conditioning for operations in the Far East.

Fraser and the other new skippers were sent to the factories at various times to watch the construction. As well as being able to provide valuable input, it was an excellent way for the young men who would have to take these new vessels to war to 'bond' with these inanimate machines of destruction, to fully understand them inside and out. They learned a lot from the artisans who designed and built them, knowledge that made their operation even more effective.

A few weeks later Tich Fraser found himself aboard a blacked-out London Midland & Scottish Railway train rumbling and squeaking its way north to an American base on the Clyde. He was sitting in a first-class carriage, the collar of his naval greatcoat turned up against a cold draught from an ill-fitting window, a draught that was laced with smuts from the steam engine as the locomotive hauled its top-secret cargo to Scotland. On an enormous bogey-truck was *XE-3*, her long steel hull hidden inside a massive wooden crate. The crate was disguised to look like an enormous food container.[16] Fore and aft of the *XE-3* were empty flatbeds as spacers, as the submarine was too long and overhung its own carriage. Behind the single passenger carriage was a guard's van. If anyone wondered why a naval officer was accompanying a train that consisted of a single giant crate and a first-class railway carriage, no one said anything. It was wartime and people believed what they were told, or minded their own business.

Inside the carriage Fraser smoked a Player's and sipped from a thermos of coffee provided for the trip from a hamper of food prepared at the factory.[17] His operational crew accompanied him as always. Like the other XE-craft commanders, Fraser had taken his crew with him on every visit to the factory to watch the building of 'their' submarine. It would hopefully be a smooth transition for all of the crews from the old X-craft to the new XEs.

Mick Magennis felt very proud to be among the special group of men who would crew them. He was grateful that Fraser had chosen him for his main operational crew. A bond of friendship had grown up between the officers and the few ratings in the programme. They were risking their necks together, and shared adversity had broken down the usual naval conventions.[18]

Occasionally, the train would slow down as it passed through blacked-out stations, the steam whistle giving a lonely blast, but for the most part Fraser sat, lulled into a drowsy state by the train's rhythm. He had little idea of his specific destination beyond *Varbel*, but it was clear that wherever it was, it was going to be warm. The XEs were designed for tropical operations and that could only mean one thing – sooner or later Fraser and his crew would be facing the Japanese. A sudden chill ran down his spine at the thought, for, like all servicemen, he had read in the newspapers and heard stories about Japanese barbarity and atrocities since their invasion of China in 1937. But first he would have to work up his crew on *XE-3* in the safer waters of the Western Isles, and prepare them for whatever lay ahead. He stubbed his cigarette out on the floor, leaned his head back against the vibrating seat rest and closed his eyes. But sleep stubbornly refused to come.

CHAPTER FOUR

Westward Ho!

'I remember Mick Magennis and other X-craft men.
We thought very highly of them. They were brave
men to go to sea in such small submarines.'

—Able Seaman John Clarke, HMS *Bonaventure*

The bang was very loud inside the *XE-4*, which veered violently off course, her trim and buoyancy shot to pieces as the little submarine was thrown around in the wake of whatever had hit her. The *XE-4*'s commanding officer, Lieutenant Max Shean, was ashore at the time. One of his crew, a tough Scot named Adam Bergius, had taken her out for a routine run when the accident had happened. 'Jock' Bergius, then an Acting Sub-Lieutenant, had joined the navy as a rating in 1943. He was trained as an X-craft diver, but in all the crews the junior officers were given opportunities to take command of the submarine to gain vitally needed experience. On operations, if the skipper and first lieutenant were incapacitated, any remaining officer among the crew would be expected to assume command.

An accident was the last thing that Captain Banks's carefully worked-out training programme needed. The six XE-craft of the first division were being hastily readied for transfer to the Far East aboard the *Bonaventure*, and their crews had been working up their new boats hard since they had been delivered from the makers in November 1944. Banks had been given only a six-week window for the crews to become completely familiar with the new type. Then the boats were to be winched aboard the *Bonaventure* and she

43

would sail for the Panama Canal. There would be little opportunity for training once the depot ship was under way, and everyone expected the flotilla to arrive in the Pacific ready for action.

Bergius grabbed the small brass handles of the periscope and pressed his face against the eyepiece. He saw only blackness. 'Stand by to surface. Shut main vents,' ordered Bergius, cursing his bad luck. As soon as *XE-4*'s flat deck was above the water he threw open the main hatch and clambered up the short ladder. 'Christ, the periscope's bust,' he called back down into the submarine's hull. The periscope was still raised, but it was twisted over to one side, its delicate head smashed to pieces. 'Hand me the Aldis,' said a dispirited Bergius, taking the large signal lamp as it was passed through the hatch by the ERA below. Steaming away from the stationary *XE-4* was an American-built LST (landing ship tank), a big, grey-painted amphibious warfare vessel used for beach assaults. She had barely registered the contact with the little submarine and had declined to stop.

Ashore at HMS *Varbel II*, Shean had been looking across the loch at the exact moment his submarine had suddenly surfaced in the wake of the large transport ship. Kames Bay had become a very busy waterway in the months before and after D-Day. Assault craft of all sizes and shapes were continually travelling to and from the adjoining Kyles of Bute. Many were loaded with army commandos in training on Loch Fyne a few miles to the west.[1] The new XE-craft exercised close to this busy channel, and good care had to be taken while submerged to keep within their allotted area. It was apparent to Shean that young Bergius had just made a very serious mistake.

As Shean watched he saw the Aldis lamp flash a message in Morse code to *Varbel*'s signal tower. Shean could read it. 'Run down by landing craft. Periscope bent.' Shean, cursing under his breath, started for the tower and ran straight into Captain Banks who was coming in the other direction. The flotilla commander was not happy either.

'Bergius is exercising in *XE-4*, sir,' said Shean to Banks, whose face was like thunder. 'He's had a minor accident.'

'Yes, I read his message,' replied Banks. 'What was he doing outside the exercise area, Shean?'

'I don't know, sir, but he has some inexperienced crew under training. Possibly he overran his area. I'll talk to him as soon as he berths, and let you know.' Shean knew that damage to such sensitive equipment as a periscope, a submarine's eyes, was very serious indeed.

'Right, Shean. I will leave that to you.' Shean turned to go but Banks grabbed his arm. 'And Shean, tell him that I am *bloody* annoyed!'[2]

Apart from the slight delay caused to the already tight training window while *XE-4* was being repaired, such an error on an operation could prove fatal. The periscope was the only way the submarine could visually navigate in enemy territory, and a blind boat was a dead boat. An accidental ramming by an enemy vessel would merely have alerted the enemy to the submarine's presence, which was also tantamount to a death sentence for the XE's crew. If the boat had been hit any harder major flooding could have occurred down the periscope well, a potentially fatal situation for the crew. Captain Banks worked the men of 12th Submarine Flotilla hard in order to minimise such life-threatening errors. Shean knew that; all of the XE-men did. Six weeks working up was not long and it was inevitable that under pressure-cooker training accidents would happen.

Nothing was left to chance. First came speed trials, followed by turning circles with the rudder set at different degrees to find out each boat's turning radius. The XE-craft's maximum safe depth was 300 feet, and each new vessel was harnessed to a boom defence vessel that lowered the submarine down to this depth so the crew could check the boat for leaks. The submarine was winched down rather than free diving to avoid accidents – a single telephone line meant the crew could speak to the boom vessel above.[3]

In Holy Loch the navy had set up a sound range.[4] This consisted of hydrophones slung on buoys down the length of the loch. The XE-craft raced up and down on diesel engine or electric motor while the boffins ashore recorded their sounds. Then the submarines would moor up between a couple of buoys, dive with the engine stopped and, in telephone communication, run each of the pumps, motors and other devices to see how much noise they made.[5] At the end of the exercise the crews would come ashore and the technicians would give them their recorded signatures and tell them which items to run, which not to run and which to get adjusted or repaired.

The final test was passing the submarine over indicator loops, special cables that had been laid on the seabed that detected the magnetic signature made by metal objects passing overhead. In order to prevent their detection by enemy indicator loops each XE-craft was fitted with degaussing equipment that demagnetised the vessel.[6]

*

It already seemed an age since the commanders and crews had brought their brand-new XE-craft to Scotland by train from England, such was the hectic pace of the training programme. But naval tradition dictated that each boat had a proper naming ceremony and Banks and his staff had laid this on.

'I name this boat *Sigyn, XE-3*,' announced Melba Fraser in a loud voice, her husband Tich standing atop the X-craft in his best uniform alongside David Carey and the rest of his crew. Melba, pregnant with her first child, had just left the Wrens. 'Godspeed to all those who sail in her,'[7] she said, and then she broke a bottle of champagne over the bow of HMS *XE-3*. Everyone applauded loudly as the submarine slipped into the water. The little naming ceremony had been arranged at a slipway at Ardmaleish on the Isle of Bute as commanding officers of X-craft were traditionally given the privilege of nominating the person to launch their boat. Fraser had naturally chosen his wife.

The day before, Fraser had brought the *XE-3* up to Bute from a prefabricated harbour run by the Americans on the Clyde after his train ride from the makers. But it had been a far from glorious entry into the loch. The *XE-3*'s diesel engine had seized up shortly after starting out from the Clyde and Fraser's new command had had to be towed to *Varbel* by a scruffy little fishing trawler. A spare engine would be fitted in her after the naming ceremony was over.

A few days later on 15 November 1944 the XE-men and their wives gathered again at Ardmaleish, where Max Shean's new English wife Mary went through the same ceremony and christened *XE-4*, hauled up on a cradle. Shean had chosen the name '*Exciter*' for his boat, thinking it very appropriate considering the job he was expected to do. The fizz, this time Australian as befitting the submarine's new commander, had been salvaged from Shean's hasty wartime wedding a few months before.[8]

One man taking part in this ceremony was probably one of the most experienced midget submariners in the service: Engine Room Artificer 4th Class Vernon 'Ginger' Coles, who had joined the navy in 1938 at the age of eighteen to escape a tedious apprenticeship in a tin box factory in Reading. He had served in Norway in 1940 aboard the destroyer HMS *Faulkner* and later in the Mediterranean. After a short course in Portsmouth Coles had qualified as an ERA. He had joined submarines after being egged on by a Glaswegian friend over several convivial pints, but after five combat patrols Coles decided that regular submarines were not exciting enough. Then he saw the Admiralty request for volunteers for 'Special and Hazardous Service'. 'I looked at this and thought "Shall I or shan't I? Shall I or shan't I?" In the end I thought, yeah, I'll have a go.'[9]

A tall, rangy man with thick side-parted hair and a gap-toothed grin, Coles possessed first-rate technical knowledge as well as an astounding facility for finding the humorous side of mishaps that would have completely upset most people.[10] During the *Tirpitz* operation in 1943 he had served as ERA aboard the ill-fated *X-9*, which had been scuttled on passage. Aboard the *X-22* Coles had conducted training operations in British waters before he joined Pat Westmacott's *X-24* during the successful attack on the floating dry dock at Bergen in March 1944.[11] Now he would be going to war for the third time aboard the new *XE-4*.

Ginger Coles was not unusual – the X-craft programme attracted men from all across the navy, and for a variety of reasons. As one historian has written, 'There was no easily definable sort of person. What did bind them together was a certain restlessness, a taste for adventure and a willingness to take mighty risks.'[12]

Within a week, the first six XEs had been christened and formally inducted into the submarine service. The crews' wives and sweethearts had been confronted with the reality of their loved ones' secret work in Scotland when they had first seen an XE-craft. For several of them, including Melba Fraser, they were less than impressed by the new boats, and more than a little alarmed. 'But it's so small,' Melba exclaimed as she approached the boat sitting in its cradle at Ardmaleish with Fraser, Mick Magennis, and the other two crew members, David Carey and ERA Maughan. Against the backdrop of the gorse-covered hills that framed the large loch *XE-3* did indeed look tiny. Fraser smiled at his wife's comment. 'That's the idea, darling. Small in this case is an advantage.'[13] Fraser hadn't told his wife much about what he was doing up in Scotland, and as a servicewoman herself, she knew better than to ask too many questions. Whatever the work, it was evidently important for the war effort. The other wives and sweethearts were all in exactly the same position.

A few weeks earlier Melba had managed to get leave from the Wrens and had stayed with Fraser for a weekend at *Varbel*. She had got her first brief look at an older X-craft quite by accident during lunch when she and Fraser were dining with Captain Banks and his wife Audrey. She had glanced out of the wardroom window and spied two X-craft floating on the still waters of the loch.

'What on earth are those?' exclaimed Melba, pointing out of the window. Fraser's eyes met Banks's, who said nothing but raised one eyebrow.

'They're, um, they're motorboats, dear,' said Fraser innocently.

'I've never seen motorboats like those before,' said Melba, staring intently at the X-craft at their moorings.

'But you've never been in Scotland before,'[14] said Fraser, smiling innocently. Fortunately for all concerned Audrey Banks neatly changed the conversation and nothing more was said about the strange craft on the loch. Fraser tried to keep Melba in the dark about X-craft for as long as possible. He knew that she would be deeply worried by the prospect of her new husband riding in such a craft to war, and that went for all of the wives.

*

If Melba Fraser had been privy to the highest echelons of command she might have slept a little easier at night. Operation Dracula, Mountbatten's masterstroke against Rangoon that would open the way for a British invasion of Singapore, was cancelled. Hitler had remained a more formidable foe than either Churchill or Roosevelt had reckoned on, and the German Army was far from defeated by October 1944. The promised landing ships, infantry divisions and aircraft to support Mountbatten's invasion could not be released from the European theatre.[15]

The new XE-craft already had orders to sail for the Far East in support of Mountbatten's Southeast Asia Command. But with Dracula's cancellation the future employment of the new machines was looking uncertain.

*

The six weeks leading up to Christmas 1944 was a very hectic time for the XE-men. The training had produced two types of officer. The first were the 'Tigers', who trained until they were as fit as big cats. They would rise early, run along the Dunoon road or up into the hills, returning for a lean breakfast of thin toast and ersatz scrambled egg. Hunger mounted day by day, the Tigers concomitantly becoming progressively leaner. The other school of thought argued that the best way to prepare for life aboard a poorly ventilated submarine was to take all the rest available. The second group consisted of officers who were likely to be found during their off-duty hours lounging before the wardroom's log fire sipping gin, a thick fug of tobacco smoke giving the room the impression of a cosy public house or gentleman's club.[16]

The six weeks were also marked by a lot of parties as the men let off steam. The rather ascetic life at *Varbel II* was considerably enlivened by the launching ceremonies, and by the cocktail parties that accompanied each launching. The XE-men soon had a renewed taste for the stuff that comes in bottles. Six weeks out on Loch Striven with the new boats was interspersed with a succession of monumental hangovers.[17]

The final operational crews were sorted out. Max Shean's first lieutenant Joe Brooks, a good-looking leisure-time artist, departed to be replaced by an Irishman, Sub-Lieutenant 'Ben' Kelly. A second diver, Sub-Lieutenant Ken Briggs from Orange, New South Wales, joined diver Jock Bergius. Shean was very pleased to have a fellow Aussie among his happy little crew.[18]

The only change to *XE-3*'s crew was a new Engine Room Artificer, Charlie Reed in place of ERA Maughan. Jack Smart's *XE-1* crew consisted of Sub-Lieutenant Harold Harper as second-in-command, ERA 4th Class Henry Fishleigh and diver Leading Seaman Walter Pomeroy. Pomeroy had been passage crew on Smart's *X-8* during the *Tirpitz* operation.[19] There were plenty of first-rate men to choose from, but final operational crews were the closest knit of all, and often the best of friends.

*

The CO of *Varbel II*, Lieutenant-Commander Beaufoy-Brown, paid particular attention to net cutting, pushing the divers to the limits of their underwater endurance. The original X-craft crews trained for Operation Source had mastered the method of cutting through anti-submarine and anti-torpedo nets back in 1943, and it had not been changed since. But it was extremely hazardous work for the divers who had to do it. Max Shean had originated the chosen method. One evening when he was sitting before a roaring log fire in the wardroom at *Varbell II* he had sketched out a cutting plan for the *Tirpitz* operation commander, fellow Australian Henty Henty-Creer.

Anti-submarine nets were constructed from steel mesh arranged in a diamond pattern, and the problem the early X-craft crewmen had faced was how to stabilise their submarine in an underwater current while hovering in front of the net as the diver worked to cut a hole.

Shean realised that if the X-craft hit the net its bow would nestle in one of the diamond-shaped spaces. The submarine's motor could be kept running on 'dead slow ahead' to keep the X-craft's nose lodged in the net. The diver would then go out through the W&D compartment, collect hydraulic cutters from the craft's stowage bay and proceed to carefully cut a large hole for the submarine to pass through.[20]

As the crews practised this procedure in the few weeks remaining before Christmas, the commanding officer, Lieutenant-Commander Beaufoy-Brown took to donning a DSEA and diving down twenty feet beside the cable to watch. It was a strange experience, watching as the XE-craft approached out of the gloom, pushing its bow into the net. Silently, a hatch would open for'ard and a figure dressed in black, wearing a cumbersome diving rig, would slowly emerge and make the cuts before disappearing silently back inside the submarine. 'It was like watching something out of a science fiction film come to life,' recalled Beaufoy-Brown.

Between the six new boats a healthy competition developed over who could cut a hole the fastest, with nearly fatal results. The record was seven-and-a-half minutes and Mick Magennis decided to try to break it.

'How's the trim,' asked Tich Fraser, as the *XE-3* approached the practice net.

'Pretty good, Tich,' replied Carey, turning the hydroplane wheel slightly to keep the submarine just below the surface.

'Fifteen feet, slow ahead,' ordered Fraser.

'Aye aye, fifteen feet, slow ahead,' repeated Carey.

'Steer two-seven-oh,' said Fraser.

'Steering two-seven-oh,' replied Carey.

'Depth fifteen feet,' announced Fraser.

'Ship's head on two-seven-oh,' said Carey.

Fraser pressed his eyes to the night periscope. 'Should be nearing the net soon now.'[21]

With a grinding noise, the *XE-3*'s bow came to rest in the net.

'She's riding quite steady, it seems,' said Fraser, the *XE-3* remaining against the net. 'Right, Magennis, off you go.'

Inside the *XE-3*'s W&D Magennis flooded the chamber, equalised the pressure and opened the hatch. He eased his body into the position for rising out of the compartment. With his torso half out of the submarine, he held himself by the knees within the compartment and vented.[22] The surrounding water was dim and freezing cold.

Once clear of the hatch and horizontal, the power of the tide pushed him aft along the submarine. Quickly, Magennis grabbed the periscope standard. Tidal pressure on the upper part of the DSEA breathing bag half-emptied it, causing Magennis to breathe much harder and faster than usual, what the divers called 'guffing'. He moved along the submarine to collect the cutters, which were attached to a long pressurised cable, giving Fraser the thumbs-up as he passed by the night periscope. The skipper could respond to the diver's hand signals by wiggling the periscope. After retrieving the big grey cutters, shaped like an oversize pistol with metal jaws, he made his way over to the net, dragging the water cable behind him.

Working quickly, Magennis made his cuts, his breathing laboured as he worked flat out and the tidal pressure continued to push upon him. As he completed cutting a hole for the *XE-3*, he started to feel tingling in his lips and limbs. Gulping air like an exhausted horse, Magennis slowly stowed the cutters, his wrists aching badly.[23]

I can't make it, he thought as he tried to reach the open W&D hatch. His breathing was becoming more and more constricted. The heavy labour, coupled with working in the current, had exhausted his oxygen supply to the point where he was poisoning himself with every breath. Suddenly Magennis gave up, letting go of the *XE-3*'s hull and rushing towards the surface, kicking his fins wildly. He couldn't breathe; he was suffocating. He might black out and drown. Magennis hit the surface of the loch and tore off his face mask, spitting out the DSEA mouthpiece before gulping down beautiful, clean fresh air. The rescue boat quickly came alongside him. But Magennis waved the launch away. 'I'm going back,' he declared breathlessly as he bobbed on the surface. Replacing his mouthpiece and face mask, Magennis dipped beneath the water and swam down to the still-stationary *XE-3*. As he struggled into the W&D the straps on his DSEA caught on the hinge of the hatch. Completely exhausted, Magennis broke the straps and breathlessly slipped into the compartment. With his last reserves of energy he flooded down and crawled exhausted into the boat, lying on the deck like a half-dead black fish.

'All right, Mick?' asked a concerned Fraser.

Magennis smiled gravely. 'Fine,' he said, rather unconvincingly. 'Everything's okay, sir.'

*

'Let this be a warning,' said Captain Banks once Mick Magennis was back on dry land. 'Don't be too clever.' He was angry that divers were trying to break nonsensical time records and nearly killing themselves in the process. Beaufoy-Brown stood beside Banks, his face serious as he listened to his superior upbraid Magennis and the other divers. 'If this had happened on an operation it would have given the whole job away.'[24] From now on, there would be no more competitions. The divers were ordered not to over-exert themselves.

*

As the last Christmas of the war arrived, the crews had managed to achieve a high state of readiness for whatever missions, if any, lay ahead. They had become very close, their teamwork second nature. The *Tirpitz* veterans and the newcomers were virtually indistinguishable.[25] There was a natural democracy among them that would have horrified senior officers, but due to the dangerous nature of their jobs and the claustrophobic, cramped confines of the XE-craft, distinctions of rank, education and social class, so important to the surface navy, were largely irrelevant. Their loyalty was to each other, their boat and to the 12th Submarine Flotilla. Their comrades had become their family. Their beloved leader, Captain Banks, was returned to regular duties in November 1944. His replacement was an officer who had already been intimately involved with the earlier X-craft programme, Captain P.Q. Roberts, DSC.

*

Christmas is a time for real family, and Captain Roberts granted everyone leave over the holiday season. Those that could contrive to spend a few days with their wives or sweethearts did so. Word had already come through that the first division of the new flotilla, consisting of *XE-1* to *XE-6*, was to be shipped to the Far East in February 1945. Named the 14th Submarine Flotilla (thereby avoiding unlucky thirteen[26]), another familiar face from the original X-craft operations would be taking the new unit operational.

Captain William 'Tiny' Fell had earned his nickname because of his diminutive stature, standing just 5ft 7in, but to those who knew him or served under him, Tiny was a giant of a man. 'He thought the world of his crew,' said Able Seaman Ken Clements, an electrician on board HMS *Bonaventure*.[27] Fell would assume full command of *Bonaventure* and the new flotilla on 22 January 1945.

A sympathetic type of man who was considerate to a fault in his dealings with other people, Fell was proud of his New Zealand parentage and of his long service in submarines.[28] He was 48 years old, slightly built with a striking nose and a strong chin. He had first come to England in 1914, spending a term at Charterhouse where a relative of his mother was headmaster, and then two terms at Crediton Grammar School in Devon before joining the navy in 1915. He had fought as a midshipman in the First World War's most famous naval engagement, the Battle of Jutland, before transferring to submarines in 1917.[29] In the interwar period Fell had seen service in the Mediterranean and on the China Station. Made an OBE in 1937, he was due to retire when the outbreak of war propelled him back into the front lines. He would always feel that he had been very well served by the war.[30] Fell had gone on to win a DSC in 1940 before seeing action in the Vaagso Raid on occupied Norway the following year.

Fell, whose son also served in submarines, had drifted into secret operations almost by accident. One day in March 1942 he was seeking out old friends at Northway House, a converted block of luxury flats in London that formed the wartime headquarters for the Submarine Service. Fell was asked whether he would consider rejoining 'boats' in an unusual capacity. When he replied that he would, Fell was immediately whisked in to see Admiral Sir Max Horton who told him all about Italian human torpedo operations against the British in the Mediterranean.

'Are you interested in starting something similar?' asked Sir Max.

'I am, sir,' replied Fell enthusiastically.

'Well, get down to Blockhouse, find Sladen and two or three madmen he has collected, and build and train a team of charioteers.'[31]

From this beginning emerged the British Chariot programme of human torpedoes, and Fell would move on to play an instrumental role in the early development of the X-craft midget submarine alongside 'Slasher' Sladen. Fell's 'partner in crime' could not have been more different, both physically and in personality. Sladen stood over six feet tall – big for a submariner – weighed 13 stone, and had four England rugby caps to his name. His personality was likened to a whirlwind. Before joining the Experimental Submarine Flotilla in early 1942 Sladen had commanded the regular submarine HMS *Trident* in which he had managed to torpedo the German heavy cruiser *Prinz Eugen*.[32]

*

The decision to send the XE-craft to the Far East had been taken at the Quebec Conference in September 1944 in private meetings between the chiefs of the Royal Navy and US Navy.[33] There was a strong belief at the time that the ingenious little submarines would be able to play a vital role against the Japanese now that the war against Nazi Germany was winding down. Lord Mountbatten was marshalling as many forces as possible under his control for forthcoming operations against the Japanese, and the new XE-craft would find no useful employment if they were left behind in Europe. The fighting had shifted on to land in both France and Italy. Hitler's navy had been reduced to a mere shadow of its former self, with only the U-boats continuing to operate in the open seas, and those with much-reduced effectiveness. But Fell and 14th Submarine Flotilla, though they didn't yet know it, would face less than plain sailing in making the dream of X-craft operations in the Pacific theatre a reality. For it was sorely evident to everyone in higher command that the war with Japan was primarily an American fight, and not everyone in Washington was happy to include the British in their plans. But in early 1945 the officers and men of 14th Submarine Flotilla had no inkling that they were going to be sailing into such a politically sensitive new theatre when they left Scotland. Instead, with Christmas over and the New Year chimed in, it was a time for goodbyes.

Partings were never easy, but partings during wartime were particularly painful. The uncertainty over whether husbands would ever see wives and children again was agonising. Max Shean's moment, like nearly everyone else's, came on a railway platform. He was at Glasgow's main station on New Year's Day 1945. He held his wife Mary in his arms while all around them bustled servicemen and their families, many others going through the same riot of emotions that Shean felt at that moment. Trains shunted and wheels squealed on the tracks while carriage doors slammed and guards' whistles blew shrilly. Shean pulled away slightly and looked down into his wife's damp eyes. He smiled, though there was a knot of emotion in his throat. It was such a wretched place to say goodbye, a smoky railway platform in cold, wintry Glasgow. He said the things that all husbands have said during such partings, soothing things, hopeful things. But he knew that this might be the last time he would ever see his new wife. Mary was going home to await world peace, while Shean was sailing to war in the Pacific.[34] Their parting was suddenly interrupted by a shout of 'all aboard!' as the last passengers for his train hastily clambered into their carriages. He gave his wife one final embrace, feeling her warmth against him, the coldness of her frozen cheek against his neck. And then he climbed into his carriage, dumping his kit into the overhead rack. He stood at the compartment's open window and held his wife's hand as she reached up from the platform. She was crying.

CHAPTER FIVE

'Their bird'

Tridenti stimulabimus hostem –
'With trident, stimulate the enemy'
—Motto, HMS *XE-4* '*Exciter*'

Mick Magennis's eyes grew large inside his round diving face mask. *Jesus fucking Christ!* his mind screamed, his left hand dropping down to his ankle where a large diver's knife was lashed to his leg. His breathing had increased dramatically and his hands were shaking. But he had not fallen prey to 'Oxygen Pete', the mythical monster that hunted divers. Rather he had succumbed to a very old, and very real, human fear. Swimming towards him was a large grey-coloured shark, its head moving from side to side as its tail propelled it silently through the water. The shark's two dead black eyes were looking straight into Mick's. Magennis's hand tightened around the knife's handle as he prepared to defend himself. Suddenly, with a swish of its large tail, the shark changed direction and cruised away.

Magennis felt very exposed, perched atop Lieutenant Terry-Lloyd's *XE-5*, the hatch to the boat's W&D compartment still wide open. The submarine, not Magennis's usual ride, was hovering in the shallow tropical waters off Trinidad in the Caribbean while the divers practised the new technique of attacking enemy ships with limpet mines. It had proved hard work, with the sea choppy and the undercurrents strong. They were using the *Bonaventure* as the target vessel, and her large keel loomed above Magennis's head.[1]

Magennis couldn't concentrate. He kept turning his head from side to side; conscious that somewhere out there was a predator. He felt very exposed and very frightened. This was an entirely different ball game from the cold but safe waters of Scotland. In fact, he was more scared than at any time since he had joined the midget submarine flotilla. Dealing with enemy warships was one thing, but tangling with potentially hostile wildlife was quite another. Something flashed in the corner of his visor – Magennis turned his head quickly. It was back. And it had company. Some distance beyond the shark, at the limit of his vision where the water grew dark and indistinct, Magennis could make out another cruising along in almost stately fashion. *Holy Mary!* Magennis thought. He seriously considered getting back into the W&D, closing the hatch and flooding down. But 14th Submarine Flotilla had stopped at Trinidad for a reason – so that the XEs and their crews, particularly the divers, could be tested in tropical waters, regardless of the local fauna.[2] As the first shark cruised by, Magennis realised that actually it wasn't all that big, certainly no maneater. In fact, it appeared to be losing interest in the strange black-clad man. Summoning up his courage, Magennis took his hand off the haft of his knife and made a conscious effort to get on with his job. He moved to the limpet mine carrier and pulled out the first of the six 200lb mines stowed inside. But his eyes still flicked nervously backwards and forwards.

*

On 21 February 1945 HMS *Bonaventure* had weighed anchor and departed from Port Bannatyne, Scotland, bound for points west. Trials and working up had been completed by New Year's Day and the first six XE-craft hoisted inboard.[3] The journey out to the Pacific theatre would encompass several stops and last eight weeks. The XE-men were buoyed up with dreams of plenty of targets; the harbours in the islands occupied by the Japanese were understood to be much less heavily defended than those of German-occupied Europe.[4]

When the *Bonaventure* set out, the Pacific War was at its height. General Douglas MacArthur had fulfilled his much-vaunted promise made to the Philippine people in 1942 when he had declared, 'I shall return'. On 9 January 1945 his forces had stormed ashore at Lingayen Gulf on the island of Luzon. By 3 February they were at the gates of Manila. Two days before the *Bonaventure* sailed, American forces had landed on the first piece of sovereign Japanese territory to be reached – the black volcanic island of Iwo Jima. A terrible and murderous battle had ensued.

For the XE-men, the voyage out was a pleasure cruise in comparison to the months of intensive training that they had endured in Scotland. Morale was sky-high. The men were full of enthusiasm for the important role they hoped to play in destroying the huge fleet of merchant ships taking ammunition and food to the Japanese forces on the islands and mainland of Asia and unloading in relatively lightly defended harbours. The battle cry of 14th Flotilla was 'Six a night!'[5] – the number of vessels they hoped to sink or immobilise. They had no idea of the political storm that they were sailing into.

Six XE-craft had been loaded aboard *Bonaventure*, with four placed inside a large 'house' that had been built over the vessel's after well deck to shield the top-secret weapons from prying eyes. Two more XEs had been placed in the ship's hold. Along with the submarines came sixteen Mark XX side cargoes packed with high explosives and their complex firing mechanisms. Tons of stores had been packed into every conceivable space, the entire ship almost bursting at the seams.[6] Every clock and firing mechanism was carefully tested before being stowed in a specially sealed compartment.[7]

In total, the *Bonaventure* sailed for the Far East with 92 officers and 540 men aboard. She joined a fast convoy off Liverpool, sailing at top speed through an area where German U-boats were still hunting, before joining more ships in the Bristol Channel. Thirty-six merchant ships with escorts then charged out into the Atlantic.[8]

At 3.00am on 25 February the *Bonaventure* received the signal to part company from the convoy and proceed independently to Porta Delgada in the Azores for fuel. By 4.00 the next afternoon the *Bonaventure* was on her way again, heading southwest at 15 knots, rolling heavily in strong trade winds and zigzagging to avoid U-boats.[9]

*

Tich Fraser was soon feeling guilty. While all around him the crew of the overcrowded *Bonaventure* worked hard, he and his fellow XE-men had nothing much to do. As the ship sailed into warmer climes after the Azores, the pleasure cruise atmosphere only intensified. XE-men could be seen lounging around on deck dressed only in shorts, working on their suntans. One day, when Fraser was leaning on the rail looking out to sea and ruminating upon the enforced idleness, Pat Westmacott, who was lying flat on the deck sunbathing, an unread newspaper over his face, stirred to life.

'Not to worry, Tich,' murmured Westmacott from beneath his newspaper. 'Our turn will come.'[10] And he was perfectly right. While the *Bonaventure*'s crew bustled about, the whole ship a hive of productive activity, they were not expected to go to war. The XE-men, on the other hand, could only look forward to hair-raising missions against a brutal enemy. The voyage west was the calm before the storm.

*

'Strong smell of dusky maiden with flowers in her hair,' yelled out the starboard lookout one evening as the *Bonaventure* entered the Caribbean Sea. The officer of the watch was about to strongly rebuke him when everyone's nostrils were assailed by a rich scent. It was the smell of tropical landfall somewhere ahead in the darkness.

'Thank you,' replied the officer of the watch, before the signal 'stop' was rung down to the engine room.

'Listen for breakers,' was the next order issued.

Captain Fell was already on the bridge and the navigating officer joined him. But it was a false alarm; they were still many miles from the nearest land.[11] The engines were restarted, a fix taken off the stars and a new route plotted towards Trinidad, the southernmost island in the Caribbean and less than seven miles off the northeast coast of Venezuela.

The *Bonaventure* arrived off Trinidad on 6 March 1945, anchoring twelve miles offshore in the Gulf of Paria.[12] All contact with the shore was strictly forbidden and to make sure that this was enforced, a pair of armed navy motor launches maintained a constant patrol around the perimeter of the 14th Submarine Flotilla's exercise area.[13] The ship's movements and plans remained top-secret, so Captain Fell could not risk allowing the crew or the XE-men ashore to fraternise with the locals. Tich Fraser described the situation, which was encountered several times during the voyage to the Pacific, as like being inside a train carriage stopped just outside the station. People on the platform could be seen and waved to but no contact was possible.[14]

Word reached 14th Submarine Flotilla shortly after arrival in Trinidad of a terrible tragedy back at HMS *Varbel II*. The six boats of the Flotilla's second division, numbered *XE-7* to *XE-12*, were busily working up preparatory to joining Tiny Fell and the rest of the flotilla aboard the *Bonaventure*. It was intended that the remaining six XE-craft would be sent to the Far East in three groups of two, stowed aboard American Liberty ships.

On 6 March *XE-11*, under the command of South African Lieutenant Aubrey Staples, with Sub-Lieutenant Bill Morrison as first lieutenant, was exercising with an ERA and two junior ratings from her passage crew, the idea being for the latter pair to gain more experience. But, in a disastrous replay of the collision between Max Shean's *XE-4* and an LST, Staples's boat was struck by a warship when it strayed out of its assigned exercise area.

The *XE-11* hit the bottom of Loch Striven at 180 feet. She was partially flooded and without power. The crew donned escape gear and waited until the submarine had completely filled with water and the pressure on the hatches was equalised. Then they tried to swim to the surface. Staples, Able Seaman Carroll and Stoker Higgins died.[15]

*

Aboard the *Bonaventure*, Lieutenant Terry-Lloyd's *XE-5* and Bruce Enzer's *XE-6* were hoisted out into the choppy Caribbean Sea so that the crews from all of the boats could conduct tropical trials. But the sea state, with constant swells and a running tide, made the training difficult. Neither XE-craft could safely lie alongside the *Bonaventure*. For the divers, practising placing limpet mines proved arduous and hazardous.[16] But one thing was discovered – the limpets lived up to their names. Placed on the *Bonaventure*'s bottom at the start of the exercise, they were all still firmly in place four days later.

The *XE-5* and *XE-6* each completed prolonged dives under hot-weather conditions, remaining submerged for 23 hours and seventeen hours respectively.[17] It was a taste of the conditions the crews could expect when they did it for real against the Japanese.

One afternoon the crew and the XE-men were finally permitted to go ashore, to a small, palm-fringed and uninhabited island controlled by the US Navy. After being cooped up aboard the ship for weeks, on a vessel totally lacking in exercise or entertainment facilities, being able to swim in the ocean, play football on the beach, stroll through the scrub or just sit and read a book was idyllic. Some men gathered coconuts to take back to the ship.[18] The American canteens and clubs were opened to the *Bonaventure*'s crew and passengers and were placed out of bounds to US personnel. Every crewman managed at least two hours ashore.[19]

Captain Fell received two important visitors while lying off Trinidad. Commodore Stewart, Senior British Naval Officer Trinidad, and Commodore Baughman, US Navy, spent a happy afternoon clambering in and out of Pat Westmacott's *XE-2*, which was uncrated on the *Bonaventure*'s deck for this purpose. Westmacott and his crew fielded questions expertly while Fell and his second-in-command Commander Derek Graham hovered in the background like anxious parents. Then, standing by the ship's rail, the dignitaries watched a diving demonstration by Bruce Enzer's *XE-6* into the choppy waters.[20] The top brass was suitably impressed and two more converts were added to 14th Flotilla's growing list of fans.

*

The *Bonaventure* passed through the Panama Canal on 19 March – 'a wonderful sight, it puts the Suez into the shade,' noted Magennis – and spent the night alongside a jetty at Balboa.[21] Fell went ashore for orders and ended up at a party in Old Panama City, eventually making it back to his ship at 5.00am.[22] Sailing a couple of hours later, the *Bonaventure* arrived at San Diego, home to a massive American naval base and a major hub of defence activity, on the 28th. But again, because of security precautions, Fell forbade shore leave. The *Bonaventure* was tied up in San Diego for two days while certain stores and a consignment of top-secret intelligence material were embarked, and word soon spread in southern California that a British ship was in residence.[23] Invitations from British stars in Hollywood flooded the *Bonaventure*'s wardroom, asking the crew to take the train 120 miles north to Los Angeles for parties and dinners in their honour. But the only reply that Fell and his officers could give was to tender their regrets.[24] As Fell noted drily, 'hearts were nearly broken.'[25]

Less formal invitations arrived daily from the main office of the Mattheson Shipping Line, located directly opposite the

Bonaventure's berth. The American office girls opened their windows and chatted with the frustrated British sailors. They scrawled messages to the crew on the office windows using their red lipstick, asking the British sailors to meet them at such-and-such a place at such-and-such a time.[26] For the single men among the crew, for most of whom this was their first experience of America, it was a torture that continued until the *Bonaventure* sailed. Morale plummeted, and Max Shean was reminded of Admiral Nelson's dictum: 'Harbours rot good ships and good men.'[27]

On 31 March the *Bonaventure* sailed up the West Coast past Los Angeles and then set a direct course for Hawaii. Heavy weather for two days threatened to sweep the false house that concealed four of the XEs into the sea, but it somehow held.[28]

Pearl Harbor was a different matter entirely from the previous ports of call. The *Bonaventure* had entered a secure naval base and Fell finally granted shore leave. The locals were friendly and the crew and the XE-men were sent to a US Navy rest camp for two days R&R at Scotland Bay on the other side of Oahu.[29] There were girls to chat up, photo opportunities under swaying palms and homemade hooch to imbibe.[30]

America was the land of plenty; a far cry from the austere world of cold Britain with its rationing, blackouts and bombsites, and this was graphically illustrated for the British sailors when they visited the service canteen at Pearl Harbor. 'It was like Christmas again,' recalled Shean. All kinds of high-quality articles were available at very low prices. None of the Britons had seen such plenty for five years.[31]

While the XE-men rested, their redoubtable commanding officer was summoned to a meeting with Fleet Admiral Chester W. Nimitz's staff at Honolulu. Sixty-year-old Nimitz was commander-in-chief of one of the three operational areas created by the British and American Joint Chiefs of Staff in order to coordinate operations against the Japanese. Nimitz's fiefdom, Pacific Ocean Areas, encompassed, as the name suggested, most of the Pacific Ocean and island groups. The powerful US Seventh Fleet and its attached Marine Corps divisions were the main offensive weapons available to Nimitz, and his efforts were directed towards mainland Japan in concert with Operation Starvation, the US Army Air Force's hugely successful strategic bombing campaign against Japanese cities.

General MacArthur commanded South West Pacific Area, encompassing the Philippines, Borneo, the Netherlands East Indies (excluding Sumatra), East Timor, Australia, Papua New Guinea and the western part of the British Solomon Islands. Lord Mountbatten, Supreme Allied Commander South East Asia, controlled the third area, encompassing all operations in India, Burma, Ceylon, Malaya, Sumatra, Thailand and French Indochina. Though it appeared an equal three-way division, in reality the two American commands dominated the relationship.

The XE-craft of 14th Submarine Flotilla had originally been destined for Nimitz's theatre, but there was a problem. Captain Fell's visit to Nimitz's staff at Pearl Harbor was a disaster.

The Seventh Fleet Headquarters was in the process of transferring forward to Guam, and Fell found the Americans direct and to the point. Fell hadn't counted on Nimitz's antipathy to the little XE-craft submarines, born out of unfamiliarity with the technology and little idea of their operational value, an attitude that had started with Admiral Ernest J. King, head of the US Navy, after he had viewed the very first X-craft in 1942.

After Fell had pleaded his case to Nimitz's representatives, the Americans told him that his XE-craft appeared to be similar to those used by the Japanese, and basically no better than suicide boats. Fell, his face flushed with anger, held his tongue. The Americans added that XE-craft were too dangerous for their crews and, to cap it all, 'inappropriate' weapons for a civilised nation like Great Britain to use.[32] When Fell was eventually permitted to speak he vigorously defended his little flotilla and its equipment, pointing out the X-craft's success in Norway against the *Tirpitz* and the Bergen targets.

'Would that be the operation where half of your men were killed and the rest were taken prisoner?' asked one American officer quizzically.

'Well, that's a slight exaggeration, sir,' muttered Fell, but before he could continue the senior American officer cut him off.

'No, I'm sorry Captain. We're going to have to carefully consider what to do with your flotilla. We'll not be responsible for throwing away lives needlessly at this point in the war on operations that can be more economically completed by our own aircraft or surface warships.' The American paused. 'It just "wouldn't be cricket", isn't that how you guys put it? Admiral Nimitz has already discussed this matter with your Admiral Fraser.'[33] Admiral Sir Bruce Fraser had recently been appointed to command Churchill's attempt to shoehorn a British naval presence into the vast assemblage of American warships and marines taking on the Japanese in the North Pacific. Christened the 'British Pacific Fleet', it had already ruffled Mountbatten's feathers, as the First Sea Lord, Admiral Sir Andrew Cunningham, no friend of Mountbatten's, had diverted many of the aircraft carriers needed for British operations in southeast Asia to Fraser's new show force instead of to Eastern Fleet. The British Pacific Fleet would be serving under American command, in an American theatre and pursuing primarily American strategic goals. To many, it seemed to indicate just how far Britain's Asian star had fallen in the three years since the surrender of Singapore.

'Take your ship to the Ellice Islands, Captain,' The American said to Fell. 'We will send word of Admiral Nimitz's decision.'[34]

Fell was dismissed. He was crushed. Months of hard work were now threatened by what appeared to be American intransigence and ignorance. Though the Americans had agreed at the Quebec Conference to send the 14th Flotilla to the Pacific, now that they had actually arrived they were not to be permitted to assist Mountbatten. The Americans had a poor opinion of X-craft technology and seemed determined to shelve the whole flotilla for the duration. How could Fell face his men and tell them this news? Morale would be destroyed when they realised that they had been judged surplus to requirements.

Though no senior American naval officer had said it out loud, it was suspected, rightly as it turned out, that the Americans didn't want the British muscling in on 'their bird'. The defeat of Japan was to be an American victory. It was also later suspected by members of 14th Flotilla that the Americans were more than a little irked to discover that the British had an ingenious weapon that they didn't themselves possess.[35]

But the one thing Admiral Nimitz and his staff didn't know about William Fell (whereas the men who served under him knew it only too well) was that he was not the type to take a beating lying down. In the car on the way back to the *Bonaventure*'s berth, Fell had already determined that, if Nimitz decided not to use his unit, someone would give him a mission worthy of his flotilla's talents and that he would not rest until he had secured it. He would, if necessary, hawk his wares around the three Far Eastern commands like a travelling salesman until he secured a customer.

On 11 April the *Bonaventure* departed from Pearl Harbor. The tension felt by Fell and his men was slightly relieved when they crossed the Equator on the 16th. A 'crossing of the line' ceremony was laid on. A canvas swimming pool was rigged up on deck amidships. Captain Fell was appointed King Neptune, with other officers as Queen Amphitrite, Clerk of the Court, Barber, Physician and attendant Bears.[36] Anyone unable to produce a certificate proving that he had already been initiated into the Comradeship of the Deep was summoned before King Neptune, tried, found guilty, shaved, forced to eat a soap pill and finally given a good ducking by the Bears. Resistance was futile. One man, however, managed to fight the Bears off. Ken Briggs, the big, physically powerful Aussie diver on *XE-4*, held the Bears at bay for an impressive five minutes before they finally got a soap pill into him.[37]

*

Funafuti in the Ellice Islands consisted of a large lagoon around which were dotted 29 tropical islets. With its white beaches, coconut palms, and thin patches of scrubland standing just a few feet above sea level around the azure lagoon, this tropical paradise had become an unlikely way station for Allied ships heading for the war zone. The *Bonaventure* chugged into the huge lagoon on 18 April. If 14th Submarine Flotilla was going to become operational its next destination would be Manus in the Admiralty Islands north of Japanese-occupied Papua New Guinea. An Allied naval base had been established there in Seeadler Harbour. If the flotilla was not required, then the *Bonaventure* would be directed to Brisbane in Australia. Fell was instructed to stand by for a coded radio message from Nimitz's staff in Oahu.

Frustratingly, the first coded message from Pearl Harbor was corrupted and illegible. Fell was forced to wait 24 hours before a repeated signal finally came through. But when the clerk handed him the signal flimsy he cursed loudly after quickly scanning it: 14th Submarine Flotilla was ordered to proceed to Brisbane.[38] Nimitz had decided that the British XE-craft were not going to play a part in defeating Japan after all.

The rather intransigent American attitude continued at Funafuti, where the US Navy initially refused to even refuel the *Bonaventure*. Only with the intercession of Lieutenant-Commander Peter Phipps, commanding the Royal New Zealand Navy's 25th Minesweeping Flotilla in the Solomons, did the attitude change. Thirty-six-year-old Phipps was one of few foreigners awarded one of America's highest military honours, the Navy Cross. In 1943, as captain of the HMNZS *Moa*, Phipps had sunk a Japanese submarine after an incredible battle, securing a Bar to his DSC and the

American medal. Phipps' intervention secured *Bonaventure* sufficient fuel to reach Brisbane.[39] The truculent American attitude was, however, an ominous sign for Fell and his men.

*

Though there was perhaps a trace of sour grapes in the US Navy's refusal to usefully employ 14th Submarine Flotilla in the North Pacific, there was a strong element of practicality backing up Nimitz's decision to dispense with their services. The strategic picture had changed dramatically between the *Bonaventure* leaving Scotland in late February 1945 and finally dropping anchor in Brisbane on 27 April. The Pacific submarine war was undeniably drawing to a close.

In Mountbatten's SEAC, Allied submarines had started running out of worthwhile targets by January 1945. In October 1944, due to horrific losses caused by Allied submarines and aircraft, the Japanese had abandoned the convoy route from Singapore to Rangoon, Burma. Only strategically vital oil shipments continued from Sumatra to Singapore, Saigon, Formosa and Japan. During the last four months of 1944 the Japanese had lost 187 ships to Allied submarines. That was over 834,500 tons sent to the bottom.[40] American submarines were now mostly operating north of Borneo, around the Philippines, Indochina and Japan. The US Eighth Flotilla, based at Fremantle in Australia, sank hardly anything. They were eager to move north to the Philippines and join in the killing.

By April 1945 the Eighth Flotilla had left Australia, replaced by the British 4th Submarine Flotilla, transferred from the Eastern Fleet at Trincomalee in Ceylon. But in the north the number of targets continued to dwindle – in the first three months of 1945 US submarines sank only 60 Japanese ships for 200,200 tons. Japan's merchant marine had been reduced to a quarter of what it had been in 1941. What was left fearfully hugged the Japanese coastline.

One small chance remained for 14th Flotilla and its midget submarines – the kind of mission that the X-craft were already famous for. The last Japanese capital ships still afloat consisted of five battleships and a handful of aircraft carriers hidden in coves in Japan's Inland Sea. They had little fuel left and were not expected to sortie against the Americans. Before Fell had left the Seventh Fleet's offices at Pearl Harbor he had pleaded with the staff to use his XEs for what they had been specifically designed to do – to penetrate enemy anchorages and blow up capital ships. He had suggested launching his XEs against the concealed battleships and aircraft carriers in the Japanese Home Islands. It would be a win-win situation for the Americans, for no diversion of their own resources would be necessary – the flotilla of T-class British submarines of 4th Flotilla had already been ordered to Australia and they could tow the XEs to Japan.[41] The risk would be entirely British. But when Nimitz's staff referred somewhat caustically to the *Tirpitz* operation and labelled the XEs 'suicide craft', they were not alone in making this comparison. Most senior American officers considered the XEs to be foolishly dangerous and any operations using them against the remaining Japanese warships in the Inland Sea grossly wasteful of lives when the war was almost over.[42]

Had the *Bonaventure* and her cargo arrived in the Far East just a year earlier the Americans would probably have happily employed them against the still-active Japanese fleet, particularly the anchorage at Lingga. The Lingga Roads, a secure anchorage between Lingga Island and Singkep south of Singapore, was where the Japanese kept their southern striking force, close to a reliable source of fuel oil in Sumatra. But Japan's last really dangerous vessel, the super battleship *Yamato*, had been sunk by US carrier aircraft on 7 April 1945 while the *Bonaventure* was still on her way from Hawaii to Brisbane and the rest of the striking force dispersed into hiding.

*

HMS *Bonaventure* tied up in Brisbane at 3.00am on 27 April. She had steamed an impressive 14,888 miles, but it had begun to look as though it had all been for nothing. Morale among the XE-men was disastrously low: 'our tails were right down, in black despair'[43] was how Max Shean put it.

While the XE-men had been in transit, the Americans had made further gains. On 3 March, MacArthur's forces had recaptured Manila, the capital of the Philippines. On the night of 9–10 March the USAAF had levelled fifteen square miles of Tokyo and Nimitz's forces had landed on Okinawa on 1 April. President Roosevelt had died on 12 April, and his successor, Harry S. Truman, pressed his generals and admirals to end the war in the Pacific quickly.

The means of achieving this was taking shape far away in the New Mexico desert. There, in total secrecy, the United States had sunk $2 billion into developing a new kind of bomb, a bomb it was hoped would bring the Japanese swiftly to their knees and bring the boys back home in time for Christmas.

CHAPTER SIX

Zipper

'That night ... I dined with Admiral Fife, and he made me feel that I had known and served under him for years.'

—Captain William Fell, 14th Submarine Flotilla

Captain Fell's eyes widened as his jeep came to a jarring halt. 'Good grief,' he muttered under his breath as the Japanese soldiers turned and stared at him. Their eyes were full of undisguised loathing, and, thought Fell, contempt. Fell stepped down from the jeep with the American general and his escort and approached the rudimentary wire enclosure.

'How many are there?' asked Fell, his shoes slipping on the muddy path.

'One hundred and thirty, Captain,' replied the general cheerfully, dressed like all of the other Americans in olive green fatigues and a helmet with camouflage cover. 'Took the bastards prisoner this morning.'[1]

Fell surveyed the scene, fascinated to be face-to-face at last with the dreaded Japanese. The enemy POWs stood around or squatted on their haunches in the mud, their tan or green uniforms filthy and ragged. Most had shaved heads or closely cropped black hair under soft peaked caps or steel helmets adorned with a yellow star. Red and gold rank tabs adorned the collars of captured officers and NCOs; their sword frogs hung empty, their prized samurai swords having been surrendered.

Fell was struck by how small the Japanese were – an army

of children next to the hulking figures of their US Marine Corps guards, who menacingly fingered Thompson sub-machine guns. The Marines looked as though they would happily kill every single prisoner without a thought, and after the appallingly bloody battles on the island of Peleliu it was understandable.

Fell looked at the Japanese, the soldiers who had been built up into a race of jungle-fighting supermen in the imagination of the Allied troops. Most of them looked dejected or ill, many wearing the shame of capture on their thin faces. Others stared back at him defiantly. Fell knew that given a chance, these Japanese would kill him in an instant. They didn't care whether they lived or died. In their military culture, being made a prisoner was a living death.

Fell was glad that he had seen the Japanese prisoners, but also a little unsettled by the experience. For he knew that he was intending to send his own men deep behind Japanese lines. He had taken the measure of the enemy troops that he had seen. They looked like formidable foes even in defeat. That much was obvious from the careful way in which the Americans guarded them. Peleliu was a hellhole, one of the worst places Fell had ever had the misfortune to visit, a stinking island of death. He would be glad to leave and be on his way again, continuing on his journey to the Philippines.

*

Though the news had appeared to be uniformly gloomy and unpromising for 14th Submarine Flotilla, a tiny glimmer of hope, at the time totally unbeknown to Captain Fell, had long since flickered to life in Kandy, Ceylon. There, on 3 February 1945, while HMS *Bonaventure* was preparing to leave Scotland, among the white-painted colonial buildings and immaculate gardens teeming with birds and insects, a message had arrived from London. It was addressed to Lord Mountbatten. He received new directions from the Chiefs of Staff instructing him to liberate the rest of Burma at the earliest date *and* to then liberate Malaya and open the Straits of Malacca.[2] Mountbatten was delighted – it was what he had been pressing for since his appointment as Supreme Commander. The only question that remained in his mind was whether he would be able to gather sufficient forces to make such an operation feasible. Mountbatten had Churchill's firm backing but, like Captain Fell, he was to find that his plans were being frustrated by politics and hampered by dissension among supposed allies.

*

When the *Bonaventure* had arrived in Brisbane on 27 April the crew had discovered that there were only two good things about the city. Firstly, the pubs were open – and Captain Fell granted everyone some well-earned shore leave. Unfortunately, the pubs didn't have very much beer. And, secondly, the local shops were full of the kinds of things most Britons hadn't seen for years, particularly fresh fruit.[3] But still, it was an awfully long way to come for a banana.

For the Australian members of 14th Submarine Flotilla, arriving home on the way to war was a slightly surreal experience. These men had already answered the Empire's call and gone to Britain in the early years of the war. Now they were passing through the familiar world of their pre-war lives headed towards points unknown.

When Max Shean went ashore in Brisbane he immediately rang his parents in Perth, on the other side of the continent. They had only been able to communicate by letter for years, so hearing his mother's voice after so long was strange. He felt emotionally disjointed. He was home in the land of his birth but he wouldn't have time to travel all the way to Perth to see his parents. That would have to wait until the end of the war. And his new wife remained in England, half a world away. This unsettled feeling was experienced by not only the Antipodeans among 14th Flotilla but also by many of the Britons. The feeling was brought on by being in Australia, whose cities looked so British, and whose people were so similar in personality, tastes and sense of humour.

In the meantime, word had arrived that 14th Submarine Flotilla was to be placed under the command of Rear-Admiral James Fife, an American officer based in the recently liberated Philippines who had responsibility for all submarine operations in the US Seventh Fleet.

Captain Fell had remained deeply unhappy. He positively writhed with frustration at what he perceived as the complete waste of talent caused by apparent American shortsightedness. His talented XE-men and their amazing submersibles deserved better than twiddling their thumbs in this backwater of an Australian posting, albeit a friendly one. While everyone else was enjoying some leave in the welcoming environment of Brisbane, Fell had decided to act. Putting aside the Americans for a moment, he had decided to try to persuade one of his own commanders to find employment for 14th Flotilla. Churchill's motto was 'action this day', and Fell took a leaf out of the Prime Minister's book.

*

Fell had boarded a twin-engined DC3 Dakota and flew down to Sydney, headquarters of the British Pacific Fleet, to meet its redoubtable commander, Admiral Sir Bruce Fraser.

Winston Churchill had been against the British Pacific Fleet when the Chiefs of Staff had first raised the idea. He thought that the Fleet, though large, would nonetheless be dwarfed by the enormous US Pacific Fleet, making Britain look even more like America's junior partner in the war against Japan. He also believed that the Americans would not welcome the British trying to muscle in on 'their patch'. In this opinion Churchill was probably right, as the US Chief of Naval Operations, Admiral Ernest J. King, tried to block the proposal. Churchill backed Mountbatten, believing that Britain was better served by retaking Burma, particularly the port of Rangoon, and then striking at Malaya and Singapore, in the process being seen to liberate three British colonies rather than having the Americans do it for them.

The crew of the original X-craft submarine *X-24* photographed on the bridge of the towing submarine HMS *Sceptre* after their unsuccessful mission to sink the German floating dock at Bergen, Norway, 15 April 1944. They would all play important roles in the XE-craft missions in the Far East. Pictured, from left to right: Sub-Lieutenant Joe Brooks, who was appointed first lieutenant of *XE-4* until his replacement by Ben Kelly; Lieutenant Max Shean, later commanding officer of *XE-4*; Engine Room Artificer 4th Class Vernon 'Ginger' Coles, engineer on *XE-4*; and Sub-Lieutenant Frank Ogden, who was passage crew skipper for *XE-3* during Operation Struggle, July 1945.

Some of the officers and men of 14th Submarine Flotilla photographed aboard the depot ship HMS *Bonaventure* in Scotland, late 1944.

HMS *XE-1* surfaced during training in Scotland. Lieutenant Jack Smart stands on the casing gripping the raised air induction trunk, or *schnorkel*, for balance.

An XE-craft approaches the practice anti-submarine boom in north-west Scotland before submerging to allow the diver to cut through the net.

Lieutenant Max Shean, the Australian commanding officer of HMS *XE-4*.

Captain William Fell (*right*), commanding officer of
14th Submarine Flotilla, with his second-in-command,
Lieutenant-Commander Derek Brown, HMS *Bonaventure*, 1945.

Acting Leading Seaman James 'Mick' Magennis (*left*), *XE-3*'s diver, with his commanding officer Lieutenant Ian 'Tich' Fraser.

The crew of HMS *XE-5* photographed in Scotland before departure for the Far East. From left to right: Sub-Lieutenant Beadon Dening, Lieutenant Herbert 'Pat' Westmacott, Sub-Lieutenant Dennis Jarvis and Engine Room Artificer 4th Class Clifford Greenwood.

HMS *Bonaventure* passing beneath Sydney Harbour Bridge in Australia.

The Davis Submarine Escape Apparatus (DSEA), an early rebreather modified for use by commando divers.

The commanding officers of the four XE-craft submarines
used in Operations Struggle, Foil and Sabre.
From left to right: Lieutenant Jack Smart, *XE-1*; Lieutenant Tich Fraser, *XE-3*;
Lieutenant Pat Westmacott, *XE-5*; and Lieutenant Max Shean, *XE-4*.

Churchill lost the fight over the creation of the British Pacific Fleet when the Chiefs of Staff threatened to resign en masse if he blocked them. They believed that the new fleet would strengthen British influence, and some in the US high command wanted the fleet to help finish off the Japanese quickly before public opinion at home turned against a protracted campaign and the high casualties that would surely follow. The Chiefs failed to see that by diverting British naval power away from Mountbatten's theatre, they were making it less likely that Britain would singlehandedly rebuild her Asian empire, making Britain a second-class power in the region in the postwar period.

President Roosevelt had finally settled the arguments over the British Pacific Fleet when he went over Admiral King's head and graciously accepted British help in the campaign against the Japanese mainland. The benefits for postwar America were obvious and Roosevelt's successor, Truman, continued this amicable policy.

Fifty-seven-year-old Sir Bruce Fraser, who was developing an excellent working relationship with Admiral Nimitz and his American superiors, could not help Captain Fell when he came calling, accompanied by an old friend from submarines, Commander G.S.P. Davies. Davies was Staff Officer (Operations) to the new Flag Officer Submarines, Rear-Admiral Sir George Creasy, whose headquarters was in London. Admiral Fraser had simply repeated Nimitz's mantra that the targets that the XE-craft had been designed to sink were no longer available. Instead, Fraser had ordered Fell to meet the British Pacific Fleet's chief of administration, Vice Admiral Charles Daniel, in Melbourne to discuss how the *Bonaventure* could be usefully employed in the 'fleet train'. Fell was horrified. If Fraser was to have his way the XEs would be offloaded and placed into storage and the *Bonaventure*, a dedicated midget submarine depot ship full of highly skilled crewmen, would be forced to become a simple transport vessel reduced to hauling supplies to the British Pacific Fleet's aircraft carriers and battleships fighting off Okinawa.

Fell's protests had fallen upon deaf ears in Sydney. But he was not completely outsmarted. Gleaned from the intelligence material that the *Bonaventure* had taken aboard at San Diego was, believed Fell and his second-in-command Derek Graham, the kernel of a mission. Fell changed tack and decided to lay his idea on the line.

'Hong Kong, sir, is where my boys could do a lot of damage,' said Fell enthusiastically to Admiral Fraser.

'Go on,' said Fraser, his face expressionless.

Fell explained that Victoria Harbour in Hong Kong was full of Japanese merchant ships. 'A couple of my XEs could make short work of half a dozen Jap transports, sir,' said Fell. He wanted Fraser's permission to work up a plan and present it to Admiral Fife in the Philippines. Though dubious, Fraser acquiesced.[4] He was impressed by Fell's salesmanship and determination and saw no harm in letting him try a few doors, even though he personally believed that they would all be shut firmly in his face.

*

With each passing day the jungle campaign in Burma sped towards a British victory. Following the important battles of Kohima and Imphal in late 1944, the Japanese army in Burma was in full retreat. General Sir William Slim's Fourteenth Army was hot on its heels. The strategically vital city of Mandalay had fallen on 20 March 1945 and by mid-April British forces were only 300 miles from the Burmese capital, Rangoon. Capturing this port would provide the British with a major supply base to strike at the remaining Japanese forces in the country and perhaps also springboard Mountbatten across the border into Thailand and even Malaya. The sooner Japanese resistance in Burma could be crushed the more likely it was that Mountbatten would launch an assault on Malaya and eventually the great prize of Singapore.

The British were determined that His Majesty's forces would liberate Singapore, their greatest pre-war naval base in Asia. It was a matter of national pride after the humiliating surrender in February 1942. Such an undertaking was going to need the support of every available British unit in the theatre, particularly now that the best naval assets had been hived off into Admiral Fraser's new British Pacific Fleet.

Mountbatten's plan was christened Operation Zipper. It was to be Mountbatten's Overlord,[5] his D-Day, when Britain would strike decisively at her most important colony outside of India and simultaneously place Britain in a much stronger position vis-à-vis the strategic balance in the Pacific. With his background in Combined Operations in Europe, Mountbatten knew he needed a bold strategy against the Japanese that would also bring the added bonus of operational equality with the United States.

The British identified two strategically important ports on Malaya's west coast as possible future landing sites, each possessing large beaches. The first, Port Swettenham, was, after Singapore, the most important port in Malaya, located only 24 miles from the capital, Kuala Lumpur. The second target, Port Dickson, lay almost 55 miles south-east of Kuala Lumpur, and therefore closer to the main target, Singapore.

The plan would involve seizing a beachhead or beachheads, possibly both ports, and using them as a springboard for an attack on Singapore. Mountbatten intended on landing 182,000 men in the first seven weeks after the invasion, along with 18,000 vehicles and half a million tons of supplies in an operation to rival the American efforts at Iwo Jima and Okinawa. He would then advance south and assault Singapore in the same way the Japanese had in 1942, by making assault crossings of the mile-wide Johor Strait onto Singapore's northern shore.

Mountbatten expected to encounter the usual stiff and suicidal Japanese resistance that British forces were already well used to in Burma. The Japanese had identified Malaya's west coast as vulnerable to just the sort of operation that Mountbatten intended to launch, and they had taken steps to create a strong defence. Lieutenant-General Teijo Ishiguro's 29th Army, consisting of one infantry division and four independent brigades totalling 26,000 men, had been created in January 1944. They were well trained and well equipped and psychologically prepared to fight to the death.

Singapore Island was garrisoned by the Imperial Army's 26th Mixed Brigade and, due to the importance of the captured British naval base to the Japanese, a very large number of well-armed Imperial Navy Landing Troops from the 10th (Singapore) Special Base Unit, 7th and 101st Guard Units. But as Mountbatten was shortly to discover, the Japanese also had a couple of formidable aces up their sleeves if the British were considering assaulting Singapore from the north. These were to come as a very nasty shock to the Zipper planners.

*

Captain Fell's journey out to meet Rear-Admiral Fife at Subic Bay in the Philippines had turned into a marathon of endurance. On 15 May, HMS *Bonaventure* had arrived in Townsville, Queensland. The big ship occupied most of the quay space and was met enthusiastically by the locals. As a party kicked off that night, Fell, accompanied by Commander Davies, had been driven to the local aerodrome and had boarded a DC3. The plane was packed with sharp pieces of machinery and had no seats. The two British officers had nothing to eat and, dressed only in naval shirts and shorts, had suffered in the bitter cold as the plane cruised at 11,000 feet.[6] Fell carried with him detailed plans for the proposed XE-craft attack on Hong Kong.[7]

The DC3 had flown on until noon over heavy cloud cover and the pilot had a job finding a hole to come down through at recently liberated Milne Bay, Papua New Guinea. The plane spent only an hour on the ground refuelling before taking off in stifling heat, affording the passengers a breathtaking view over the mountains.[8]

Fell's DC3 had touched down at 4.30pm at Manus in the Admiralty Islands. Met by an American jeep, the two officers had been driven to their accommodation, given meal tickets and told where the beer was kept. A meal was taken on well-scrubbed tables alongside 1,000 US other ranks and 200 officers.[9]

The following day Fell and Davies had been airborne again, heading for Biak off the coast of New Guinea at 6,000 feet, passing by the formidable Owen Stanley Range. Below, fighting continued between Australian and Japanese forces, though Fell saw only some ground fires from the plane. At noon, Fell had landed at Wewak, the plane crunching along a black coral strip.

Fell saw impromptu film tents, ice cream, doughnuts and crates of tinned SPAM, comforts for the troops. His plane was met by smiling American Red Cross girls carrying cartons of reviving sweet, tepid syrup and packets of dry biscuits or tins of warm and runny SPAM. The airstrip was battered and scarred, littered with the wrecks of Japanese planes and the occasional American one, unceremoniously pushed clear of the runways by US Army bulldozers. Trees in the surrounding area clearly showed the effects of artillery fire and aerial bombing, while large khaki tent encampments had sprung up next to enormous piles of oil drums and packing crates. It rained frequently, hardly alleviating the enervating humidity, turning the airstrip into a muddy affair.[10]

At 1.00pm Fell had been off again, landing next at Peleliu in the Palau Islands. Here the conditions had been even worse than at Wewak. The whole island stank. The latrines were 'unspeakable', the food 'unpleasant', and the tent where Fell and Davies were billeted 'pretty nauseating'.[11] Fortunately, an American general had asked the two Britons to dine with him. It was after this that Fell was taken to view the recently captured Japanese prisoners and watch them being interrogated.

Fell and Davies were shaken awake at 3.00am ready for their flight, which frustratingly didn't leave Peleliu till 7.00am. Packed aboard a DC3 that was full of boxes of sanitary towels, Fell and Davies endured another seven hours in the air without seats or comforts. Once they had disembarked at Leyte in the Philippines they were met by several harassed American officers who tried to secure for them onward transportation to Subic Bay. The Britons were forced to stand by and witness several heated arguments until they were given seats on a Dakota that was full of recently arrived US Army colonels and their mountain of baggage.[12]

As his plane circled over Manila, Fell could see the devastation caused by the Japanese resistance in the city. Fell's DC3 touched down in a cloud of dust and flies at Nichols Field. Fell and Davies could find no one to answer their question of how to get to Subic Bay. Eventually, five of the American colonels, Fell and Davies were piled on to a jeep and driven for miles through what remained of Manila.[13]

After a fruitless search for the British Consul, Fell and Davies pitched up at US Navy Headquarters, a bombed-out and largely floorless skyscraper. A thousand American sailors were preparing a rudimentary supper of SPAM, doughnuts and ice cream before watching a film and the two Britons joined them. It proved almost impossible to freshen up as the building's only water supply consisted of a single tap on the road in front of the building. Sleep was also largely impossible as constant loud explosions rocked the skyscraper all night long as US Army engineers detonated Japanese booby traps and abandoned ordnance while growling bulldozers worked under artificial lights clearing the streets of debris from collapsed buildings. At the same time the grim business of clearing up the dead was well under way – the bloated corpses were shovelled into mass graves without ceremony.[14]

The next morning a weary Fell and Davies boarded a US Navy landing craft that took them out through a maze of sunken ships, past Corregidor Island and on to Subic Bay, which was reached in late afternoon. Waiting to meet them was a very welcome sight

– the Royal Navy submarine tender HMS *Maidstone*, base ship for the 8th Submarine Flotilla. Her skipper, Captain Lance Shadwell, greeted Fell and Davies warmly and had them conveyed below for a cup of tea and a chance to shower and change before the *Maidstone*'s motor boat took them all over to meet Rear-Admiral Fife.[15]

*

'I fear your trip to see me has been a wasted one, Captain,' announced Rear-Admiral James Fife, the 48-year-old commander of submarines in the US Seventh Fleet, shifting in his rattan chair on the pleasant veranda of his headquarters building. Fife, who bore a slight resemblance to Humphrey Bogart, though with a pair of steel-framed spectacles, lit a cigarette and looked across at the rather crestfallen faces of his British visitors.

'But, sir, I just know that my chaps can be of use to you, real use,' replied Captain Fell. His two companions, Commander Davies and Captain Shadwell, shifted uncomfortably in their seats.

'I could have used your guys two months ago, but the big picture has unfortunately changed,' said Fife, sipping from a white porcelain coffee cup. 'The targets are just not around any more.'[16] Fife replaced his cup in its saucer with a clink and leaned back in his creaking chair.

The news was hard for Fell to take in. He lived and breathed 14th Submarine Flotilla. He was becoming almost frantic in his efforts to prevent it being broken up. The one thing that he was determined on was that his flotilla would not end the war running stores – that would have been the supreme indignity.[17]

The air was sultry and heavily scented with the flowers growing in the garden. Fell and the other British officers wore tropical kit: a white shirt, white shorts and black shoes with rank lace on their shoulder boards. Fife, in contrast, was dressed in army khakis, his senior rank indicated by two stars on each collar of his open-necked shirt. All of the men's medal ribbons provided a flash of colour above their left breast pockets, indicating long service and experience. An orderly had set out a tray containing a coffee pot and cups on the cane table between them. Insects and birds chirruped and buzzed in the warm air. It was easy to forget that there was a war on in such bucolic surroundings.

The Hong Kong operation had appeared perfectly sound to Admiral Fraser, hence his support. The plan was for one XE-craft to enter Victoria Harbour by the Mun Passage while another would simultaneously creep in through the mined East Lamma Passage. 'Numerous merchant shipping targets are reported to be present in Hong Kong daily,'[18] read a British Naval Intelligence summary confidently.

Fell had also decided to expand the plan by including Amoy, a busy Chinese port city on the Formosa Strait.[19] After all, his flotilla contained *six* XE-craft, so finding useful employment for all of them was a must. At Amoy it was planned to use one XE-craft to penetrate the harbour. Three or four Japanese merchant ships, including one tanker, were reported to be present daily. An additional advantage to the Amoy operation, in comparison with that at Hong Kong, was a complete lack of anti-submarine booms and defensive minefields. Apart from a few Japanese motor patrol boats the place was wide open. 'The two operations are considered to be both profitable and reasonably easy,'[20] wrote Naval Intelligence to Fell.

But Fife, after listening to Fell, had immediately stymied both operations, informing Fell that the 'hot intelligence' that he had based his plans on was now more than eight weeks out of date and the number of Japanese ships in both ports had dwindled.[21] It would be a waste of time and resources bringing only a minimal return, and, perhaps more importantly, a waste of British lives if anything went wrong.

As for the idea of using the XE-craft against the remaining

vessels of the Imperial Navy in the Japanese Home Islands, that idea, said Fife, was also sadly unrealistic. The Imperial Japanese Navy had practically ceased to be a serious threat to the Allies since the Battle of Leyte Gulf, appropriately nicknamed the 'Great Marianas Turkey Shoot' by the Americans, in late October 1944 when the remaining surface fleet had lost four aircraft carriers, three battleships, ten cruisers and most of its experienced naval aviators. It was certainly true that what remained of the once-formidable Imperial fleet was bottled up in harbours from Singapore to Japan. But whether these ships were worth the risk of attacking was another matter entirely. American doctrine during the so-called 'Island Hopping Campaign' was to simply bypass pockets of Japanese resistance and allow them to wither on the vine, cut off from relief or resupply. Concomitantly, the surviving Japanese capital ships could be similarly left to wither in port.

But Fell refused to give up. He, Fife, Davies and Shadwell talked for three hours, or rather Fell did most of the talking while Fife listened patiently, smoking and sipping coffee. Fell carefully explained the history and development of the X-craft, how they had been used successfully in Norway against the *Tirpitz* and the floating dry dock at Bergen. How they had helped to guide in the massive invasion fleet during the Normandy landings, of the competence and training of the crews and of how useful employment should be found for them in the Far East. And of the criminal waste if no jobs were forthcoming. Eventually, the captain fell silent. He had run out of arguments. But he had, through his eloquence and enthusiasm, gained a new friend.

Above his row of medal ribbons James Fife wore a gold badge that depicted a dolphin flanking the bow and conning tower of a submarine. The Admiral was a submariner just like Fell, and before the Japanese attack on Pearl Harbor he had even served three tours in British submarines in 1940–41, seconded from the US Navy. He was an admirer of the famous British fighting spirit and

CHAPTER SEVEN

Number Disconnected

'Long and gloomy faces are in fashion.'

—Captain William Fell, 14th Submarine Flotilla

'Shall we have a go then?' asked Tich Fraser. The *XE-3* was at the surface in Hervey Bay, 180 miles north of Brisbane. A warm tropical sun beat down on the submarine's rough black casing. David Carey, Fraser's first lieutenant, grinned. 'Rather,' he said excitedly.

'Okay,' replied Fraser. 'Off you go then.' Carey, dressed in blue working overalls, quickly pulled on a diving suit over his clothes and fitted a DSEA rig to his chest as Fraser submerged the boat into the azure sea. Carey clambered into the W&D and closed the door firmly, giving Fraser a little wave through the tiny inspection window. Little did Fraser realise that he would never speak to Carey again.[1]

*

The long voyage out from Scotland to Australia had taken the edge off the submarine crews' skills. On 14 May 1945, while Captain Fell was in Sydney discussing operations with Admiral Fraser's staff, the *Bonaventure*, under the command of Fell's deputy Commander Derek Graham, had set sail from Brisbane and the XE-craft were finally all uncrated. The engineering crews had gone to work testing all systems and readying the submarines for the water while the operational and towing crews prepared to undertake more realistic training exercises in the Pacific waters off Australia.

While Captain Fell was in the Philippines, the submarines and their crews were put through an intense period of refresher training in Cid Harbour, a place chosen as being hopefully far enough from civilisation that the chances of Japanese aerial reconnaissance were nil. It was well known that some classes of Japanese submarine were fitted with small reconnaissance planes and that these aircraft had overflown Australian territory on several occasions.

Cid Harbour was one of the most beautiful places the Britons had yet seen, nestled on the coast of Whitsunday Island, 560 miles north of Brisbane on the Great Barrier Reef. The water was crystal clear, the surrounding beaches white sand and the land an intense green canopy of jungle. All six XE-craft spent days nosing around the harbour's clear waters making dummy attacks on the *Bonaventure*, the divers practising sticking limpet mines on imaginary enemy battleships and aircraft carriers.

*

Captain Fell had bidden a warm farewell to Admiral Fife, or 'Jimmy' as he now preferred Fell to call him, on 22 May. The next morning at 5.00am Fell had landed from his temporary berth, HMS *Maidstone*, and set off with Fife's aide-de-camp and Commander Davies, plus an armed guard, over 100 miles to Manila by road. There was one nervous moment when a loud bang had sounded close by their jeep and the vehicle had come to a sudden halt. The two US Navy guards had pointed their carbines menacingly into the surrounding jungle before realising that the sound had been caused by a burst tyre.[2]

Arriving at Manila Airport coated in fine white dust, Fell's party were provided with a wash and lunch by an American admiral, while another senior officer told them that they could hitch a ride to Leyte in his own plane. The mood on the journey back to Australia was depressing. Fell had failed to secure a mission for his precious flotilla, 'with practically no hope left for our continued existence as a fighting unit'.[3]

The night of the 23rd was spent on Peleliu, and the 25th on Manus, until Fell's party finally arrived at Townsville, Australia late on 26 May. The last part of the journey had been particularly arduous. Dressed only in their summer uniforms, Fell and Davies had endured a cruise at an altitude of 14,000 feet over New Guinea's Owen Stanley Range without oxygen or pressurisation.[4] Worse was to follow. Waiting for them at Townsville was a Royal Australian Air Force Walrus seaplane that had been assigned to HMS *Bonaventure*. It was the only way to get to Cid Harbour. The Walrus had a bad takeoff into fierce crosswinds, Fell and Davies enduring two hours of severe turbulence before the pilot found the *Bonaventure* and executed a very heavy water landing that frightened his passengers half to death. Once the engines were switched off the pilot turned to Fell.

'That was fun,' he said, smiling as he pulled his leather flying helmet and goggles off. 'It's the first time I've ever flown a Walrus or landed anything smaller than a Catalina on the sea.'[5] Fell looked at Commander Davies. They said nothing.

*

Teamwork at 14th Submarine Flotilla had been tightened up, and by the time an empty-handed Fell returned to the ship on 27 May, he was satisfied that his little unit was ready for whatever mission might yet come their way.[6]

The problem was that many of the men were not at all interested in the refresher training, considering that the flotilla had been dumped in Australia while the top brass tried to decide what to do with it. Morale had sunk quite low, according to Mick Magennis. There was a feeling that their efforts were wasted and that they, an elite force, were unappreciated and little understood.[7]

The one consolation to the rather glum atmosphere that pervaded 14th Submarine Flotilla in Cid Harbour was the diving. For the divers, the time that they spent beneath those beautiful

Australian waters was memorable. Sub-Lieutenant Jock Bergius, a diver on Max Shean's *XE-4*, felt that he had entered a wonderful world of colour and light. The divers swam silently over corals and sea plants while fish of every shape and colour flitted past. No prewar diver had ever been as at home beneath the waves as the XE-men had become. The DSEA breathing apparatus did not emit any bubbles like the rigs used by hardhat divers. The fish were not frightened away and the men could swim freely among them like aquanauts.[8] But the idyllic locale soon began to lull the men into a false sense of security. As they were shortly to find out, Australia was to prove far from a safe posting. There were hidden dangers beneath those placid waters that were lying in wait for the unwary or the overconfident.

*

In late May 1945, the flotilla was struck another blow. A message arrived from Admiral Fraser at British Pacific Fleet headquarters in Sydney. Captain Fell was informed that as no work could be found for his XE-men and their ingenious machines, HMS *Bonaventure* would be proceeding to Sydney where she would 'pay off', that is, be put out of commission.

Fell stood on the *Bonaventure*'s bridge holding the signal flimsy in his hand for some time. Beside him, Commander Derek Graham watched his leader's reaction with concern. Fell didn't speak, just stared out to sea with a hard, flinty look in his eyes. Graham could imagine the riot of emotions that Fell must have been experiencing.

Morale among the XE-men, already low, sank even lower with the depressing news from Sydney. 'Nobody interested,' recorded Mick Magennis in his diary. 'Have got the impression that we have been dumped here 'till they consider what they will do with us.'[9] Magennis, like everyone else in the flotilla, had watched their commander dashing between meetings, hawking his wares and virtually 'pleading for targets'. But, after so many disappointments, none of the men thought that missions would be forthcoming. It looked as though it had all been for nothing, a complete waste of everyone's time. There would be no daring Far Eastern raid to rival the attack on the *Tirpitz*.

*

On 28 May, after talking to his ship's company and the XE-men, and full of fresh ideas for future operations, Captain Fell attended a conference in Sydney chaired by Admiral Fraser.

The meeting started on 30 May and a conclusion was reached. It was decided to ask Admiral Nimitz one last time if he had any use for Fell's unit and if the answer was in the negative, to disband the flotilla.[10] Fell was then told to fly to Melbourne and discuss the *Bonaventure*'s future employment with Vice-Admiral Charles Daniel.

On 31 May, the last day of the conference, Fell was attending the usual staff meetings. Just before he made ready to leave for the airport he was suddenly called for. The Staff Officer (Intelligence), the US Navy's Captain Claiborne, greeted a surprised Fell warmly in his office. The Americans, it seemed, were having difficulties in working out how to break Japanese submarine telephone communications between Malaya, China and Japan. Claiborne asked if Fell's outfit could provide a solution, as it was imperative to cut the underwater cables that the Japanese used to connect their headquarters overseas with Tokyo. The request had come down from the very top of the American command.[11]

Fell couldn't believe his luck – it was literally an eleventh-hour reprieve.[12] Admiral Fraser gave his immediate approval for Fell, Claiborne and Davies to fly to Melbourne to collect more information on the proposed operations. In Melbourne, Fell was forced to spend the day in his scheduled meeting with Vice-Admiral Daniel discussing the paying off of the XEs and *Bonaventure*'s reassignment. Daniel knew nothing of the American request. Fell then sat down with the intelligence staff to examine the plan to cut the cables. It was all slightly surreal.[13]

*

The United States had broken Japanese diplomatic, naval and military codes; the resulting blizzard of decrypts was codenamed 'ULTRA'. The Japanese had no idea of this enormous security breach. But with the contraction of the Japanese defence perimeter by early 1945, Tokyo was using undersea telephone cables to communicate with their forces on the nearby Asian mainland. The Allies' flow of Japanese radio intercept intelligence had abruptly ended. It was now impossible to know Japanese plans in advance or monitor the deployment of their ships and military formations. If the cables were cut, the Japanese would be forced to return to communicating using the compromised radio codes, giving both the Americans and the British the crucial information edge. It could be the difference between speedy victory over the Japanese or a protracted slog into 1946.

As well as being vitally important to the United States, an operation to sever Japanese telephonic communications would also prove to be of great importance to Admiral Mountbatten, who was already planning the invasion of Malaya and Singapore. He could plot Japanese formations and reinforcements and monitor their remaining naval forces vis-à-vis Operation Zipper.

*

On 2 June Captain Fell was seated once again in front of Admiral Fraser's desk in Sydney.

'I gather from Captain Claiborne that the two of you now have a firm plan, Tiny,' said the Admiral.

'The operation to cut the Japanese telephone cables is exactly the sort of show my submarines were designed for, sir,' said Fell to Fraser. Fell outlined his plan to Fraser, who listened patiently.

'I realise you chaps are itching to have a crack at the Japs before the show's over and I admire your persistence, Tiny,' said Fraser when Fell had finished. 'I'd like to see the plans in writing as soon as possible.'[14]

It took Fell, Claiborne and Davies three days to get everything worked out on paper. Fell immediately took the finished plans back to Fraser. After what seemed like an interminable wait Fell and his companions were ushered back into Fraser's office. Fell noticed that the file containing his cable-cutting plans lay on Fraser's desk blotter.

'Well, Tiny,' said Fraser, smiling, 'a masterful piece of work. Your plan is approved.' Fell was ecstatic. Now it just remained to persuade Admiral Fife at Subic Bay.[15]

Within the hour Fell was travelling back to the *Bonaventure* with the good news. He crossed his arms and turned to glance out of the small window beside his elbow at the shimmering sea passing by thousands of feet below. Now it was necessary for his flotilla to learn how to locate and cut undersea cables. How hard could it be? A smile formed on Fell's lips, the smile of a man who has just been given a reprieve.

*

As soon as he returned to the *Bonaventure* on 6 June, Fell convened an orders group with John Smart, Tich Fraser, Max Shean and the other XE-craft skippers and their first lieutenants. Excited, he outlined the missions that Admiral Fraser had ordered him to plan. Firstly, Commander Davies laid out a large Admiralty chart of southeast Asia onto the *Bonaventure*'s wardroom table. The officers all crowded around.

After briefly outlining the general purpose of the missions, Fell pointed to the target areas.

'We've to penetrate two separate areas,' he said. 'The Japs have the cables laid out in a triangular pattern. One line goes from

95

Hong Kong direct to Singapore,' said Fell, running his index finger down the map from the Chinese coast to the tip of Malaya. 'And a second runs from Hong Kong to Saigon,' he said, pointing at the mouth of the Mekong River in French Indochina, 'then it runs on to Singapore.'[16]

The plan was for the cables to be severed at two distinct points close to the enemy coast. The first was off Lamma Island in Hong Kong, the second close to the entrance to Saigon's Mekong River. Though only two XE-craft would be used, no decision had yet been taken concerning which ones would be chosen, explained Fell. Everyone would train for the job, and Fell would select the two ablest crews for the missions once he had evaluated their performances. Fell would write cheerfully to Admiral Fraser, predicting his return to the Philippines and a meeting with Admiral Fife: 'I am eagerly looking forward to another acutely uncomfortable journey.'[17]

But the first, and biggest, challenge was working out how a submarine telephone cable could be grabbed by an XE-craft. Fortunately the British knew exactly where the cables were located. The *Bonaventure*'s navigator had produced charts from his library that showed the position of the cables off Saigon and Hong Kong. The detail was impressive. Navigation would have to be precise, but Fell knew that his men were more than up to the task.

Fell had also had the forethought to bring with him a Cable & Wireless engineer from Manila to help settle some of the technical issues that the mission presented.

'If a cable ship were to do this job,' said the American civilian expert to the assembled XE-craft officers, 'she would drag in deep water with a large grapnel, haul the cable to the surface with a powerful winch and then cut it.'

'Well, we already have the last part of the operation covered,' said Fell. 'We use hydraulic cutters to make holes in anti-submarine and anti-torpedo nets. I don't think we would face any problems slicing through a cable.'[18] Fell turned to Chief Engine Room Artificer Ron Fisher, one of the *Bonaventure*'s senior technical crew. 'Fisher, I'd like you to start work on modifying the cutters to tackle the much thicker telephone cables. The XO will give you the cable dimensions.'

'Aye aye, sir,' replied the middle-aged chief petty officer. The *Bonaventure*'s fully equipped workshop and highly trained artisans could deal with most requests.

'What about grabbing the cable itself?' asked the engineer.

'We don't have a thing, I'm afraid,' sighed Fell. 'These submarines were not designed with this kind of job in mind. We'll have to put our heads together and create something.'

'Sure,' said the engineer, adding, 'the grapnel could be something shaped like a large anchor.'

'What sort of depth should this be performed at, sir?' asked Lieutenant Shean.

'At least 30 feet, but ideally much deeper,' remarked the engineer.

Fell grimaced. 'Depth is a problem, old boy. Our divers can only work safely at a maximum depth of 30 feet.'

'Then you have a problem, Captain,' said the American engineer, peering at the charts with the cables clearly marked upon them. 'Deeper is better because beyond 50 feet the bottom sediments no longer move. You could locate the cables easily at between, say, 50 and 100 feet. It's going to be darn difficult to find the cables in shallow water because they will be buried quite deep in all the crap on the bottom.'

'Fifty feet is somewhat beyond our safety margin, I'm afraid, especially if the divers are going to be working on the cables for more than even a few minutes,' said Fell. 'Ideally it's going to be no deeper than 30 feet for any extended period. Time is a big factor in all of this. I'd not want them operating at their maximum depth for more than 30 minutes.'

At the conclusion of the meeting Fell, though a little disappointed by how complex the operation was rapidly becoming, nonetheless suggested to his men that they start thinking about a design for a grapnel. Each crew was ordered to design something. Arrangements were made for trials to be made on a wire hawser laid on the harbour bed by the *Bonaventure*'s crew. This would simulate a cable and be used to test the different designs.[19]

Nearly everyone opted for a kind of reef anchor, all except the mechanically creative Shean. He and his crew came up with what turned out to be the most efficient design. Christened a 'flatfish' grapnel, it comprised a diamond-shaped steel plate, three feet long, with fins shaped like halves of a crescent moon welded top and bottom.[20]

'The diamond is towed by chain,' said Shean during a presentation of his design. 'It lies flat on the seabed while the lower fin digs into the mud. The second fin will dig in if the grapnel is laid the other way up.'[21] It was important that the design be just right, for, unlike using a large dredging vessel or cable cutter, the XE-craft had only a little Keith Blackman 30hp electric motor with which to drag the grapnel through the mud while the submarine was submerged.[22]

*

At this point, with missions on the cards, Captain Fell decided to put some of the officers through an *ad hoc* survival exercise. After all, if anything went wrong on either of the missions, some of them could end up stranded ashore in very hostile territory. Shean took *XE-4* and her crew close to Hazelwood Island before mooring the submarine and using an inflatable dinghy to reach dry land. They were equipped with one 24-hour ration pack, a water bottle and a poncho per man, together with one shotgun and some fishing lines. Fell ordered them left to fend for themselves for five days.[23]

The party's food was quickly supplemented when one of the officers shot a very elderly goat. They lived mainly on this rather tough meat and rock oysters. On the evening of day three an accident occurred. While the party was scavenging for oysters in the shallows in a flat area behind a coral reef, Jock Bergius trod on a stingray. The startled fish stung him on the ankle. Bergius was in agony and Shean became concerned for his welfare. Shean, ERA Ginger Coles and Sub-Lieutenant Ben Kelly carried Bergius over to the dinghy. It was pitch dark when, after boarding the *XE-4*, they started out for the unlit *Bonaventure*. Navigating through deep water, Shean used the Aldis lamp to warn the *Bonaventure* to stand by. 'Bergius stung by stingray. Coming to starboard gangway,'[24] he flashed in Morse code. Bergius, limping in agony, refused to lie down on a stretcher and instead hobbled painfully under his own steam to the quarterdeck. He was determined to show what stuff Scots were made of.[25] For a day, Bergius was semi-conscious, and Coles never left his side, carrying out primitive but efficient first aid using a tourniquet and much blood-letting to get rid of the poison in Bergius' left side.[26]

Fell spoke briefly with Shean, who agreed to return to Hazelwood Island to complete the exercise. The nocturnal visitors, Fell wrote, gave an appearance of being 'already half way back to the state of aboriginals'.[27] Once safely returned to the *Bonaventure* on day five, all the officers professed to have enjoyed themselves, but no one approached the flotilla second-in-command with a request to be included in the next similar exercise.

*

While Shean, Fell and the other XE-men had been labouring to perfect a technique for underwater grapnelling, the strategic situation had continued to evolve. The most momentous development had been Germany's surrender on 8 May 1945. Just over a month earlier the US Chiefs of Staff had rejected Lord Mountbatten's planned invasion of Malaya and Singapore, Operation Zipper, even though planning was by now well advanced.[28]

Mountbatten had argued forcefully and cogently that the longer the delay, the stronger Japanese defences became in Malaya, and the greater the sufferings of Allied civilian internees and prisoners-of-war. The Americans relented soon after and the operation was back on, but Zipper was still hamstrung by a lack of light fleet carriers to provide air support over the landing beaches. But Mountbatten, like the erstwhile leader of 14th Submarine Flotilla, simply refused to give up the operation, regardless of the logistical and equipment shortages that were forced upon him by London and Washington. By hook and by crook he managed to assemble nine aircraft carriers, two battleships and an armada of cruisers, destroyers and landing ships even though First Sea Lord Cunningham continued to divert many major vessels to Admiral Fraser's British Pacific Fleet off Okinawa.[29] So, while Mountbatten lobbied, negotiated and argued Zipper's merits, 14th Flotilla in Australia began training for a mission that was, unusually for such a contentious theatre, in both the British and American interest, and requiring support from both nations. It was about the last mission that Fell or the XE-craft commanders had expected to receive, but beggars can't be choosers.

*

'Make your depth 20 feet,' ordered Lieutenant Fraser, *XE-3* submerging from the glassy surface of Cid Harbour into the crystal-clear depths below. The target once again was a steel hawser that had been laid on the seabed to mimic an undersea telephone cable. Mick Magennis was already struggling into his diving suit beside the Wet and Dry Compartment, preparing himself for another practice at cutting the cable.

'Twenty feet, Tich,' sounded off first lieutenant David Carey.

'Right, stand by diver,' ordered Fraser, turning to the night periscope for a quick look underwater. 'Okay, Magennis, away you go, and good luck,' said Fraser as the diminutive Magennis went through the small door into the W&D chamber. Inside the control room the other crew could hear Magennis turning valves and flooding the compartment. Fraser peered through the chamber's little window and saw Magennis breathing steadily into the DSEA bag as the water rose around him.

Fraser watched through the night periscope as the W&D hatch came open and Magennis emerged awkwardly.

'Diver out,' said Fraser, his eyes never leaving the periscope. Magennis turned briefly to the periscope and gave Fraser the thumbs-up signal before swimming over to the stowage compartment outside the submarine where he selected the grapnel that was attached to a 50ft length of stout manila rope. Magennis dropped the grapnel, letting it fall to the seabed, the rope paying out behind it. Then he re-entered the W&D and flooded down.[30]

Once Magennis was safely aboard, Fraser submerged *XE-3* to within ten feet of the bottom, Carey adjusting the boat's trim with the compensating tanks fore and aft. This depth would be maintained by carefully watching the sounding apparatus in front of Fraser's position in the control room. Slowly, the submarine crept forward until it was brought to a sudden jerking halt as the grapnel caught on the cable, pulling it several feet off the seabed.

This was the signal for Magennis to enter the W&D again. But first, Fraser landed the submarine on the seabed. Once Magennis was outside the *XE-3* he collected the special hydraulic cutters normally used to cut through anti-submarine nets, followed the rope to the grapnel and made his cuts. When he had finished he felt his way back along the rope to the *XE-3*, stowed the cutters and re-entered the W&D. It was a simple enough process in clear water, and against a cable that was not buried by silt, glutinous mud or sand. But divers had to go slow. Over-exertion even at safe depth was dangerous when working on pure oxygen.[31]

*

On 12 June the XE-craft were hoisted aboard the *Bonaventure*. The next day she sailed from Cid Harbour to Townsville to embark stores and provisions.

Training shifted to Hervey Bay on 15 June, where there was a disused telegraph cable. This would more closely simulate the real conditions that the two selected crews would encounter in their missions against the Japanese. The cable, stretching for a mile, was up to 50 feet deep in places and partly buried in silt and mud. It would test the divers to the limits of their endurance.

On 17 June, Mick Magennis was not available to dive. Instead, Tich Fraser took aboard a spare diver from one of the passage crews. While *XE-3* was still surfaced and close to shore the diver suddenly reported to Fraser that there was something wrong with his equipment. He said there was a defect in his breathing apparatus. Fraser took the DSEA from him and tested it himself. He could find nothing wrong with it. But the reserve diver was adamant – it *was* defective and he wouldn't dive. Fraser had no choice but to send him back in the safety boat to the *Bonaventure*. After all, if there were something wrong with the equipment, the diver would be the one to suffer, not Fraser.[32]

Fraser and his best friend David Carey were determined to continue with the exercise. When Fraser suggested that Carey have a go, the younger officer jumped at the opportunity. Once Carey was dressed and inside the W&D, the compartment was flooded and Fraser took his position at the night periscope to watch his friend. Carey disappeared off the stern of the submerged *XE-3*, following the line down to where the grapnel had snagged the cable. As Fraser watched, his friend reappeared and gave him the thumbs-up sign. Kicking his swim fins, Carey moved over to the stowage compartment and collected the hydraulic cutters before swimming back down the rope. After a few minutes Carey reappeared, stowing the cutters and giving Fraser another thumbs-up. Fraser glanced at the depth gauge – 47 feet.

'Prepare to surface,' ordered Fraser, as Carey re-entered the W&D after stowing the grapnel. Fraser stood by while the valves began to open as Carey prepared to flood down. Suddenly, with a bang, the hatch to the W&D flew open and Carey shot out. Fraser pressed his eyes against the night periscope and saw Carey atop the submarine's casing, giving him the thumbs-down sign.

'Surface the boat!' yelled Fraser. Something was dreadfully wrong. As the little submarine broke the surface, Fraser was watching his best friend carefully through the night periscope. But before Fraser could open the main hatch Carey suddenly dived over the side into the ocean and disappeared beneath the surface.[33]

He didn't reappear.

CHAPTER EIGHT

Operation Suicide

*'These second divers are not properly coursed divers,
they are merely blokes who are very keen.'*

—Acting Leading Seaman James Magennis, HMS *XE-3*

When Tich Fraser stepped back aboard HMS *Bonaventure* from the *XE-3* on 25 June 1945 his white, strained face and red-rimmed eyes betrayed the emotions that had surged through him following the death of his best friend. Captain Fell had had as many divers as he could muster search the area where David Carey had last been seen, but to no avail. His body was never recovered.

Fraser felt responsible for his friend's death. He had allowed him to make the dive. His heart felt cold inside of him.[1] Fell assured him that what had happened was a tragic accident, and not his fault, but a lingering doubt would remain with Fraser for the rest of his life. Carey had been his first lieutenant and was not the boat's assigned diver. Unlike Mick Magennis, Jock Bergius and the other highly trained divers, it was never intended that Carey should undertake a combat dive, so his time and experience under the water had been very limited.

Fell ordered Fraser back out the next day to complete the exercise with a different diver.[2] Fraser knew that Fell was not a heartless or cold man, and that his decision was the right one under the circumstances. They were at war, and casualties were sadly to be expected, even in training. The nature of their job was extremely hazardous as it was. The missions had to take precedence over personal feelings. Fraser and the other men would mourn Carey when the job was done.

The other five XE-craft were also ordered out on exercise on 26 June. Aboard Pat Westmacott's *XE-2* the diver for the day was Bruce Enzer, normally the skipper of *XE-6*. Fell felt that it was important that commanders as well as assigned divers all gained plenty of practice cutting the cable. But the commander would only ever leave the submarine under the direst of emergencies. His job was to command the boat and his crew.

When *XE-2* broke the surface of the bay on 26 June off Mon Repos Beach, Bruce Enzer was atop the submarine. He had been trying to retrieve the towed grapnel when something had gone wrong. The safety boat immediately pulled up alongside, a concerned officer leaning over the gunwale.

'Are you all right?' the officer shouted at Enzer, who was still fully dressed in his diving suit, DSEA and round facemask. Enzer didn't even remove his mouthpiece, just leaned over and suddenly punched the officer on the chin, sending him sprawling into the bottom of his boat. Then, without a pause, Enzer dived headfirst into the sea and disappeared beneath the surface.

Pat Westmacott opened the *XE-2*'s main hatch a second later, in shock. 'What the hell just happened?' he called out to the officer in the launch, who was standing rubbing his jaw, a confused expression on his face, his eyes frantically scanning the surface of the water for some sign of the diver.

It had happened again. Enzer was gone, his body never recovered. Two highly experienced submariners had drowned in as many days. Fell and everyone in the flotilla was appalled. The reason for the deaths soon became clear.

Neither Carey nor Enzer had dived every day during the training in Hervey Bay. The assigned divers had managed to build up tolerance to breathing pure oxygen whereas Carey and Enzer, a first lieutenant and a skipper respectively, had not. Fell also discovered that both of the dead divers had overexerted themselves during their final dives, and had exceeded safety limits.

Although Carey and Enzer were the only deaths suffered during the working-up training, two other divers came close to being killed, highlighting just how hazardous 'Special and Hazardous Duties' were fast becoming. One diver bailed out of a W&D compartment while his submarine was submerged and only just made it to the surface. Another blacked out in the W&D but was saved by his colleagues.[3]

'It was unthinkable that these two athletic men should be lost under the ideal training conditions of Hervey Bay,'[4] wrote Max Shean of Carey and Enzer's deaths. If they could lose men when everything was perfect, what might befall the rest of them in combat?

In light of the two tragedies, Fell imposed stricter controls over diving. The cause of the two deaths was provisionally noted as 'oxygen exhaustion'.[5]

That night Tich Fraser went to David Carey's cabin to pack up his best friend's gear to send home to his mother. It was the saddest moment of his life.[6]

The gloom of the two deaths cast a long shadow over the other XE-men. They were considerably shaken up by the tragedies and some felt that the whole set-up was too risky. Two of the officers decided to leave the flotilla, which came as a further surprise to everyone. Lieutenant Terry-Lloyd, the South African commander of *XE-5* requested a transfer to general service, as well as Sub-Lieutenant A.J. Renouf.[7] Fell granted their requests without animosity but, with Terry-Lloyd's departure and Bruce Enzer's death, he was now minus two skippers. Sub-Lieutenant William Smith, the New Zealander first lieutenant of *XE-6*, was appointed to the same post in Fraser's *XE-3* to replace Carey. *XE-2* and *XE-6* were now both minus commanders and first lieutenants. As there was only one XE-craft skipper and one first lieutenant in the pool of spare crew this created a serious problem for Fell and the operational efficiency of his flotilla.[8]

*

Seven days after Bruce Enzer's tragic death, Captain Fell sent a signal to Admiral Fraser's headquarters. It read 'Success', indicating that his flotilla had perfected locating and severing an underwater telephone line. Fraser cabled back that Fell was to proceed to Subic Bay and lay his plans before Admiral Fife for his final approval.[9]

*

With trials completed for the two cable-cutting operations, now codenamed 'Sabre' and 'Foil', the *Bonaventure* arrived in Brisbane on 27 June under the temporary command of Derek Graham.[10] Fell had ordered that the crew and the XE-men enjoy seven days' shore leave. It would raise morale and hopefully allow them to start to get over the deaths of the two popular officers. After the second night the majority of the *Bonaventure*'s ship's company found good homes to go to. The locals showered liberal generosity on the visiting 'Poms'.[11] While his men relaxed, Fell was ushered into Fife's office at Subic Bay. It was make or break time for 14th Submarine Flotilla.

*

Fell had made another long and arduous journey by several planes to Manila, eventually arriving at Subic Bay. He returned once more to HMS *Maidstone* for a wash and a quick cup of tea before setting out for Admiral Fife's office. Fell was in a considerable state of nerves when he sat down opposite Fife. The American took the binder from Fell containing the operational plans for Sabre and Foil and settled down to read them. Fell and Commander Davies, the staff officer, both nursing cups of coffee, sat in silence watching as the Admiral carefully read through everything. It was impossible to read anything from Fife's face. After what seemed like an eternity, Fife looked up over his spectacles and spoke.

'What about having a crack at the two cruisers in Singapore while we are at the cables?'[12]

Fell was astonished by Fife's suggestion, so astonished that he didn't say anything for a few seconds. Then he smiled, a broad grin forming across his face.

'I don't see why not, Jimmy,' said Fell, 'I don't see why not at all.'

*

Admiral Fife took his British guests to his new mess, 'giving me an old-fashioned [whisky-based cocktail] that nearly knocked my head off,'[13] recalled Fell. Then with one of Fife's staff officers as liaison and with *Maidstone*'s staff Fell got down to the new plan to take out the heavy cruisers and worked solidly for 36 hours until he felt it was ready to show Fife.

Fife approved the plan in principle and Fell immediately returned to Australia, a journey of 5,000 miles in 46 hours, to obtain Sir Bruce Fraser's blessing and to get the *Bonaventure* under way for the operations.[14]

In Sydney, Fraser approved the new plan and Fell spent two days and nights collecting information, making adjustments and tying up loose ends before boarding a plane for Brisbane.

On 7 July, Fell assigned the boats for the cable-cutting operations. A rather casual conference was called aboard the *Bonaventure*.[15] Apart from Fell and his second-in-command Derek Graham, the commanders of *XE-1*, *3*, *4*, and *5* were all present.

Because of the amount of underwater work that would be involved in the cable-cutting operations, and taking into consideration the fear of oxygen exhaustion when working at depth, the two selected XE-craft would each be assigned two divers instead of the more usual one. In this way, the workload could be shared.

'Max,' said Fell, turning to the Australian skipper of *XE-4*. 'I'm assigning you Operation Sabre.' This was the mission to cut the cable off the mouth of the Mekong River in French Indochina. Shean's crew would consist of Lieutenant Ben Kelly, his Irish first lieutenant ERA Ginger Coles, and two divers, Sub-Lieutenants Ken Briggs and Jock Bergius. Two Australians, two Celts and an Englishman. It was a happy crew.

Operation Foil, the plan to sever the undersea cable off Lamma Island, Hong Kong, went to the New Zealand skipper Pat Westmacott and the *XE-5*. Apart from the regular crew of his XO, Beadon Dening, and ERA Clifford Greenwood, his two divers would be Lieutenant Bruce 'Nobby' Clarke and Sub-Lieutenant Dennis Jarvis.

*

Mountbatten's Operation Zipper was now scheduled for the second week of August. Therefore, the Japanese communication cables needed to be severed by the end of July or the beginning of August.

The *Bonaventure* arrived at Manus on the morning of 13 July. After embarking fuel and fresh water, she left the Admiralty Islands at 5.00pm and set course for Subic Bay in the Philippines. Morale could not have been higher. 'D-Day' was scheduled for 31 July.[16] On 20 July she arrived and anchored close to HMS *Maidstone*, depot ship for 8th Submarine Flotilla. This unit would provide the big 'mother' submarines that would tow the little XE-craft into action.[17] The cable-cutting and heavy cruiser mining operations had both been laid once more before Admiral Fife, and he had approved both without any alterations.[18] The green light was now well and truly on.

*

The next task was to assign operational crews and XE-craft to the attacks on the Japanese heavy cruisers at Singapore. They looked on the face of it to be targets as formidably well hidden and defended as the *Tirpitz* had been.

'These, gentlemen, are what we've got to put out of action.' Captain Fell placed two black-and-white prewar profile photographs of the Japanese warships onto the wardroom table. 'Somehow the *Takao* and the *Myoko* have got to be neutralised before early August,' he said to the small gathering of XE-craft skippers and their first lieutenants aboard the *Bonaventure* as she rode at anchor off Subic Naval Base.

'How does that appeal to you, Tich?' asked Fell, looking directly at Fraser.

'All right, sir,' replied Fraser, somewhat taken aback at being chosen without preamble by Fell. He thought that he'd have preferred pretty much any job to that which Fell had just sprung on him.

'Tich, your target will be the *Takao*,' continued Fell, his index finger landing on the photograph of the ship as he spoke.

'Jack,' said Fell, turning to Lieutenant Smart, commander of *XE-1*, 'how do you feel about going after the *Myoko*?'[19]

Smart, who was stroking his beard, stopped and looked up from the photographs, his eyes briefly flashing.

'Marvellous, sir,' he said, in a tone of voice that sounded somewhat less than convincing. Smart's face had taken on a very serious expression, and Fraser, when he glanced at him, knew exactly what his friend was thinking. Compared to cutting telephone cables, attacking two huge Japanese warships deep inside a heavily defended harbour was one of the most dangerous jobs any X-craft skipper could expect. Memories of what had befallen the three X-craft submarines that had managed to get close to the *Tirpitz* in 1943 were seared into the flotilla's collective memory. For Fraser, there was a certain horrid inevitability about the whole thing. While Fell talked, his mind flashed briefly back to March 1944, when he had first arrived at Rothesay with David Carey after the two of them had fled the boredom of 'pinging' duties aboard the *H.44* for the tantalising unknowns of 'Special and Hazardous Service'. He had always had the buried knowledge that a day like this would finally arrive, and that he should have to do that for which he had been trained. But he had always secretly hoped that he would not have to do a harbour penetration.[20]

Another officer had joined the *Bonaventure* at Brisbane shortly before she sailed. Lieutenant G.C. Potter, DSC, was a member of Admiral Fraser's British Pacific Fleet Staff.[21] A naval intelligence officer, his task would be to brief the crews conducting the forthcoming operations on the latest British naval and RAF assessments.

Fraser leaned forward and carefully examined the photographs Potter had brought with him from Sydney.

'Potter,' said Fell, 'you'd better fill them in on the latest intelligence.'

Potter nodded and began to speak. The *Takao* and *Myoko*, he explained, were practically the sum total of Japan's surface warships in the Singapore region. They formed the 5th Cruiser Division, part of Vice-Admiral Shigeru Fukudome's 10th Area Fleet, headquartered in Singapore. The only other surface combatant left in Singapore was the 1,700-ton destroyer *Kamikaze* as well as a few auxiliary patrol and minesweeping vessels. The *Kamikaze* was to be considered a target of opportunity for both XE-craft.

'The Japs have been using their remaining heavy cruisers to bring troops into Singapore from outlying territories,' continued Potter. 'As you know, so far the Yanks and our good selves have managed to bag three of the blighters.'

Admiral Fukudome had watched his once-mighty fleet wither away. In early April 1945 the American submarine USS *Char* had torpedoed and sunk the cruiser *Isuzu* in the Java Sea. The most spectacular action had been on the night of 16 May when the five vessels of Captain Manley Power's British 26th Destroyer Flotilla had encountered the heavy cruiser *Haguro*, the newest vessel of the

Myoko-class, escorted by the destroyer *Kamikaze* in the Malacca Strait 50 miles off Penang. The *Haguro* was acting as a supply vessel for Japanese garrisons in the Netherlands East Indies and the Bay of Bengal. In what would turn out to be the last ship-versus-ship naval battle of the war, 26th Flotilla had attacked the giant *Haguro*, damaging her with gunfire, and then managed to slam three torpedoes into her side. Nine hundred Japanese sailors went down with the ship while the damaged *Kamikaze* managed to rescue 320 men from the sea before fleeing back to the safety of Singapore. British casualties amounted to just two men killed.

On 8 June the Royal Navy had scored another major victory when the submarine HMS *Trenchant* had torpedoed the *Ashigara*, another of the *Myoko*'s sister ships. At the time the *Ashigara* had been transporting 1,600 Japanese troops through the Bangka Strait from Batavia to Singapore.

With the destruction of the *Isuzu*, *Ashigara* and *Haguro*, Japanese naval power in the Malayan Peninsula region had been reduced to only three vessels: the heavy cruisers *Takao* and *Myoko* and the destroyer *Kamikaze*, all neatly bottled up in Singapore.

'They're both armed with eight-inch guns with a range of about eighteen miles,' continued Potter, describing the *Takao* and *Myoko*. 'The problem for us is where the Japs have moored them.'

He picked up a manila folder from a side table and took out several aerial reconnaissance photographs and laid them before Fraser and Smart. They were stereoscopic photos prepared by the RAF Photographic Reconnaissance Unit, and when a pair of pictures was viewed through a special tabletop stereoscopic device the images appeared three-dimensional, vastly increasing the detail that could be seen.

'Here's the northern shore of Singapore Island,' said Potter, pointing with his finger. 'And here's the southern edge of Johor,' he said, pointing to the southern coast of Malaya. 'Between them is the Johor Strait, a mile or so wide at its widest point,' said Potter, running his finger along the thin waterway that separated Singapore from the mainland. 'You'll enter from the eastern end here,' pointing to a narrower series of channels that threaded past a collection of small islands off Singapore's northeast coast.

Reading the reports and perusing the photos soon gave Fraser and Smart the impression that the *Takao* and *Myoko* were floating fortresses that constituted very formidable obstacles to British designs on the region. But no one standing around the *Bonaventure*'s wardroom table could deny that it was a mission that the XE-craft had been specifically designed for.

The ships were impressive targets. The oldest of the pair was the 13,500-ton *Myoko*, launched in 1927. She had fought in China, the Philippines, Java, the Coral Sea, Midway, the Aleutians and Guadalcanal. Damaged by an American torpedo in December 1944, the *Myoko* had been towed to Singapore for repairs. In February 1945 the Japanese had decided to keep her in harbour as a floating flak battery to counter American air raids.

The 15,500-ton *Takao*, 668 feet long and launched in 1930, had taken two torpedoes at Leyte Gulf in October 1944. Limping into Singapore, her wrecked stern had been cut off and shored up.

Apart from the flak guns, the two enormous warships' turreted main guns cast long shadows on the fast-flowing waters of the Selat Johor, or Johor Strait. The *Takao*'s ten 8in guns could deliver 280lb high-explosive shells, allowing her to dominate the sea approaches to Singapore as well as southern Johor. *Myoko* had ten 7.9in guns. Combined, the two warships could pump out 60 shells a minute across a 20-mile radius. The damage such gun platforms could inflict upon Mountbatten's Operation Zipper troops as they advanced south towards Singapore would be incalculable. As Potter explained, though both ships had been damaged, the British didn't know whether the Japanese had managed to make them seaworthy again, and whether they might even sortie in an attempt to either reach Japan or try to disrupt any British landings on Malaya's west coast at Ports Swettenham or Dickson. But the positioning of the ships suggested that the Japanese were intending to use them to dominate the land approach to the northern coast of Singapore Island. To all intents and purposes, they were as immovable and impressive as medieval castles.

The *Takao* had been positioned close to the old British naval base at Sembawang, while the *Myoko* was two miles further west near the Causeway, the narrow concrete and rubber roadway that connected Singapore to mainland Malaya. A prewar British anti-submarine boom closed off the eastern end of the channel, accessible only through a large gate that was guarded by a boom defence vessel.

'Can't the air force bomb them?' asked Smart.

'No. We'd need Lancasters armed with Tallboys to sink these behemoths and we've only got light carrier aviation in the region,' said Potter. 'The best they could do is to scorch the paintwork a bit. The Yanks can't help either.' The USAAF had redeployed its B-29 Superfortress heavy bombers from a base in India to the recently captured Marianas Islands in May 1945 to concentrate on turning Japanese industry and cities into piles of ashes. Before the move, the B-29s had made some raids on the naval base infrastructure and oil tanks, but Singapore had been at the bombers' extreme range, limiting their usually huge payload to just four 1,000lb bombs per aircraft.

'Anyway,' continued Potter, 'the bally things are bristling with ack-ack guns, not to mention the whole area is laced with protective flak batteries.' He paused and rubbed his tired eyes. 'An aerial torpedo strike has also been ruled out as the channel is too shallow. The only practicable way to get at them is for a couple of XEs to creep down the strait and basically emulate Operation Source. Try and break their backs using your side cargoes and limpet mines as we did with the *Tirpitz* in '43.'

'What kind of defences against submarine attack do the Japs have in place?' asked Fraser.

'There's a contact minefield at the eastern entrance to the strait, and then the old British boom. We think that there may be hydrophone posts or indicator loops in the channel, but this hasn't been confirmed. Of course, there will be patrol boats. I've prepared these reports for you on both ships,' said Potter, passing across two bulging manila folders containing photographs, charts, target descriptions and assessments. The front covers were marked with the words 'TOP SECRET' and below 'OPERATION STRUGGLE' printed in bold letters.

'"Struggle", sir?' said Fraser.

'I thought it appropriate after what I've been through obtaining this mission for us,' replied Captain Fell wryly.[22]

Fell leaned over the table and patted an enlarged photograph of the *Takao* with the flat of one hand. 'You're on big things now, chaps,' he said to Fraser and Smart. 'Things are humming up, and you must be ready to slip on the 26th. D-Day for both the cable-cutting operations and your ops is the 31st. Brief your crews and formulate a plan of attack.'[23]

'Yes, sir,' said Fraser. When he spoke he found that his mouth had gone rather dry.

*

Back in his cabin, Fraser had time to reflect upon the forthcoming mission. He had been worried for weeks already, a constant nervous strain buzzing in the background of his everyday duties like static. Every night-time worry about how he would perform on a mission was about to be transformed into reality. Now there was no turning back. There was no denying that David Carey's death had hit Fraser hard, harder than he realised at the time, and brought home the full, ghastly reality of what he had volunteered for. Fraser, like all the other XE-men, submerged his private feelings into the job at hand. Keeping busy was the best defence against the jitters.

Fraser called his crew together to brief them on the mission and begin preparing a plan in concert with Smart. He kept his fears to himself, appearing calm and untroubled in front of Kiwi Smith, Mick Magennis and Charlie Reed. To Fraser, the crew of the *XE-3* had always seemed so imperturbable to him, and he drew enormous strength from that.

*

Captain Fell ordered the four midgets that would take part in operations against the Japanese to be swung out immediately into Subic Bay to commence working up for the three forthcoming missions.[24] Fell also laid on lectures on the intricacies of towing and communications for the operational and passage crews. Lieutenant B.J. Tonks, a highly accomplished New Zealander from the *Bonaventure*, delivered these vital talks.[25]

*

Although the targets had been identified and methods of attack settled upon, further detailed planning for the three operations continued in between practical training in the Bay. The crews of *XE-1*, *XE-3*, *XE-4* and *XE-5* spent hours cloistered in their skippers' cabins aboard the *Bonaventure*, hunched over intelligence reports, Admiralty charts and RAF aerial photographs. Nothing was left to chance. Jack Smart and Tich Fraser required detailed maps of the Straits of Singapore and the Johor Strait, but the only available ones were large and designed for the normal-sized chart table found on surface warships. They did not fit on the small awkward area of the XE-craft chart table. Like schoolboys involved in a homework project, Smart and Fraser spent hours making their own smaller charts by cutting out the areas they wanted to the size that they wanted, and then sticking on a compass rose for measuring off direction.

CHAPTER NINE

Siamese Blood Chit

*'Most people think that the crews are a bunch
of madmen volunteering for a most dangerous
job in a Heath Robinson type of submarine. In
reality they are very good small submarines.'*

—Lieutenant G.C. Potter, Staff Officer (Intelligence)

Ian Fraser narrowed his eyes against the glare of the sun and tried to hold the big Colt .45 pistol on target. He aimed carefully at the figure's chest and took first pressure on the trigger. The American automatic was heavy and cumbersome in Fraser's small hand. The sights danced across the figure's head and chest as Fraser tried to control his breathing. The longer he waited, the heavier the weapon became. He pulled the trigger, the automatic jumping in his hand, its loud report echoing across the sea as the ejected shell case tumbled to the deck with a metallic clatter.

'Don't jerk at it like that, sir,' said the chief petty officer instructing him. 'Remember what I said. You squeeze it like a lemon, sir.'

Fraser sighed and lowered his aching arm.

'Try again, sir, and this time remember to breathe out as you squeeze. It'll help you keep the weapon on the target.'

Fraser was standing only fifteen feet away from the makeshift target, a thick sheet of cardboard that had been cut into the shape of a man's head and upper torso. The target had been tied to the *Bonaventure*'s guard rail.[1] Behind Fraser was his own crew from the *XE-3*, as well as the crews of the other three submarines that would take part in Operations Struggle, Sabre and Foil. A trestle table covered with a grey blanket had been set up on the deck beside the group. Several other Colt .45s were neatly arranged on it, alongside small cardboard boxes of shiny brass-cased bullets.

Fraser, sweaty with concentration, raised the weapon again and fired.

'Bad luck, Tich,' said Jack Smart as yet another bullet missed the target and whined off into the open sea.

'I don't think I could hit a barn door with this damned thing,' said Fraser irritably. He could never understand why the navy insisted on issuing such large and cumbersome weapons instead of smaller and lighter Webley .38 revolvers.[2]

The target practice was in aid of the unthinkable, but something that everyone involved in the raids was starting to seriously consider. They were all going deep behind Japanese lines, and the navy had decided, in its wisdom, to make sure that every XE-man had kit that he could use to survive if he was forced to abandon his submarine. No one was under any illusions about their probable fate should they fall into Japanese hands. After what had happened to Lieutenant-Colonel Ivan Lyon's men on Operation Rimau in 1944, more precautions would be taken this time. It was felt by those in the know that mistakes had been made on Rimau that had contributed to the grim deaths visited upon Lyon's surviving men who had been taken prisoner. Avoidable mistakes.

*

'Welcome aboard, Jimmy,' said Captain Fell, shaking hands vigorously with Rear Admiral James Fife as the American, accompanied by his flag lieutenant and Lieutenant H. Crooms, his communications officer, stepped smartly onto the *Bonaventure*'s quarterdeck on the morning of 22 July.[3] Fell's subordinate officers stood in a neat line, their navy whites starched, the whole occasion having an air of ceremony about it. History was about to be made.

'It's great to be here, Tiny,' replied the genial Fife, before he introduced Fell to the senior members of his staff who followed him on to the British ship.

For the first time in history an American admiral would hoist his flag on a Royal Navy ship.[4] Fife had decided to accompany the *Bonaventure* to Brunei, the starting point for Operations Struggle and Foil. Pat Westmacott and the *XE-5* would begin Operation Sabre directly from Subic Bay and would remain aboard HMS *Maidstone* until departure.

It was a reflection of how Fife felt about 14th Submarine Flotilla that he insisted on being aboard the *Bonaventure* when the XE-men left on their missions. It was also an indication of how important the cable-cutting missions were to the American high command. Fife brought his entire 80-man staff with him, accommodation and office space having to be found on the already fully manned British ship.

Fife had a surprise for Fell. Behind the scenes the American submariner had been talking up 14th Submarine Flotilla among his own colleagues and a surprise visitor arrived at the quayside. Fifty-five-year-old Vice-Admiral Charles A. Lockwood was 'COMSUBPAC' – Commander Submarines Pacific – and was Fife's immediate superior. Known to his men as 'Uncle Charlie', Lockwood had revolutionised the US submarine service, turning it into the hard-hitting, highly aggressive and successful organisation that was defeating Japan. Beloved of those who served under him, Lockwood had a sterling reputation for looking after his submariners. Fife had persuaded Lockwood to come and inspect the little British unit, sure that his superior would find the experience an education.

Captain Fell, anxious to please such an important and influential figure, ordered a demonstration to be laid on in Subic Bay. Admiral Lockwood decided that he wanted to play an active role in the demonstration and get a good feel for an XE-craft, so he would sail with the submarine during the demonstration. Fell was a little unsettled by this turn of events because, casting an eye towards the skies, something was wrong. The day had broken oppressively hot and still, 'with a most sinister feeling in the air of some impending cataclysm.'[5] That cataclysm began to reveal itself shortly after Lockward boarded the *Bonaventure* when the heavens opened. It rained so hard that it was difficult to breathe, but Lockwood decided to go out with Max Shean regardless and soon disappeared into the downpour aboard the *XE-4*.

Shean and his operational crew would demonstrate a simulated attack on the *Bonaventure*. After a run on the surface on the diesel engine, Shean dived the boat quickly, doing what was termed a 'crash dive'. Lockwood had never been in such a tiny submarine before and he didn't look entirely comfortable. It was a steep learning curve, and Lockwood watched Shean's crew carefully, noting their efficient teamwork and easy familiarity with each other. But having a VIP onboard made Shean's crew nervous, and nervousness in a submarine can lead to accidents.

'I forgot to shut the engine exhaust and muffler valves till we were well down,' whispered Ben Kelly, Shean's first lieutenant, trying not to alert Admiral Lockwood who was sitting close by. Shean winced and nodded, saying nothing. The diesel engine was now full of seawater. As long as they didn't try to run it, they should be all right, thought Shean. The *XE-4* was running smoothly on its electric motor. But Kelly seemed to take Shean's silence to mean he hadn't been heard. So, in a slightly louder whisper, he repeated what he had just said.

'Alright, Ben, I heard you,' hissed an embarrassed Shean. 'Just carry on.'[6] Unfortunately, by now Lockwood had got wind that something was amiss and had begun to ask questions. Fortunately, the rest of their simulated attack went like clockwork and Lockwood was duly impressed. He, like Fife, could see just how useful these little British subs could be to a variety of different types of operation where stealth was required.

Later that day, Lockwood would formally approve Operations Foil, Sabre and Struggle.[7] He had been surprised at the capabilities and efficiency of the XE-craft and their crews, in comparison with the horror stories doing the rounds among the Americans that were largely based on the earlier trials and tribulations of X-craft operations in Europe. Captain Fell couldn't stress enough that the new XE-craft was a completely different animal from the original X-craft, the latter having been virtual prototypes that had been pressed into frontline service before all their design faults had been addressed. The XE-craft design was the next generation of small submarine, incorporating all of the lessons learned during the earlier operations in Norway and Normandy.

Captain Fell sent a report on the visit to the Admiralty in which he admitted that this stigmatisation of his submarines was unfortunately well entrenched. 'The fallacy that X craft are unreliable, dangerous and altogether "stunt craft" dies hard.'[8]

*

Once the *XE-4* was moored in the Bay and Admiral Lockwood safely offloaded, Ginger Coles went to work pumping out seawater from the flooded crankcase. Shean and Kelly were back aboard the *Bonaventure* when the ship's public address system suddenly blared into tinny life. 'All hands, all hands, a cyclone is approaching. Repeat, a cyclone is approaching. All XE-craft must leave their moorings and lay off immediately.'[9]

The wind picked up, whipping the water's surface into steep, tumbling peaks. The wind tore the crests off the waves and within minutes the *Bonaventure* was straining at her anchor cables, threatening to break free at any moment. Captain Fell ran to the bridge and ordered 'slow ahead both engines' in an effort to gain some slack on the anchor cables.[10] The *Bonaventure*'s cutters were soon working hard trying to rescue sailors from the water, while stacks of timber on the *Bonaventure*'s decks were blown off. HMS *Maidstone*'s six submarines had all cast off and were milling about the harbour, attempting to ride out the tornado-like conditions.[11]

Max Shean turned to Ben Kelly and yelled 'Come on!' as the wind and rain almost drowned out his words. Further out in the bay the tiny *XE-4*, with Ginger Coles still aboard, was rolling heavily, waves breaking over her deck. Tich Fraser and Pat Westmacott were standing on the *Bonaventure*'s deck with an assortment of their men, all of them frantically scanning the rough water. There wasn't a moment to lose.

The sea's turmoil increased with long rolling whitecaps surging through the bay while horizontal rain swept down in soaking sheets. Nature had opened hostilities and there was nothing to do but to run for cover.

When the order went out aboard the *Bonaventure* for all crews to stand by their XE-craft, the challenges of trying to secure the small submarines in a raging tumult of wind, rain and high waves soon became all too obvious. It was the weather, rather than the Japanese, that suddenly seemed to conspire to dash 14th Submarine Flotilla's chances of ever seeing action.

The wind speed was soon fluctuating between Force 8 and 9, smashing, ripping and tearing at every man-made object in the bay with phenomenal power. American sailors struggled to secure their ships, tiny figures crawling about like ants under nature's fury.

The *XE-4* started to drift away on the rising waves, the force of the surge breaking her free from the floating boom used to moor the midget submarines. Unfortunately ERA Ginger Coles was still aboard her, pumping out the flooded crankcase as she drifted off stern first. Max Shean knew that he had to act, and act fast. Inside the submarine the motion was terrible, and Coles was being bounced around like a rag doll inside of a barrel. Shean and Ben Kelly didn't hesitate but dived straight into the raging water and struck out for their submarine, fighting against the current to reach her.[12] It was a hard swim, but they made it, coughing up seawater as they grabbed hold of the vessel's trailing lines. Once aboard, Shean and the crew got themselves sorted out and then took the submarine half a mile out to sea and sat on the bottom where a bruised and battered Ginger continued pumping until the storm passed.[13]

The *XE-5* was also in serious trouble. Her skipper, Pat Westmacott, and ERA Clifford Greenwood tried in vain to release her from the pontoon. Both men struggled in the water, spending several minutes repeatedly ducking under as they worked to free the lines, the waves breaking over their heads as they struggled to gulp a mouthful of air before another immersion. Their fingers hurt from the effort of trying to work the lines loose, both of them aware that they could be swept away or crushed by the out-of-control submarine at any minute. Suddenly the lines gave and the boat was finally loose. With an effort, Westmacott hauled himself aboard, before reaching down and helping Greenwood to climb onto the lurching and swaying deck. Both men felt like they had been fighting, their hands bleeding and their bodies bruised all over from the effort. The rain that lashed their faces was almost painful as they reached down and got the main hatch open. Hardly pausing, they scrambled down the short ladder into the damp interior, grateful to start the submarine's engine and escape from the wrecked pontoon.

While Shean and Westmacott laboured to save their boats, *XE-6*, which was being used as a reserve vessel since Bruce Enzer's death in Australia had left her with no assigned skipper, was dragged away along with her mooring buoy. The rest of her crew could only watch helplessly from the *Bonaventure*'s railing as the submarine made a rapid passage towards a lee shore. Captain Fell wiped the rain out of his eyes and struggled to stand upright at the *Bonaventure*'s rail as the wind buffeted him relentlessly, strong enough to make breathing difficult, and watched as the *XE-6* sailed away on her own. He cursed and swore, convinced that one of his submarines was going to founder. Though she was the spare boat, Fell couldn't afford to lose a single vessel as he was expecting several

Once the big blow had passed, the XE-men returned to making preparations for the forthcoming missions. One important aspect was facing the unsettling possible outcome of undertaking secret missions against the Japanese – capture. Or more precisely, how to avoid being taken alive by the most brutal adversary Britain had ever faced.

'Gentlemen, sadly some of our chaps who have been captured on operations against the Japanese have not been treated correctly,' said Lieutenant G.C. Potter, the intelligence officer, with great understatement. 'As I'm sure you are aware, the Japs don't abide by the Geneva Convention in these matters.'

Potter's remarks stilled the room, previously filled with good-natured banter. Potter began to extract various items of kit from a large cardboard box on the table in front of him.

'Now, I'm not suggesting for one moment that any of you chaps are going to fall into Japanese hands, but the Admiralty have decided to take certain precautions to help ensure that you don't, if anything should go wrong.'

The room was now so quiet that one could have heard a pin drop. Potter removed a smaller carton from the box and opened its top.

'Inside here we have some badges that I would like all of you to sew on to your operational uniforms.' He reached inside and held up two examples. One read 'ROYAL NAVY' and the other was a miniature Union Flag patch.[16]

'Please sew one title patch and one flag on to each shoulder of your shirts,' said Potter, pointing to his own upper left sleeve as he spoke. 'They are to make sure that you are not mistaken for spies should you be captured.' It was illegal to conduct offensive operations dressed in civilian or unmarked military clothing. Most countries, including Britain, took a dim view of anyone caught doing so and many combatant nations routinely executed those that they apprehended as spies and/or saboteurs. Identity discs worn around the neck might not be sufficient to convince some nations that the wearer was conducting a legal wartime mission. This was an argument used by the Japanese to attempt to justify the execution of Colonel Lyon's captured Force Z commandos a few weeks before.

In fact, with the Japanese, most of the accepted Rules of War did not apply. They could be quite arbitrary in their treatment of prisoners, torturing and imprisoning some, while often executing others at the point of capture or soon afterwards. The treatment meted out to captured Allied personnel often depended on the mood of the soldiers who apprehended them, and the Japanese were mercurial at best. Whether proper military identification patches would make any difference to the XE-men should they fall into Japanese hands was an unanswerable question. Judging by previous Japanese treatment of Allied POWs, particularly airmen and commandos, they should expect no mercy from their captors. It was a massive incentive to seek to remain free from capture if at all possible.

Lieutenant Potter went on to explain that extra petty officers' rank badges should be carried by the ERAs as identification, and the officers would wear rank epaulettes and also caps with the naval cap badge very tightly sewn on to them.

'All officers will wear the rank insignia of a sub-lieutenant RNVR, regardless of your real ranks or arm of service,' continued Potter. 'This is to indicate your lack of knowledge and experience to the Japanese if you are captured.'[17]

'That shouldn't be too hard to fake,' quipped Jack Smart, nervous laughter from the others breaking the tension a little.

'Don't worry, Smart, we'd make you all Snotties if we thought that the Japs would swallow it,' said Potter jovially, using the naval slang for midshipmen, the lowest commissioned rank.

'Now, if you have to vacate your submarine behind enemy lines it is likely that you will have to survive for several days or even weeks before a rescue can be attempted,' said Potter. 'This, then, may be your most important piece of kit,' he said, holding up a small, neatly folded piece of white silk that came in a little oilskin pouch. With a flourish, Potter unfolded the silk, revealing a prominent Union Flag printed in the middle, around which was a message written in Chinese, Malay, English and several other languages. It stated:

> I am a British naval officer who has been engaged in operations against the Japanese. If I am captured I cannot continue to fight against the Japanese so I appeal to you to hide me and provide me with food until I can rejoin our forces. If you will help me by giving me food and hiding me in a safe place until our armies arrive you will have the gratitude of my government who will give you a big reward. I am authorized to give you a chit to this effect.[18]

'We call this a "Siamese Blood Chit",' said Potter once everyone had read the English message. 'The Japs offer the locals rewards to hand over Allied personnel. There are loyal natives who *will* help you, particularly the Chinese, but you should remain on your guard. Some are quite unsavoury customers, and more than a few are actively collaborating with the Nips. This chit may keep you free should you need to ask for assistance. So whatever you do, don't lose it. It will probably be of more use to you than this.' He reached into the big box and placed a Colt .45 on the table with a heavy metallic clunk. His point was well taken by everyone in the room.

For the next hour the rest of the evasion and survival kit was demonstrated to the XE-men. It was a little like Christmas morning, with people passing things around and often marvelling at the ingenuity of the items provided. Aside from a holstered pistol, ammunition and the Siamese Blood Chit, there was a little cloth bag containing 25 gold sovereigns to bribe unconvinced locals, a prismatic compass, hacksaw blades, a small leather wallet containing a selection of paper currencies, silk maps, fishing line and hooks, a needle and thread, a heliograph for signalling using the sun, a tiny telescope, and a box containing emergency iron rations.[19]

'There is also this,' said Potter, placing a Fairbairn-Sykes Fighting Knife on the table. It had a mean-looking seven-inch steel blade with a black metal vase-shaped handle and a metal sheath. This weapon was ordinarily issued to Army Commandos. Several of the men stared transfixed as Potter unsheathed the knife and held it up for all to see, the deck light glinting menacingly off its razor-sharp blade. 'This is primarily a thrusting weapon for insertion between the ribs, but it can also be used to slash at an opponent,' said Potter grimly. The thought of sticking a knife into another human being was a sobering one. Several of the men winced in distaste at the thought.

'Finally, we have the "L" pill,' said Potter, holding up a small Bakelite vial that contained a single tablet.

'"L" pill?' asked Westmacott.

'"L" for "Lethal", old boy,' replied Potter, his face sober. The 'L' pill contained hydrogen cyanide, and was a last resort for those who preferred death to capture. It was the smallest item that Potter had shown them, but by the far the most shocking. All of the kit, except the pistol, which would be worn on a belt around the waist during an evasion, went into a small army haversack to be stowed inside the submarine.

*

Later that night, Fraser lay in his bunk thinking about capture. He had a dread fear of torture, and the thought of falling into Japanese hands, of never seeing his wife and daughter again, sent a chill through his body. The fear would always be with the men who embarked on missions against the Japanese. It was as though a pitiless, faceless monster was standing behind them, just out of sight but lurking in the shadows waiting for them to make a mistake.

Waiting to pounce. The monster had no compassion and didn't live by the same rules as the XE-men. And Fraser and his companions were going to try to enter the monster's domain, his lair. Get caught and his fury would be boundless.

It was very clear from Potter's escape and evasion briefing that if he and his crew had to abandon their submarine, they would be on their own. Though Potter talked about them having to survive for several days or weeks until rescue, he was fooling nobody. There was little chance that a rescue could be effected from occupied Singapore or southern Malaya. The only thing Fraser and the others could cling to was the chance that they might be able to join up with the local resistance, assuming they could even make such a contact without compromising themselves. Potter had provided the men with a short list of contacts and addresses. Before Fraser switched off the light beside his bunk and turned in for the night he thought about the 'Siamese Blood Chit' – it was, he thought, chillingly well named.

CHAPTER TEN

Night Passage

'To a considerable extent the success of an operation
depends on the condition in which the craft is turned
over to the operational crew. In no sense of the word
are the X-craft passage-crews "maintenance crew".'

—Captain William Fell, 14th Submarine Flotilla

With plans finalised and the crews mentally prepared, each of the four designated XE-craft was assigned to a 'mother' S-class submarine from the *Maidstone*'s 8th Submarine Flotilla. The S-class were the most numerous British submarines of the Second World War, some 62 entering service. At a length of 217 feet, they displaced 842 tons each and were crewed by 49 officers and men. These workhorses were armed with six torpedo tubes and a three-inch deck gun. The men who captained them were all highly experienced and often highly decorated submariners.

The four S-class captains met with the XE skippers in *Bonaventure*'s wardroom to discuss the operations and go over charts, timings and operational procedures.

HMS *Spark* would take Jack Smart and *XE-1* in tow. Her captain, Lieutenant Derrick Kent, had sunk seven small Japanese coastal craft since arriving in the Far East. Kent, 25, was already on his sixth war patrol.

HMS *Stygian* would tow the *XE-3*.[1] Her captain, Lieutenant Guy Clarabut, had been appointed one of the navy's youngest sub skippers at the tender age of just 23. Despite having a weak left eye and heart trouble, Clarabut had won a DSO after sinking an Italian submarine with a single torpedo. Now 26, he had already destroyed 20 Japanese vessels since being assigned to the Eastern Fleet at Trincomalee. Being in Ceylon had enabled him to fly up to Nagpur on India's North-West Frontier, where he had grown up, to see his father for the first time in eight years.[2]

Max Shean and the *XE-4* were placed in the hands of Lieutenant-Commander R.E. Youngman and HMS *Spearhead*. Pat Westmacott and the *XE-5* were left behind at Subic Bay when the *Bonaventure* sailed, in the care of HMS *Maidstone*, ready for his mission against the telephone cable at Hong Kong. The almost brand-new S-class HMS *Selene*, commanded by Lieutenant-Commander Hugo Newton, DSC, was detailed to tow *XE-5* towards her target. HMS *XE-6*, still without a skipper, was left with *Maidstone* as a spare craft should anything happen to the *XE-5*.

Towing presented a major problem for the S-class submarines. They had not been specially modified to do so, and the tow had had to be improvised. The result was some hasty modifications performed by the engineering crews aboard the *Bonaventure* and *Maidstone*.

There were only four days available for the little XEs and their crews to settle into a comfortable working routine with the large S-class subs that would haul them most of the way to the enemy coasts. During the tow, passage crews would control the midget submarines. A long tow was exhausting and uncomfortable, so the attack crews would remain on the mother submarines to rest while travelling to their targets.

Towing tests were completed but problems still remained. One of the greatest fears that the passage crews had was breaking the tow while under way. In one horrific example from the *Tirpitz* operation the *X-9*'s towing cable had broken away from the mother submarine. Unable to slip the line while submerged, the *X-9* had been dragged deeper and deeper because of the 600 feet of heavy line on her bow until she had fallen past her safe depth of 300 feet and been crushed like a tin can squeezed by a giant's hand. All aboard her had been killed instantly. Tich Fraser and the other skippers fretted about the lines, but because of the urgency of the missions they would have to make do with what could be provided. They could only hope that the lines would hold, or if they did break, would do so harmlessly.

*

On 24 July 1945 the *Bonaventure*, with *XE*s *1*, *2*, *3* and *4* embarked, set sail for Brunei Bay on the island of Borneo. *XE-2* would remain aboard the *Bonaventure* during the forthcoming operations as the reserve craft for Operations Struggle and Sabre. Admiral Fife was the ranking officer, his flag flying from the *Bonaventure* as she steamed along escorted by two American destroyers. The little flotilla had been designated Task Group 71.11 by the US Seventh Fleet. The three S-class towing submarines sailed separately, escorted by the submarine tender USS *Cougal*.[3] It was evident to everyone that the operations were shining examples of Anglo-American cooperation. During the voyage Admiral Fife spent hours inspecting each XE-craft and talked future plans and operations long into the night with Captain Fell and the other senior officers.[4]

Australian forces had only recaptured Brunei six weeks before the *Bonaventure* arrived at 9.00am on 26 July. She anchored off Labuan Island in Victoria Bay. *XE-1* and *XE-3* were due to depart under tow on their operation against Singapore that afternoon, with *XE-4* sailing early on the 27th. But even though pressed for time, some of the crew were able to go ashore and explore a little of Labuan, including some swimming in the safe local waters.[5] This idyll was disturbed twice by air raid warnings. The *Bonaventure*'s gun crews closed up but nothing happened. They were false alarms, but they gave notice that 14th Submarine Flotilla was very close now to Japanese territory.[6]

*

When the *Bonaventure* dropped anchor on 26 July, some 3,500 miles to the northwest another Allied warship had also arrived at a very secret destination. The heavy cruiser USS *Indianapolis* had just unloaded crates containing top-secret components at the Pacific island of Tinian. When assembled, those components made something that went by the rather charming codename 'Little Boy'.

*

The first order of business in Brunei was to obtain the latest intelligence summaries for the 14th Submarine Flotilla targets. It had been expected that fresh material would be waiting for Tiny Fell and his skippers at Labuan. But instead they learned that a terrible tragedy had struck. Commander J.W. Clark, a British officer from Admiral Fraser's HQ, who was carrying the latest intelligence briefings and photographs, had been killed when the Dakota he was travelling in crashed on 24 July. Another officer, Commander Lindsay of the US Navy, had set out with replacement materials, but tragically he was killed the very next day when his plane was also wrecked in an accident. Lindsay had been bringing with him the latest Photographic Reconnaissance Unit images of the *Takao* and the *Myoko*. But the show would go on regardless of these terrible losses. Smart and Fraser would have to make do with the material they already had while hoping that updated intelligence would somehow arrive before they left.

*

'Good luck,' said Captain Fell, pumping Fraser's hand. It was the afternoon of 26 July 1945. The crews of the *XE-1* and the *XE-3* were drawn up on the *Bonaventure*'s quarterdeck for an official farewell. Max Shean and the crew of the *XE-4* stood watching from the sidelines – they would depart on Operation Sabre the following day.

Fell walked down the line of XE-men, shaking hands with each, wishing them luck and Godspeed, passing the odd joke as he progressed. The two XEs were already joined up with their towing submarines. Rear-Admiral Fife was also present, along with his staff. He had been up since 5.00am talking to Shean and the crew of HMS *Spearhead*. Now Fife gave a brief speech to the assembled crews. It was a speech that was loaded with praise for the XE-men and quite out of keeping with British tradition. Fell and his men were acutely embarrassed by all of the attention.[7]

'You're the little guys with a lotta guts,' said a beaming Fife, concluding his rousing talk. 'Good luck!'

The men all smiled and nodded at the American's remark. They were, by and large, little guys physically, but to Fife and Fell they were giants when it came to pluck and daring. Both officers knew that the XE-men were undertaking missions from which some might not return, the kind of missions that in the past had resulted in very heavy casualties. But standing on the warm deck beneath a blazing tropical sun, the 'little guys' looked invincible. Fraser, his service cap tipped back on his head; Magennis, a slightly wry smile creasing his tough face; Smart, his blond beard bleached by the sun, his jaw set firmly; Kiwi Smith, cap at a rakish angle, eyes narrowed in concentration; ERAs Reed and Fishleigh, the old sweats with their permanently oil-stained hands; young Leading Seaman Walter Pomeroy, the diver, and Sub-Lieutenant Harold Harper, Smart's No. 2, sharing some private joke between them, their differences in rank forgotten. These were eight 'expendables' who had bravely answered the call for volunteers for 'Special and Hazardous Duties'. 'Little guys' they may have been, but they already walked tall among their peers.

*

That same day, 26 July 1945, a significant event occurred on the other side of the world, an event that had a great bearing on the XE-craft missions. Truman and Churchill released the Potsdam Declaration, demanding that Japan accept unconditional surrender, and threatening 'prompt and utter destruction' should they reject the terms offered. What form the threatened 'prompt and utter destruction' would take was as yet unknown save to a select few top military leaders and politicians, a list that included Lord Mountbatten. The Americans continued to make secret preparations at Tinian while the cable-cutting missions made ready to depart from Brunei and Subic Bay. The significance of the cable missions could not, at this stage, be linked in the crews' minds with any secret developments at Tinian.

Many XE-craft veterans who were involved in the cable operations later suspected that the sudden American about-face concerning the use of British midget submarines in 'their' theatre was linked to the ultra-secret atomic bombing of Japan.[8] With British submarines providing the only covert means to force the Japanese back on to their compromised radios, the Americans had to use the XE-men to do the job. The cable-cutting operations were scheduled to be completed by the first days of August. The Americans already knew that their first atomic weapon would be ready for deployment around the same time. Before the Potsdam Declaration had been promulgated, Truman had ordered an atomic bomb to be made ready. 'Prompt and utter destruction' was already possible before the President had written those words. Now it was just a question of timing.

Before a decision was taken by Truman over whether to authorise an atomic attack on Japan, the American government and Chiefs of Staff wanted to be able to judge the resolve of the Japanese government and military command to continue the war once they had had a chance to read and absorb the clauses of the Potsdam Declaration. If the Japanese refused to surrender and Truman went ahead and ordered the bomb dropped, in the aftermath the Japanese Imperial General Staff would immediately communicate with its most important overseas army commanders in Saigon, Singapore and Hong Kong. If the Americans had access to those communications they could then take further steps based on either opening surrender negotiations with a Japanese government prepared to capitulate, or, if not, attack Japan with a second bomb. But critically, the Americans had to have access to the secure Japanese communications to make this strategy remotely workable.

The sudden American change of heart regarding the operation of British XE-craft within the US sphere of influence, after so much resistance, could only have come about if the cable-cutting operations were primarily in the interests of the United States.

Of course, the Americans did not tell the British the whole truth about why they were suddenly so happy to use British midget submarines, and the British, desperate to find some useful employment for their highly trained submariners and frogmen, were not going to argue. All they knew was that cutting the cables was of strategic importance to *both* the Americans and the British. As for Operation Struggle, the neutralising of the two Japanese heavy cruisers in the Johor Strait was vital to the success of Mountbatten's putative invasion, and so to the future position of Britain in Asia. The ships were a clear and present danger and removing them paved the way for a glorious return to Singapore.

Unbeknown to the men of the 14th Submarine Flotilla, their missions assumed even greater and more critical importance on 28 July when the Japanese government rejected the terms of the Potsdam Declaration and opted instead to continue the war. The news was depressing to Truman. When the Americans read the words of the Japanese Ambassador to Moscow, they knew that atomic war could not now be avoided. 'We cannot consent to unconditional surrender under any circumstances,' wrote the ambassador stubbornly. 'Even if the war drags on, so long as the enemy demands unconditional surrender we will fight as one man against the enemy in accordance with the Emperor's command.'[9]

It was now imperative that the American high command obtain the best information possible about Japanese intentions, and the

British would unwittingly make this possible. Truman authorised the use of Little Boy anytime after 3 August 1945, ushering in a completely new chapter in the history of warfare.[10]

*

'Wake up, sir – it's oh-four-oh-oh,' said a voice close to Tich Fraser's head. He stirred in his makeshift bed, his eyes flicking open in the dim light. The voice belonged to the control room messenger, sent by Lieutenant Clarabut to wake him. It was 4.00am on 30 July 1945 – 'zero hour' for Tich Fraser.

The messenger placed a steaming hot enamel mug of tea on the small wooden table beside Fraser's 'bunk' in HMS *Stygian*'s seamen's mess. Fraser gradually entered the land of the living from a disturbed and agitated night's sleep. He rubbed his eyes and face, feeling exhausted.

'It's oh-four-oh-oh, sir,' repeated the messenger, adding, 'and quite a nice morning.'

Fraser yawned. 'Thank you,' he said groggily. 'Leave the others for a moment. I'll shake them myself.'[11] Close by, Kiwi Smith, Charlie Reed and Mick Magennis lay bundled up in blankets, snoring fitfully.

Fraser raised himself up on one elbow and took a sip of tea. He had butterflies in his stomach. He could hear the familiar routine of a large submarine in the background, the sounds that for the past four days had been the accompaniment to the journey towards Singapore and the commencement of Operation Struggle. The distance from Labuan to the *Takao* was about 650 miles. Lieutenant Clarabut was Fraser's old friend, so the two of them had plenty to talk about during the passage. Fraser and his crew had spent their time studying and restudying the charts and diagrams that had been prepared for the forthcoming operation while the *Stygian* had motored on at maximum speed towards the enemy coast, the *XE-3* on tow behind with her passage crew working hard.

Clarabut, like the other S-class skippers shepherding the XE-craft, was fully aware of their plans. It was important that they all work together to place the mother submarine into the most favourable release position. Whenever Clarabut had surfaced his boat to recharge the batteries or ventilate, the latter event occurring every five or six hours, Fraser had gone up to the conning tower to check that the *XE-3* was still there, its tiny dark shape being pulled through the water several hundred feet astern of the big submarine. When the *Stygian* dived the *XE-3* had followed suit.

The routine was the same aboard HMS *Spark*, where Jack Smart and the crew of *XE-1* rehearsed their infiltration of the Johor Strait and the attack on the *Myoko*.

Aboard their little XE-craft, the passage crews were exhausted. The concentration required to control a tiny submarine in tow was tremendous, the movement often jarring and uncomfortable. *XE-3* was under the command of Sub-Lieutenant Frank Ogden, a volunteer reserve officer, while *XE-1*'s passage skipper was Sub-Lieutenant Edgar Munday. Both men were earning their wages. The telephone cable that ran along the tow line to the mother submarine could not be relied upon and for large parts of the journey the passage crews were cut off and alone. They all prayed for the changeover, when they could finally get out of the smelly, damp, and cramped confines of the twisting, lurching XE-craft and into the mother submarine for food and proper rest. The only consolation was the sea state, which varied between calm and moderate.

Towing required unrelenting hard work from the passage crews, and constant vigilance. Someone had to have an eye glued to the depth gauge and inclinometer bubble all the time the XE-craft was submerged. There had to be unceasing preparations for emergency signals from the mother submarine. Hour after hour, maintenance had to be undertaken. The air bottles and batteries needed recharging. Battery readings had to be accurately taken every few hours, and insulation readings on all electrical circuits every day. And then there were the cleaning and cooking duties to perform.[12]

Mick Magennis in particular knew exactly what the passage crews were going through, having performed this role himself during the *Tirpitz* operation two years before. He was very glad to be aboard the *Stygian*, travelling in some comfort compared with the passage crews.

The *XE-4* had not left at the same time as *XE-1* and *XE-3*. The distance to her target off Saigon was shorter than those going to Singapore, and the intention was that all operations would occur on the same day, 31 July 1945.

At 7.40am on 27 July the *XE-4* had secured the towline from HMS *Spearhead*. Aboard the midget submarine the passage crew, commanded by Sub-Lieutenant Willie Britnell, settled into their positions.[13] Atop the conning tower the *Spearhead*'s skipper, Lieutenant-Commander Youngman, gave his orders and the submarine and its little companion eased out of Victoria Bay to the open sea.

For the next three days Max Shean and his crew, like Smart's and Fraser's, went over their plans carefully aboard *Spearhead*. Captain Fell had given Shean orders that once the telephone cables had been severed he was to pursue a secondary objective of destroying Japanese shipping present near Saigon.

Back at Subic Bay, *XE-5* and HMS *Selene* departed for Hong Kong on 27 July. *XE-5*'s skipper, Pat Westmacott, was confident that he could locate and sever the telephone cables off Lamma Island. He would stay on station for however long it took. In the meantime, Captain Fell had dusted off his original attack plan for Victoria Harbour in Hong Kong, and told Westmacott to try to mine enemy vessels there if he managed to complete his primary mission quickly and he believed such an attack was feasible. Fell's original plan had been added to the Operation Foil mission plans.

*

Tich Fraser sighed and looked at the sleeping forms of his friends aboard the *Stygian*. By 4.00am on 1 August 1945, thought Fraser, he would either be sitting in this exact same spot, sipping hot, sweet tea, filled with the satisfaction of having successfully blown up the *Takao* – or he would probably be dead.[14]

As Tich Fraser drank his tea his mind kept returning to his general unease at the thought of a harbour penetration. The disasters that had befallen the X-craft on Operation Source against the *Tirpitz* had cast very long shadows. Of the six X-craft that were sent on that mission, three had managed to penetrate the defences around the *Tirpitz* to attack her. *X-6*, under Lieutenant Donald Cameron, mined the battleship but was detected and sunk, with her crew of four taken prisoner. *X-7*, commanded by Lieutenant Basil Place, also dropped her charges beneath the *Tirpitz* but was likewise sunk, two of her crew being killed and the other two taken prisoner. *X-5*, the flagship for the mission under the command of Lieutenant Henty-Creer, may have dropped a charge but was most probably sunk by a direct hit from one of the *Tirpitz*'s 4in secondary guns. Henty-Creer and his three crewmen were all killed. Three X-craft attacked the *Tirpitz* and three X-craft were destroyed for the loss of six men killed and six captured. If the same odds were applied to Operation Struggle, then the chances of ever seeing HMS *Stygian* again were nil. 'Suicide mission' was perhaps too strong a description for the XE-craft missions, but 'forlorn hope' would have summed it up well.

Fraser's greatest fear, capture and torture, surfaced once more. After what had happened to the X-craft that attacked the *Tirpitz*, and more recently the fate of Lieutenant-Colonel Lyon's surviving men during the Operation Rimau debacle, his fear was well grounded. The six Allied crewmen taken prisoner during the attack on the *Tirpitz* had been well treated and sent to POW camps. It seemed unlikely that the Japanese would be so generous should any of the XE-men be taken alive after blowing up the *Takao* and

Myoko. This narrowed the odds of surviving the mission even further.

If any of them were captured alive, they could expect little mercy from the *Kempeitai*, Japan's dreaded military police, who would torture them for months in order to extract classified information. By now, enough was known of their grim methods to draw a suitably nightmarish picture.

Beatings were used to soften a man up. These beatings included 'kicking, usually in the genital region – anything connected with physical suffering.'[15] The inquisitors used pickaxe handles, truncheons or bamboo rods. 'When the questioning began, the prisoners had to remove all their clothing and kneel before their captors. When their answers failed to satisfy their interrogators, the victims were beaten on the back and legs with four-foot bamboo sticks until blood flowed.'[16] If beatings failed to loosen tongues, other more invasive tortures were used.

A copy of the *Kempeitai* handbook, *Japanese Instructions on How to Interrogate*, had been captured by the Americans in August 1944 and it corroborated many of the stories of severe ill-treatment of prisoners of war, civilian internees and local populations that had been emerging in a steady stream since the Allies began to advance on Japan.[17]

Perhaps the most feared torture was the innocuously named 'water cure'. The *Kempeitai* gave most prisoners this treatment as a standard opening gambit. This involved a pipe being jammed into the prisoner's mouth and water pumped down the throat until the prisoner effectively drowned and lost consciousness. Japanese guards jumping on the prisoner's abdomen then evacuated the water, and the process was repeated several times. Many people died during this violent and repellent procedure.[18]

Heat was viewed as an efficient method to loosen tongues, particularly its application to sensitive parts of the body. Hot irons were often used, along with lit cigarettes or pokers, pressed against feet or groin. Pokers and cigarettes could also be inserted inside the victim's nostrils, resulting in excruciating pain. Two American airmen shot down over China in 1945 a few months before Fraser left on his mission were paraded through the streets by the *Kempeitai*, beaten up and then doused with petrol and burned alive as an example to the local populace.

When not being tortured, prisoners could expect to live in a cramped and filthy cell with their comrades, forbidden to wash or shave for months, their beards and hair crawling with lice while they were systematically starved. At the end of this purgatory would come the kind of kangaroo trial that the surviving Operation Rimau commandos had endured, followed by a barbaric and often botched beheading by sword.

The Geneva Convention was of little relevance to the Japanese military, who had labelled it 'the coward's code'. Every time Fraser thought about capture a chill ran down his spine. The XE-men didn't discuss it with each other, but the fear was always there.

The alternatives to capture were equally grim. If their submarines were sunk by enemy action or scuttled by the crews, after getting ashore they might manage to survive for a few days on the food from their emergency survival packs, but then what? Before the crews left the *Bonaventure* aboard the mother submarines for the long tow to the targets, Lieutenant Potter's intelligence briefing had included a rather vague contingency plan for their rescue should the missions go awry. But it was less than inspiring. Their only means of signalling was a heliograph, about the size of a small shaving mirror. They would have no radio transmitter, and even if they did, the kind of rescue seaplanes that could pick them up were unable to fly anywhere near the targets because of Japanese air defences around Singapore. Their only chance of making it back without their XE-craft – and this was so slim as to be considered virtually impossible – was to steal a boat and try to make it to the pre-assigned rendezvous point with their mother submarine, which would be waiting for them once the mission was over. But how far would they get in a stolen boat before the Japanese navy overtook them?

As for asking for help from the locals, this was also fraught with danger. As Potter had intimated in his briefing, many Malays were actively collaborating with the Japanese in the deluded belief that they would achieve some measure of autonomy now that the Japanese had kicked the British out. Indians, particularly the large numbers of Tamil rubber estate workers, were also treated reasonably well as the Japanese hoped to foment anti-British uprisings in India. The Chinese were largely pro-British, but had suffered appalling mistreatment under Japanese rule. In 1942 the Japanese had murdered over 50,000 Chinese in Singapore precisely because of their community's support for the British and Chiang Kai-shek's Nationalists who were fighting the Japanese in China. Throughout Malaya and Singapore, ethnic Chinese remained targets. Would they risk their already delicately balanced survival by aiding Allied sailors?

The British Force 136, part of the Special Operations Executive, had infiltrated a few dozen officers into Malaya to work with the Malayan People's Anti-Japanese Army, a communist organisation that was proving quite effective. But for the XE-men, unschooled in Oriental languages and cultures, the chances that they might successfully contact Force 136 agents or friendly locals was remote. Once ashore in Japanese-occupied territory an Allied serviceman was really on his own, a white face in a sea of Asian ones, the proverbial sore thumb.

Small wonder that the Far East was the only front where Allied Special Forces were routinely issued with suicide pills.

CHAPTER ELEVEN

'Dive, dive, dive!'

*'Shean was an ideal CO. He had a very highly developed
mechanical brain and thoroughly understood all
the technical side of the craft. Then, his coolness in
difficulties and his extreme quickness of thought
made him the perfect submarine skipper.'*

—Stoker Petty Officer Jim Warren, Charioteer
and X-craft submariner

'**S**trewth!' yelled Max Shean as the strong wave broke over *XE-4*'s casing. His grip went and he rolled off the deck head-first into the choppy sea, his cumbersome binoculars still hanging around his neck. Shean struggled in the black ocean, kicking himself to the surface with difficulty, his shoes heavy. He surfaced, coughing up seawater, just as the *XE-4*'s rudders passed by his head, the propeller churning the water dangerously close. Realising that he had only seconds in which to save his life, Shean struck out for the submarine, kicking hard, one hand reaching out for the jumping wire that ran from the periscope shield to the XE-craft's rudder. If he missed it, he would be dead. Kicking wildly, he stretched his fingers out, desperately pushing towards the single strand of black-painted steel wire that was almost invisible against the moving submarine's dark flank.[1]

*

When Tich Fraser had awoken in the seaman's mess aboard

HMS *Stygian* the day before his friend Max Shean's untimely dunking, he had had to fight down his fears for the coming mission: the fear of failure, of capture and above all of torture. Getting hold of his emotions, Fraser had sighed, put down his steaming mug of tea and stood up. He decided that activity was the best cure for a case of the heebie-jeebies and he got dressed. His khaki shirt carried the rank epaulettes of a sub-lieutenant RNVR as a rather hopeful subterfuge, the upper shoulders of the shirt also adorned with the freshly sewn-on badges provided by Lieutenant Potter that declared his arm of service and his nationality. He pulled on khaki shorts and long socks, laced up his black shoes and picked up his white-topped naval officer's cap with its firmly sewn-on crown and anchor badge.

'Come on, Kiwi, wakey-wakey, its oh-four-thirty,' said Fraser as he shook his first lieutenant awake. Smith, his eyes blank, rose suddenly from a tangle of blankets, his hair in disarray, and stretched wildly.

'Give the others a shake, will you?' asked Fraser. 'We'll have breakfast when you're ready.'[2]

Fraser walked along the corridor to the control room, lit by red night lights. The helmsman was at his wheel, his eyes glued to the gyro-compass repeater in front of him. He barely acknowledged Fraser's entrance. Fraser walked over to the chart table and switched on the light. Detailed naval charts of Singapore and its approaches littered the table. For some time Fraser went over each aspect of the plan in his head, working through the complex series of courses, speeds and distances that he had memorised, knowing that they would all lead to one final destination – the *Takao*.

Once he was satisfied that all was in order, Fraser snapped off the light and requested permission to climb the conning tower ladder up to the bridge. Guy Clarabut gave his permission immediately and when Fraser emerged on to the bridge it was still night. The sea was calm with just a few clusters of stars visible through breaks in the clouds. Lookouts scanned the sea in every direction through powerful binoculars watching for Japanese aircraft and patrol ships.

'How much longer till we slip?' Fraser asked. Clarabut wasn't sure. Together, the two officers returned to the control room chart table for a final consultation.

'Officially, the slipping position is roughly about five miles from Horsburgh Light,' said Clarabut, putting his index finger on the chart, 'but it's a dark night tonight, and I'll try and get in a little closer. I want to be as near as safety will allow.'[3] The Horsburgh Lighthouse stands on Pedra Branca Island 34 miles east of Singapore and less than nine miles off the coast of Johor. It marks the eastern entrance to the Straits of Singapore.

Clarabut and Fraser discussed the situation for a little while longer. Fraser appreciated Clarabut's offer to take them in closer to the enemy coast. It was a risky venture, but it would decrease the amount of time that Fraser and his crew would have to spend aboard the cramped and uncomfortable *XE-3*.

Soon, the smell of bacon and eggs wafting along the corridor from the seaman's mess drew Fraser back to his crew and breakfast. No one spoke much as they ate. Their thoughts were elsewhere. It would be the last proper meal they would have in several days, so they savoured every delicious mouthful, or at least they tried to. More than one man found that he didn't have much of an appetite.

At 5.30am the *Stygian*'s main engines were stopped, the clutches were disengaged and she continued along at slow speed on her quieter electric motors. There was a shout from the conning tower. It was Clarabut.

'Control room, sir,' replied the helmsman instantly.

'Towing party on the bridge,' ordered Clarabut, his voice muffled.

'Towing party on the bridge, aye, sir,'[4] repeated the helmsman. The chief petty officer and four ordinary seamen in the towing party disappeared up the conning tower ladder. Fraser gathered his crew in the control room and then followed the towing party up top, the ladder cold to the touch.

Fraser and his men watched as the towing party inflated a large yellow aircraft rescue dinghy on the submarine's casing. Small waves were breaking over the deck and the party struggled to pump the dinghy up. A grass rope – that is, one which floated – was attached to the dinghy's towing bracket. Fraser looked astern and could just make out the *XE-3* about 200 yards away, the tall figure of Sub-Lieutenant Frank Ogden, the passage skipper, standing on the casing, waiting patiently for relief.

'Dinghy's ready for launching and streaming, sir,' called up the chief petty officer in a strong Cockney accent from the deck.

'Thank you, Chief,' replied Clarabut. 'Okay, Tich, we're all ready for you.'

Fraser looked at Clarabut in the dim light. 'Righto, Guy,' he said, his face tight with concentration.

Clarabut stuck out his hand. '*Au revoir*, and good luck,' he said smiling. 'See you Friday night.'

'Thank you,' replied Fraser, 'but don't forget to wait.'[5] Clarabut shook hands with Smith, Reid and Magennis, who all mumbled their goodbyes, before the four XE-men clambered down to the casing and made their way over to where the dinghy was being held with difficulty against the side of the submarine. The casing was wet and slippery, and Fraser's party made their way over to the dinghy in single file. After shaking hands with the towing party, each man jumped into the dinghy. The dinghy was released and slowly drifted towards the *XE-3*, the grass line playing out behind it. Fraser and his crew sat in silence, each preoccupied by his forthcoming duties. A lot rested on their young shoulders.

*

Aboard HMS *Spark* a few dozen miles away the same scene was being played out as Jack Smart and his crew transferred to the *XE-1*.

Like Fraser, Smart's mind was filled with mission information, but also like Fraser, apprehension lurked below the surface.

*

As the dinghy came close to the *XE-3*, Sub-Lieutenant Ogden cast Fraser a line, pulling them alongside. Fraser clambered aboard, shaking Ogden's hand. Little was said. Ogden and his men were relieved to be getting back aboard the *Stygian* and Fraser's party was focused on the job to come. Anyway, it was not goodbye, but only '*au revoir*'. At least, that's what everyone prayed for.

*

The transfer between HMS *Spearhead* and *XE-4* hundreds of miles away near Indochina was effected more smoothly. Max Shean and his crew changed over with Sub-Lieutenant Willie Britnell's passage crew, the *XE-4* brought close astern of the *Spearhead* and made fast with a short line. Britnell had been through the whole process for real once before. He had been passage skipper on the *X-24*'s first mission against the German floating dock at Bergen.[6]

The *Spearhead*'s motor was run astern to prevent contact between the two submarines. Shean and his four crewmen simply stepped from the *Spearhead* over the small gap to the *XE-4*, shaking hands with Britnell and his crew as they went the other way. The sea and swell were low, making for a quick and easy changeover.[7]

Likewise, aboard the *XE-5* heading for Hong Kong, the transfer went without mishap. The sea state was also calm, and Pat Westmacott and his crew bade farewell to HMS *Selene*. Westmacott believed that his operation to cut the telephone cables off Lamma Island would be straightforward and considerably less hazardous than making a harbour penetration. Spirits were high as the *XE-5* submerged still in tow and the crew settled into the final approach to Hong Kong.

*

Sub-Lieutenant Edgar Munday, *XE-1*'s passage crew skipper, reached down and helped Jack Smart to climb aboard his boat. The two men shook hands. 'Any trouble?' asked Smart.

'No, nothing serious,' said Munday. 'The telephone's been unreliable, but that's all.' The telephone link was intermittent aboard all four of the towing submarines involved in the operations. Though undoubtedly inconvenient, it was a minor problem.

'Well, thanks Eddie,' said Smart as the rest of his crew clambered aboard and Munday's passage crew emerged gratefully from the *XE-3* and jumped into the dinghy.

'Good luck, Jack!' said Munday, giving Smart's hand a final squeeze before he followed his men into the dinghy. Munday was glad that he wasn't going with them. No matter what was said, the chances of coming back from a harbour penetration were remote. 'See you soon!' shouted Munday, forcing a smile onto his weary face, hoping that he sounded and looked convincing.

*

Aboard the *XE-3* Frank Ogden also reported that the telephone line was intermittent. But the battery density was right up, and the boat was dry inside and recently cleaned out.

'Thank you, Frank,' said Fraser. 'You had better go now before anything goes wrong. I should hate you to be left here in the middle of this ocean in a rubber dinghy.'

'Righto!' laughed Ogden. 'Cheerio, and good luck.'[8]

The plan was for the mother submarines to tow the four attack midgets as close to their targets as they dared before releasing the umbilical lines. That meant all four XEs would be on tow for most of the day, something that most of the crews had not experienced before.

Aboard the *XE-3*, Fraser and his crew settled into their workstations. Fraser stood in the control room's periscope well while Kiwi Smith was seated aft operating the hydroplanes and pumping systems. When under way using its own power, Smith would also operate the motor and engine controls. ERA Charlie Reed was seated on the starboard side of the control room just forward of the periscope well where his attention was concentrated on the wheel and the gyro-compass repeater. Mick Magennis, the only member of the crew to have experienced towing before, plotted the course and bearings on Fraser's handmade chart.[9]

Once the crew transfer was complete, Fraser signalled the *Stygian* with a lamp to pull back the dinghy containing Ogden and the passage crew. The *Stygian* was soon under way again, pulling the *XE-3* through the water at a steady five knots. Fraser remained on deck for a few minutes until he heard Smith's voice from inside the casing. 'Casing, all ready below.' This meant that Fraser could dive the boat.

'Okay,' shouted down Fraser through the open hatch. 'I'll just check the casing before I come down.' Fraser gave the exterior of his submarine a quick once over. The side cargo containing two tons of high explosive and the limpet mine carrier were both secure. 'Stand by to dive,' he shouted to Smith.

'Aye aye, Tich. Ready for diving,' came his reply.

Fraser raised the Aldis lamp and signalled his intention to dive the submarine to the *Stygian*'s yeoman, who acknowledged receipt with a few brief flashes of Morse. Fraser turned and started down the ladder. Before he shut the heavy hatch he looked around one last time. The first fingers of dawn were lighting the horizon. It was going to be a long day and night to come. He slammed the hatch shut and took his place beside the periscope standard.

'Dive, dive, dive,' he ordered calmly. 'Thirty feet.' Fraser gave the course, adding, 'Let me know when you're happy with the trim, Number One.' Smith repeated the orders.

ERA Reed slammed open the levers controlling the three main vents to the tanks.

'Q flooded,'[10] said Reed, the *XE-3* sliding beneath the dark waves.

'Craft trimmed for diving, Tich,' said Smith shortly after.

'Very good,' replied Fraser.

They were on their way to the *Takao* and their moment of destiny.

*

A submerged XE-craft on tow behaved badly for the first fifteen minutes or so until the crew had settled her trim. The *XE-1*'s depth was initially all over the place, first fifteen feet, then 50 feet, then 20, as first lieutenant Harold Harper struggled to sort out her trim with the fore and aft tanks. Eventually she settled down, the submerged HMS *Spark* dragging her along at a sedate two knots. It was expected that both the *XE-1* and *XE-3* would slip from their mother submarines around 11.00pm.[11]

*

Aboard the *XE-3* Fraser studied his charts again. He already knew every course change and bearing off by heart. Kiwi Smith constantly monitored the distance that had been run using the Chernikeeff Log, an instrument used to measure distance at sea. When a turn came up, Smith would inform Fraser and then monitor the next run for the agreed distance. When he had planned his mission, Fraser, like Smart, Shean and Westmacott, had taken into account water currents and wind speeds. But no matter how accurate the chart navigation, all of the skippers had to occasionally take bearings on lighthouses and other prominent landmarks during the run in and report any deviation to the mother submarine via the telephone link. A change in current or wind could set them off course by miles and it was the only way to be absolutely sure. But it was inherently risky. They were already deep into enemy waters, and popping up the attack periscope presented the constant risk of detection and/or attack.

When Fraser wanted to check his position Smith would bring

the *XE-3* up to periscope depth. Near the periscope standard was a bearing indicator with a swinging needle for taking the bearings of any objects in relation to the submarine's bow; so the captain could take a bearing 180 degrees on either side of the boat. As Fraser called out, his eyes pressed to the periscope, Reed called out the ship's heading on the gyro-compass repeater, and after Fraser had given the appropriate bearing of the ship's head to Smith, he would work out the true bearing to be noted on the chart.[12] But this method was by no means accurate because of the bearing indicator's swinging needle. Generally, the XE-craft skippers knew that they were within a ten-square-mile patch of ocean after each peek outside.

'Minefield ahead, Tich,' stated Smith flatly. Fraser knew they were about to nose into every sea captain's nightmare. The approaches to Singapore and Johor were protected by a series of minefields that had been laid by the British, Dutch and Japanese. The charts were not completely accurate, so a cautious skipper would normally take the long route and work around the minefield into one of the safer swept channels. But Fraser in *XE-3* and Smart aboard the *XE-1* did not have the luxury of time. They had to reach the anti-submarine boom protecting the eastern entrance to the Johor Strait by first light the following day. After talking to the captains of the towing submarines *Stygian* and *Spark*, it had been decided to simply sail straight through the minefields to save time. The mines, great steel balls with magnetic detonation arms giving them the appearance of scaled-up medieval maces, were suspended from thick chains and anchored to the seabed by weights. The submarines could pass safely over the tops of the mines, which were set deep to strike the hulls of large warships. Everyone tried not to think about the possibility that one might have broken its chain and be bobbing about near the surface. A collision would mean instant death.

*

The day wore on. Aboard the XEs the crews tried to eat, but mostly they just picked at their 'proper' food. The submarines carried mostly tinned food and a steamer for heating it up, actually a carpenter's glue pot.[13] Because everything aboard an XE-craft was in miniature, the food came in small, sample-size tins. Into the pot were poured the contents of any tins that the crew wanted to eat. It was then heated up and served as a glutinous stew. It was very much an acquired taste.

Lacking much appetite, the crews instead drank pint cans of American orange juice and nibbled tinned American peanuts. Conversation was limited to technical issues.

*

The *XE-3* surfaced at 10.30pm. When Fraser opened the hatch warm tropical air wafted into the stuffy craft. Fraser climbed out on deck and looked around. He immediately spotted the Horsburgh Lighthouse flashing a couple of miles away, marking the eastern end of the Johor Strait. Lieutenant Clarabut had been true to his word, bringing the *XE-3* in much closer to the Malayan mainland than the agreed five miles. As Fraser strained his eyes in the gloom, he could make out dark hills. 'Johor,' he muttered to himself. It was almost time to slip the tow. He could feel the excitement building inside him. Taking the blue Morse lamp, he flashed the *Stygian*.

'Casing – control room,' he said down the open hatch.

'Control room,' replied Smith.

'Raise the induction,' ordered Fraser. A few seconds later the *schnorkel* pipe slowly cranked up to fifteen degrees. Fraser closed the hatch, remaining on deck. He would use the open pipe to speak to his crew.

'Stand by to slip the tow,' Fraser shouted down the induction trunk.

'Aye aye, Tich,' came Smith's voice, as if from far away.

A few seconds later Smith spoke again. 'Ready to let go now, Tich,' he said.

Fraser signalled the *Stygian*, asking for permission to slip.

S-L-I-P, came the Morse code reply.

'Okay, let it go, Kiwi,' shouted Fraser.

'Tow line released, Tich,' shouted Smith a few seconds later.

'Slow astern,' ordered Fraser. The electric motor thrummed into life, the beating propeller noisy after the silence of towing. The towing line came completely free as the *XE-3* backed away from the *Stygian*.

'All gone for'ard,' shouted Fraser. 'Stop the motor.'[14]

The *XE-3* was free of the *Stygian*. She was on her own. Now there was one final farewell to make to 'mother'. *XE-3* motored close alongside the *Stygian*. Lieutenant Clarabut stood atop the conning tower and yelled out the latest position to Fraser – oh-three-six degrees, two-and-a-half-miles from the Horsburgh Light.[15] Clarabut had come in much closer to land than his orders had specified. Clarabut raised his hand and Fraser did the same.

'Thank you!' yelled Fraser, whose tiny, toy-like submarine looked terribly small beside the *Stygian*'s long menacing hull. 'Cheerio, see you later,' said Fraser.

He turned back to the induction trunk and ordered the diesel engine engaged.

'Full ahead. Steer two-four-oh degrees, 1,500 revolutions!' he shouted to Smith, the little submarine vibrating as the propeller bit into the water.

As the *XE-3* pulled away from 'mother', Fraser heard a subdued cheer from the *Stygian*'s darkened deck. In the time-honoured tradition of warriors, they were saluting those who were about to go into battle.[16]

*

When Max Shean lost his grip and tumbled into the sea from the

XE-4 he knew that he had only seconds to save himself. The submarine was running on the surface at two knots. The sea state had changed since Shean had slipped the tow and bid farewell to HMS *Spearhead* at 9.00pm on 30 July. The ocean was shallow over the Formosa Bank, and the wind had whipped the night-time waters into waves that broke over the submarine's casing. This had become more problematical to Shean as the night had worn on, as he needed to take a visual sighting off the Cape St Jacques Lighthouse to accurately establish his position. But the lighthouse had not been lit and Shean couldn't make it out from his position atop the surfaced *XE-4*. Instead, he had managed to take a rough fix on a range of mountains called Nui Baria.[17]

With a rising wind and sea, Shean had experienced difficulties even using his binoculars. Salt spray kept fogging up the lenses and he was forced on several occasions to climb back inside the submarine to clean them. Getting in and out of the craft had also become increasingly hazardous. Because of the choppy sea Shean would open the hatch and quickly leap up to sit on the casing, swing his legs out and over the side, then shut the hatch before a wave broke over the casing and poured down inside the submarine.

With the hatch closed down, Shean had been communicating with his crew using the partly raised induction *schnorkel* trunk, just like Tich Fraser had been aboard the *XE-3* approaching Johor.

Shean had thought that he could see one of the casing bolts breaking loose, forward of where the waves were buffeting worst. He had gingerly left the induction trunk to investigate, slipped on the wet deck and been washed overboard by a strong wave.[18]

When Shean went into the sea the *XE-4* sailed on oblivious to her commander's sudden departure. Fortunately, his outstretched hand grasped the jumping wire and he was able to slowly pull himself back aboard the submarine's deck, where he lay exhausted for a time, coughing up seawater and thanking God for his deliverance. If he had not managed to grab the wire the *XE-4* would have sailed on at a stately two knots. Coupled with the sea state, Shean would not have been able to catch up with her.[19]

It would have been around fifteen minutes before his first lieu-tenant, Ben Kelly, noticed that all orders had ceased from the casing and gone to investigate. In fifteen minutes on a dark ocean in the middle of the night Shean would have been long gone. Kelly would have undoubtedly brought the *XE-4* about and tried to search for Shean, but the chances of finding him would have been remote. Shean would have tried to swim in the direction of the submarine, or trodden water, until he either drowned or was eaten by sharks – either way, a terrible, lonely death best not thought about.

When Shean clambered down the main hatch ladder to sort himself out after his impromptu swim, he tried to make light of the drama in front of his crew, but no one was under any illusions about the seriousness of the incident. Ben Kelly would not have aborted the mission if he had failed to locate the missing Shean. He could not have afforded to linger for too long conducting a futile search, dangerously flashing lights on the water's surface in Japanese ter-ritory, but would have been expected to take command and push on and complete the mission without Shean. It was what they were trained to do, and this was the real deal, not a training mission. The mission always came first, not the man. Shean knew that more than anyone. It was a brutal fact in their line of business.

CHAPTER TWELVE

Enemy Coast Ahead

*'The courage and determination of Lieutenant
Fraser are beyond all praise.'*

— *The London Gazette*, 9 November 1945

Tich Fraser sat on the edge of the *XE-3*'s open main hatch, his legs dangling. A slight red glow came from the special night lights inside the submarine. It was the early morning hours of 31 July 1945. The *XE-3* was motoring on the surface while Fraser checked his position. Gentle waves slapped against the submarine's black pressure hull, a slight bow wave glowing with green phosphorescence. Fraser was looking for a large buoy that was clearly marked on his Admiralty chart. He wanted to reach the anti-submarine boom that protected Singapore's old British naval base at first light, so there was a sense of urgency in taking a bearing and hurrying on.

Fraser had a pair of binoculars clamped to his eyes as he scanned the darkness looking for the outline of the buoy, a tall metal structure with a large light mounted on top. It was supposed to be lit; yet he could see no light. Ever cautious, Fraser ordered a reduction in speed.

Straining his eyes into the darkness, Fraser espied an object in the sea ahead of him. It was where the buoy was supposed to be, but it was unlit. Fraser cursed Lieutenant Potter and his damned 'intelligence'. Potter had assured him aboard the *Bonaventure* before he left Brunei Bay that the buoys that marked the eastern approach to the Johor Strait would still be lit. Intelligence was wrong.

The distance between the *XE-3* and the object decreased until only 50 yards separated them. Suddenly, the indistinct image that was hidden in darkness and shadow resolved itself without warning into the shape of a boat, its tall mainsail raised. It was a Malay fishing boat. In the stern Fraser could make out two men looking over the side, watching their fishing lines.[1]

'God Almighty,' said Fraser in a loud and strained whisper, 'hard a'starboard!'

'Wheel hard a'starboard, sir,'[2] came the reassuringly calm voice of ERA Charlie Reed from inside the submarine. The *XE-3* swung around until her stern was pointing at the fishing boat, showing as little silhouette as possible, and quietly crept away. *Did the fishermen see us?* Fraser's mind screamed. They were close to Singapore now, and blundering into a vessel that could report the encounter to the Japanese might jeopardise the whole mission.

Fraser continued to watch the fishing boat until it was swallowed up by the darkness. The Malays aboard her never moved, just sat like statues watching their fishing lines. Fraser let out a long breath, rubbed his eyes and issued fresh orders to the helm. If they had been anyone other than sleepy native fishermen the *XE-3*'s stealthy approach to Singapore would have been blown. Fraser lifted his heavy binoculars back to his tired eyes and started scanning the darkness for danger. It was proving to be the longest night of his life.

*

'We're sinking!' shouted Sub-Lieutenant Beadon Dening to Pat Westmacott aboard the *XE-5*.

'Depth?' yelled back Westmacott, who up until that moment had been resting in the control room.

'Seventy feet, Pat ... 75 ... 80 feet,' replied Dening, his eyes fixed to the big round depth gauge. The motion of the submarine had suddenly and dramatically changed. HMS *Selene* had been towing them towards their target in Hong Kong when the sudden emergency had occurred on 29 July.

'She's still falling, Pat,' said Dening urgently. The submarine was going down by the head. 'Depth one-five-oh feet,' said Dening. That was halfway to safe depth.

An XE-craft could safely dive to 300 feet. Occasionally they could reach 400 feet for very short periods, but this was not encouraged. Postwar tests showed that XE-craft imploded between 520 and 540 feet, where the pressure was equivalent to 250 pounds per square inch.[3] As the *XE-5* began to free-fall down into the dark depths Westmacott knew that in this location the ocean was 1,000 feet deep. If he couldn't arrest the dive, he and his crew were dead.

'Shit. The tow must have parted,' exclaimed Westmacott. 'Slip the rope!' Still attached to the submarine's bow was 350 feet of sodden rope weighing hundreds of pounds and this was dragging the submarine deeper and deeper at an increased velocity.

But Westmacott's order was easier given than followed. The releasing mechanism was in the XE-5's bow, a tight squeeze for a crewman sent forward to try to manually release the tow.

'Depth?' shouted Westmacott, as ERA Clifford Greenwood struggled with the release mechanism.

'Two hunded and fifty feet!' exclaimed Dening, his eyes never leaving the depth gauge.

'Come on, Greenwood, release the damned thing,' Westmacott called through the control room door.

'I'm almost there, skip,' shouted back Greenwood, his voice strained and muffled.

'Depth?' demanded Westmacott.

'Three-oh-oh feet, skipper,' replied Dening.

'Stand by to blow all tanks,' ordered Westmacott.

The *XE-5*'s hull began to groan and rumble as the submarine continued its death dive. It was the worst sound in the world for a submariner – it meant that the outside water pressure was building up around the hull like a vice that was being inexorably tightened by a giant unseen hand. As the pressure built, the groaning turned into a long rumbling that was interspersed with weird metallic cracks and thumps as the hull started to contract.

Westmacott instinctively glanced around him, waiting for leaks to spring in the hull, cold jets of water lancing into the crew's dry inner domain as joints began to separate at their weakest points.

'Tow line released!' suddenly yelled Greenwood triumphantly from the bow.

'Blow all tanks,' shouted Westmacott. 'Full speed ahead. Hydroplanes hard to rise.'[4]

Westmacott intended to drive the *XE-5* to the surface as fast as possible. The submarine's hydroplanes, the fins that steered her through the water, were set at their maximum elevation.

'Depth?' yelled Westmacott.

'Three-five-oh feet, skipper,' replied Dening instantly.

The crew was thrown back hard as the submarine started to rise, its bow pointing up sharply towards the surface. She was coming up fast, very fast, like a cork.[5] The crew grabbed hold of fixtures and pipes to steady themselves as the propeller bit into the water and the depth gauge started running anti-clockwise.

*

Once Westmacott had the main hatch open he clambered out onto the deck. The sea was heavy and running hard, the little submarine rolling erratically in the chop. There was no sign of HMS *Selene*. This was the last thing he needed. The tow to the slipping position was 560 nautical miles.[6] The *XE-5* was hundreds of miles from anywhere, a tiny submarine in the midst of a hostile ocean. Westmacott immediately started to scan for the *Selene*. He knew that her skipper, Lieutenant-Commander Hugo Newton, would realise that the tow line had parted and would retrace his course to try to find them.

Two-and-a-half anxious hours later and HMS *Selene* reappeared. But the sea state was still rough. Westmacott and Newton decided against reattaching the tow rope. Instead, it was agreed that the *XE-5* would continue independently towards her target, with *Selene* heading for the rendezvous area to wait for her.[7] The carefully timed plan was now shot to pieces. A 24-hour postponement was imposed, meaning that the *XE-5* would not arrive in the West Lamma Channel until late on 31 July. Westmacott cursed his bad luck and stared fixedly at his charts. He now realised that he would not be in position and ready to begin searching for the cables until the early morning of 1 August 1945.

*

Tich Fraser had smelled Singapore long before he saw it. It was a peculiar aroma that was indicative of the Far East, a mixture of overripe mangoes, spices and oily cooking. Fraser had had the *XE-3* trimmed down low in the water and was making about five knots in the darkness. The sea was flat calm, but this had actually caused both Fraser and Lieutenant Smart aboard the *XE-1* a few miles away some problems. The movement of the two submarines had stirred up the natural phosphorescence in the water, particularly on the bow and in the wake, leaving them thumping along in their own peculiar halos of colour.[8] Fraser in particular had been pushing his XE-craft hard and taking a calculated risk by running at top speed in this manner, but he was determined to arrive at the anti-submarine boom that was strung between Singapore Island and Pulau Ubin Island off the Johor coast no later than 7.00am on 31 July. His eyes and arms ached from constantly scanning the darkness with his binoculars, perched between the periscope standards. Inside the submarine all was silence.

At 1.36am Fraser had fixed his position as three-and-a-half

miles southwest of Pualmungi Lighthouse on the southeast corner of Johor. On the *XE-3* went, eating up the miles towards the *Takao*, further and further into Japanese territory.[9]

Fraser's mind kept wandering as he perched on the submarine casing staring into the darkness. His mind kept returning to his obsessive fear of falling into Japanese hands. All of the XE-men involved in Operations Struggle, Sabre and Foil were thinking about it. You wouldn't have been normal if you hadn't.

As he had continued to scan the darkness with his binoculars – made, according to the manufacturer's plate, in 1908, twelve years before he was born – Fraser also thought about his wife Melba, who was back in England with their month-old daughter. He had never seen his child, and he wondered morbidly whether he ever would.

Fraser took a deep breath and lowered the binoculars for a second. 'Brew up?' he shouted down the induction trunk, and a few minutes later he was nursing a mug of steaming hot tea that tasted a little of engine oil. But it restored his confidence and he resumed his lonely vigil a little more at peace with himself.[10]

*

Aboard the *XE-1*, Jack Smart had been having a rough night of it. Like Fraser he had spent virtually every minute on the submarine's casing since he had slipped the tow from HMS *Spark* at 11.00pm on 30 July. Like Fraser, his binoculars had hardly left his eyes, as he constantly scanned for trouble or landmarks. Three times he had been forced to take evasive action when unidentified vessels had been encountered. The area was littered with Malay and Chinese fishing boats, and who knew how many Japanese patrol craft. Smart couldn't risk a single encounter, but the evasive manoeuvres were starting to eat into his carefully timed schedule.[11] The *XE-1*, which had the greater distance to cover to reach the heavy cruiser *Myoko*, was expected to pass through the anti-submarine boom in advance of Fraser's *XE-3*, but in fact Smart's boat was falling behind, a fact that he was very much aware of .[12] He was beginning to develop an uncomfortable feeling in his stomach, a knot of anxiety and frustration that he was going to be late for the party.

*

'Looks like a small armada of junks,' said Pat Westmacott as he scanned the surface through the *XE-5*'s raised attack periscope. 'I'd say at least 20 to 30 of them.'[13] Westmacott's target, the submarine cable linking Hong Kong to Singapore, was located off the west coast of Lamma Island, in West Lamma Channel. The third largest island in the colony, Lamma is a hilly, rocky, jungle-covered island 4.3 miles long lying southwest of Hong Kong Island. The West Lamma Channel, one of the main shipping lanes into Victoria Harbour, passes between the island and the larger Lantau Island to the west.

Apart from the submarine telephone station, the occupying Japanese forces had constructed a series of caves near one of Lamma's dozen small villages at Sok Kwu Wan. The Imperial Navy was preparing for a final battle with the Allies and had hidden small one-man *Shinyo*-class suicide attack boats in these caves ready to assault any invasion fleet. Each was armed with 700lbs of high explosives.

As Westmacott's submarine motored in on the surface towards Hong Kong during the early predawn hours on 31 July he could make out the mountainous backdrop of jungle-covered low peaks and rocky islands. Pinpricks of light were dotted across the darkened land. Already, during his run in, he had had to take evasive action on several occasions when Chinese junks, appeared. Nothing was seen of the Japanese navy, though British Intelligence knew that they had several patrol vessels operational around the islands.

Before leaving the comfort of the *Selene*, Westmacott and Beadon Dening had carefully gone over the subsidiary operation that they had been ordered to undertake. If they located and cut the cable on time Westmacott and the *XE-5* were to proceed into Victoria Harbour and mine as many Japanese ships as they could find before exfiltration and heading for the rendezvous with 'mother'. But the approaches to Victoria Harbour were well protected. The Japanese had incorporated the original British anti-submarine defences into their own plan.

The British defence boom remained in place blocking Tathong Channel, the main shipping lane into Victoria Harbour from the eastern side of Hong Kong Island. Stretching from Tathong Channel south and then west in a great arc terminating at Lantau Island were eight sets of submarine indicator loops installed by the Royal Navy in the 1930s.[14] They were designed to pick up the magnetic signature of a large underwater object passing over them. The British had destroyed some of the control stations before Hong Kong was overrun in December 1941, but the Japanese might have repaired them.

Finally, the old British contact minefields remained in place and had probably been supplemented by the Japanese. The north end of West Lamma Channel was sown with 371 mines, while the narrower East Lamma Channel was blocked with 96.[15] Westmacott knew that penetrating the small and well-protected Victoria Harbour without being detected was as difficult a proposition as getting into the Johor Strait and sinking the *Takao* and *Myoko*. But Westmacott would try. After all, he had done this kind of thing before when he successfully crept into Bergen Harbour in Norway aboard the *X-24* on 15 April 1944 and blew up the Germans' prized floating dock. Of the four XE-craft skippers attacking the Japanese, the tall New Zealander was the only one to have any experience of harbour penetration.

*

At 2.17am Fraser aboard the *XE-3* had ordered a 'slow down' in order to pass suspected Japanese listening posts off the southern end of Johor. The diesel engine was stopped and the quieter electric motor switched on for 30 minutes. Naval Intelligence had been unable to verify whether the Japanese had hydrophone stations in operation but it was wiser to err on the side of caution. If the roles had been reversed the British most definitely would have installed this equipment.

After he felt that the danger of sound detection had passed, Fraser had ordered the clutch engaged and the main engine restarted. The XE-3 had suddenly picked up speed, lurching forward in the water, her bow wave growing. Fraser was still relaying his orders by shouting down the raised induction trunk, and he had begun to feel rather foolish. The night was so quiet that he suspected his voice must be carrying for quite some distance. He opened the main hatch and sat with his legs dangling inside. Due to the noise of the machinery Fraser still had to raise his voice to be heard by the crew, but he was no longer bawling at them like a parade-ground sergeant major.

At 3.50am Fraser had sighted the dark outline of an unlit buoy. He immediately asked Charlie Reed for the direction of the submarine's bow.

'Two hundred and eighty degrees, sir,' had come Reed's reply from below.

'Steer ten degrees to port two-seven-oh degrees,' Fraser had ordered.[16] He intended to pass close to the buoy to be certain of his position on the chart. It was at this point that the 'buoy' had resolved itself into the Malayan fishing boat, necessitating an emergency course change before the two natives who were peering over the stern spotted them.

After steering around the fishing boat the XE-3 continued across uncharted minefields and past listening posts without further incident. Every so often Fraser permitted each member of the crew to put his head out of the open hatch for some fresh air.

*

Max Shean, following his dunking in the sea, managed to establish the *XE-4*'s position. They were close to the cable and there was plenty of work to do while the darkness held. The *XE-4* stopped and Shean ordered a standing charge of the batteries and compressed air used for blowing the buoyancy tanks. Shean went back topside, where small waves continued to wash over the submarine's deck. He extracted the 'flatfish' grapnel from its storage compartment. It was already attached to 20 feet of stout chain and 30 feet of very strong sisal rope. The grapnel's line was attached to a bridle that went around the *XE-4*'s hull, designed to make sure that when the submarine began 'ploughing' for the cable the grapnel would be pulled from just aft of the propeller, so as not to upset the craft's delicate trimming.[17]

The major problem facing Shean was locating the right cables to sever. Several emerged from the shore station, but only two were still in service. The only way to identify the right ones was by very accurate navigation. The *XE-4* was in the correct position according to the charts to begin grappling, now Shean had to wait for dawn to break so that his two divers, Ken Briggs and Jock Bergius, could see what they were doing when they swam out of the submarine to start work.

After preparing the grapnel Shean remained on deck, his binoculars clamped to his eyes. The Mekong River delta was a major waterway, with plenty of traffic into and out of the port of Saigon.

'Prepare to dive,' shouted Shean down the partially raised induction trunk at 3.30am. Two junks were on a direct course for the *XE-4*.[18] Shean didn't want to take his submarine out of position and have to waste lots of time navigating back to the correct place so he dived the stationary boat where it was. The *XE-4* came to rest on the bottom with a gentle bump.

'We'll stay here till oh-six-hundred hours,' announced Shean to his crew.

'Righto, skipper,' said Ben Kelly. 'Tea break?'

Shean smiled. 'A brew sounds bloody marvellous, Ben.'

*

By the early hours of 31 July, the *XE-3* and *XE-1* were creeping along only half a mile to a mile from the southern coast of Johor. When Fraser and Smart trained their binoculars into the gloom they could make out the palm-fringed shoreline on their starboard side. Apart from the hum of the engine and the slapping of water against the bows of the submarines, the only other sound was the occasional shriek or caw of some tropical bird ashore. The land appeared dark and deserted, with no lights visible anywhere. Then the eastern end of Singapore Island began to take shape in the gloom, the reaches of the Johor Channel gradually appearing to starboard.[19]

Singapore Island is shaped like an elongated diamond, 20 miles from east to west and about ten miles north to south at its widest point in the middle. The main population centre, Singapore City, lies on the south coast around Keppel Harbour. This was where Lieutenant-Colonel Ivan Lyon and his Force Z commandos had successfully sunk Japanese merchant ships during Operations Jaywick and Rimau. Tich Fraser and Jack Smart's targets, the heavy cruisers *Takao* and *Myoko*, were in a much less accessible and more easily defended location off the island's north shore. On this northern side of the island was the old British naval base at Sembawang, a vast collection of dry docks, cranes, and huge workshops, acres of barracks and railways. Shortly before Singapore fell to the Japanese in mid-February 1942, the British had extensively damaged the facilities in a vain effort to deny them to the enemy, but the Japanese had managed to repair them and Seletar had been used as a major fleet base for most of the war. At this point, the Johor Strait is about one mile wide.

Three miles west of the dockyard is the Causeway, a concrete and rubber bridge that carries the only road and railway links to mainland Malaya over the Strait. In 1942, the Royal Engineers had blown a 60ft gap in the Causeway to prevent the Japanese from using it to invade Singapore. The Japanese had instead launched successful amphibious assaults either side of the Causeway and later repaired the structure after the British defeat.

At the eastern end of Singapore Island is Changi. Under the British, Changi Cantonment had been a vast modern barracks complex that housed 10,000 troops and their families. The Japanese had turned it into a huge prisoner-of-war camp, originally accommodating 50,000 British and Australian POWs. But, by the time Fraser and Smart sailed past, the number of POWs was down to less than 20,000 after drafts had been shipped off as slave labourers to complete the Burma–Thailand Railway or sent down the mines in Japan, Formosa and Manchuria.

Adjacent to the Cantonment was Changi Jail, a large, modern prison. It was being used by the Japanese as an internment camp for British and Allied civilian men, women and children. Conditions were dire.

The heavy cruiser *Takao* was moored slightly east of the dockyard, so Fraser would need to travel eleven miles up the Johor Strait from the old British anti-submarine boom that was located at a point east of Pulau Ubin Island and Singapore Island. Eleven miles through a narrow and shallow channel deep within the Japanese backyard.[20] Jack Smart had slightly further to travel as his target, the *Myoko*, had been moored two miles west of the *Takao*, and a mile east of the Causeway.

Once inside the Johor Strait, the *XE-3* and *XE-1* would be like rats trapped in a barrel if they were discovered. The channel was in effect an enormous *cul-de-sac*. They could not escape west as the Causeway blocked the strait, and returning east would mean getting through the defence boom for a second time.

As far as Fraser was concerned, Smart and the *XE-1* should already have passed ahead of his boat. But having encountered more surface vessels than *XE-3*, Smart was falling further and further behind schedule. The *XE-3* had unknowingly taken the lead.

*

Fraser intended to pass through the anti-submarine boom at around 7.00am, when visibility through the attack periscope should be adequate. At 4.13 he obtained a good land fix but he had no confidence that he would be able to find the buoy that was supposed to mark the limits of the Johor Strait – the Japanese had probably removed or sunk it with its flashing red light long before.[21] He altered course, steering the *XE-3* towards the north, designed to take him past Pengelly, a promontory, on the starboard bow. His speed was four-and-a-half knots. Everything was going as planned.

*

'Dive, dive, dive!' yelled Tich Fraser suddenly.

'All main vents open, "Q" tank flooded, induction shut and lowered,' said Charlie Reed, spitting out the words like a machine gun.

'Take her to 40 feet, number one,' Fraser ordered Kiwi Smith.[22]

As the *XE-3* slid beneath the Johor Strait, Fraser braced himself. A few seconds before, he had been on the submarine's deck, his eyes fastened on two indistinct shapes coming towards him. He had taken a fix on them, and it was clear that they were closing the distance. Two vessels. Fraser's eyes strained through his binoculars. The bigger ship looked like some kind of tanker. The smaller must be an escort vessel. An escort meant trouble. It was a Japanese navy motor launch and it would be armed with machine guns and possibly depth charges.[23] Fraser didn't hesitate. He clattered down the ladder and sealed the main hatch, simultaneously giving the order to dive.

'Thirty feet,' said Smith, calling out the depth. 'Blow "Qs".'

'"Q" tank blown, sir,' replied Reed. He had hardly finished speaking when the *XE-3* smashed into the bottom of the Strait with an almighty crash, short of the depth Fraser had ordered. The lights flickered as the crew was thrown violently towards the bow.

Fraser instantly demanded a depth reading. 'Thirty-six feet, sir,' replied Reed.

The impact had broken the sensitive Chernikeeff Log, vital for navigation; the speed and distance needles on the dials in the control room were no longer giving readings. Fraser swore loudly. They would just have to manage as best they could without it.[24]

'Stop the motor,' said Fraser, and the submarine suddenly went dead quiet. The four men stood or sat virtually motionless for half an hour, their eyes looking upwards as they listened for the sounds of propellers passing overhead. But there was nothing, no sound at all. Fraser decided to surface for a quick look.

Fraser would use the Wet & Dry Compartment for his look-see. It would remain dry. Fraser would wait until the *XE-3* had surfaced and then quickly open the compartment's hatch and stand up. This would mean that his head and shoulders would present a lower profile than if he clambered out onto the submarine's deck. But the manoeuvre was very risky. The XE-craft were not fitted with hydrophones so Fraser had no way of knowing whether enemy vessels were close. The submarine would head for the surface essentially blind and deaf. Fraser could find himself surfaced in the midst of the Imperial Japanese Navy. But he couldn't stay submerged – time was of the essence. He had to get the *XE-3* running fast on the surface to have any chance of arriving at the defence boom at 7.00am.

Fraser ordered the main ballast tank partially blown, which should ensure that when the *XE-3* surfaced, only the top of its deck would broach the water. Fraser tensed, both hands on the W&D hatch release clip. Kiwi Smith started counting off the depth from his post at the hydroplanes.

'Thirty feet, skipper ... twenty feet ... ten feet.' Fraser's hands tightened on the clip. *What if I've made a mistake and those vessels are still up there?* he thought as he listened to Smith's countdown.

It was a submarine's moment of greatest vulnerability. *Christ, let my luck hold!* Fraser thought fiercely.

'Nine feet, eight, seven, six, five, four, three … surface!'[25] yelled Smith, as Fraser flung open the hatch, cold spray smacking him in the face as he scrambled awkwardly to his feet. As soon as he raised his binoculars to his eyes he knew that he had just made a very big mistake.

CHAPTER THIRTEEN

Heart of Oak

'War is, of course, a folly, peculiar to humans, who nevertheless describe it as 'inhuman'. For the individual faced with it, as we all were, it was a fact to be reckoned with.'

—Lieutenant Max Shean, HMS *XE-4*

'**O**h, Jesus Christ!' exclaimed Tich Fraser, standing in the open Wet and Dry Compartment hatchway, his binoculars raised to his eyes. The Japanese tanker and her escort were practically on top of him, both vessels cutting through the sea directly towards the half-submerged *XE-3*, white bow waves visible in the darkness, the deep throb of their engines clearly audible.

'Dive, dive, dive!' screamed Fraser down the opening before he dropped into the chamber, slamming the hatch shut behind him. 'Half ahead, group down,' he yelled to his crew. The *XE-3*'s bow plunged steeply into the sea, her stern rising clear of the water, propeller whirling for a few seconds in fresh air until it bit into the sea and powered her deep beneath the waves in a fluid movement.[1]

'Steer three-six-oh degrees!' Fraser shouted at Kiwi Smith manning the hydroplanes.

'Aye aye, skipper, three-six-oh degrees,' repeated Smith purposefully.

'Nine-seven-five revolutions,' Fraser said breathlessly to Charlie Reed, who automatically repeated the order.[2] Mick Magennis braced himself as the boat pitched violently beneath the surface.

With their hearts in their mouths, the crew of the *XE-3* made good their escape. They could only pray that the Japanese escort wasn't equipped with hydrophones or particularly alert lookouts.

*

Dawn was fast approaching on 31 July 1945. Max Shean glanced at his watch for about the thousandth time. 6.00am. The *XE-4* was sitting on a shallow bank in the perfect position to begin the first pass in search of the Saigon to Singapore telephone cable.

We'll surface and ventilate the boat, Shean said to himself. The air was becoming thick, and the crew drowsy. Shean gave Ben Kelly and Ginger Coles their orders, and the *XE-4* rose silently up to the surface where it was still gloomy. Shean popped the main hatch, taking a deep breath of jungle-scented air, and climbed out to scan the horizon with his binoculars.[3] Within seconds he caught sight of three junks that were sailing close by. One was coming straight for him, its big angular sails unmistakable in the pre-dawn gloom.[4]

Shean didn't hesitate. He scrambled back down the hatch commanding that the boat dive at once. The *XE-4* slid silently back beneath the water and Shean gave orders for her to proceed at slow speed towards the Indochinese coast.

Shean was careful not to get off the assigned track and end up ploughing up the wrong cable, so accurate navigation remained critical. Every so often Shean would order his boat to periscope depth for a quick look to check his position against known geographic features ashore, but even this was very risky. A junk, unlike other craft, had no engine, so before surfacing the submarine it was not possible to listen for the noise of propellers droning by above. Shean had to come up to periscope depth deaf and blind. The chance of a collision was always uppermost in Shean's mind. Although a collision with a wooden sailing junk would probably not sink his submarine, it would wreck the attack periscope, just like the collision that had occurred in Scotland when Jock Bergius had been in command of the boat during a training exercise. If the same happened off the enemy coast Shean would be unlikely to complete his mission, or even to escape and rendezvous with HMS *Spearhead*.

The waters off Saigon were very busy with native craft. It was a safe assumption that the Japanese had watchers or sympathisers on some of these boats, not to mention a few motorised patrol vessels of their own in the vicinity. The city was of major strategic importance to the Japanese. Shean knew that he must make sure that no one, not even potentially friendly locals, guessed that an Allied submarine was operating so close to such a sensitive port.

Saigon, colonial capital of Cochin China – modern-day Vietnam – had been since the loss of the Philippines to General MacArthur the headquarters for the Japanese Southern Expeditionary Area Army. In July 1945 this vast organisation still controlled over 668,000 troops who were garrisoning Indochina and also Malaya and Singapore, Thailand, the Netherlands East Indies, Sumatra, Borneo and New Guinea under the command of Field Marshal Count Terauchi. Lieutenant-General Yuitsu Tsuchihashi's Thirty-Eighth Army garrisoned French Indochina and was head-quartered in Saigon, the famed 'Paris of the Orient'. The Japanese had suddenly taken complete control of Indochina from the collaborationist Vichy French administration in March 1945 following the liberation of France by Allied forces.

The Imperial Japanese Navy maintained large numbers of patrol and minesweeping vessels in the Mekong River Delta, guarding the approaches to Saigon. Shean and the *XE-4* were poking a stick into a hornet's nest, as Japanese naval and military power in the country remained unchallenged even during the dying days of the Second World War. Outside of the Home Islands, Terauchi's Southern Expeditionary Area Army was Japan's most important force, so severing its telephonic communications with Imperial General Headquarters in Tokyo would provide the Americans with a massive intelligence boon as Terauchi and his commanders were forced to confer with their superiors by radio, using codes long since compromised.

Shean came in close to the shore and conducted a periscope reconnaissance of the rocks and beaches off Cap St Jacques.

'The Japs are at home,' he said to his crew as he slowly swung the attack periscope along the shore where the telephone cables emerged. He could see gun emplacements and searchlight positions, as well as Japanese sentries wandering about.[5] It was surreal to be so close to the enemy and yet remain completely unseen.

At 7.48 Shean fixed his position as being on the northwest edge of the sandbank off Cap St Jacques. He was now ready to make his first attempt at snagging a cable. 'Steer oh-nine-oh degrees,' he ordered Coles at the wheel. The *XE-4*'s depth was ten feet clear of the sandy, gravelly bottom.

'Right boys,' Shean announced, 'let's go to work.'

*

Charlie Reed was apparently indestructible; at least, that was the conclusion that Tich Fraser was coming to aboard the *XE-3*. Reed had forgone any rest since the changeover with the passage crew. He had remained resolutely welded to his post, the steering controls. By 6.00am on 31 July, Fraser, Smith and Magennis were all feeling exhausted. The spartan seaman's mess back aboard HMS *Stygian* seemed like a first-class state-room on an ocean liner compared with the cramped, stuffy, damp and increasingly hot interior of the *XE-3*. But the navy had provided an alternative to sleep – something designed to keep men awake and alert well beyond normal human endurance.

'Right, men, I want each of you to take a Benzedrine tablet,' ordered Fraser. Each crewman took out a small cardboard box filled with pills and swallowed one. Benzedrine is an amphetamine that produces a euphoric stimulant effect. The armed forces commonly used them to counteract natural exhaustion. Without these 'uppers' the XE-men would have eventually passed out from exhaustion and fallen asleep at their posts. The pills initially had no effect, indicating just how worn out the crew actually was. Magennis even managed to sleep for 30 minutes in amongst the spaces between machinery in the engine room. Smith nodded off at the hydroplanes, the *XE-3* hanging motionless at a depth of 30 feet. There was a bunk in the control room and space for two men to lie down on the battery cover boards in the fore ends. But it was very cramped.[6]

At 7.00 Fraser determined that the *XE-3* was about half a mile from the defence boom. He would wait another hour before attempting to get through the barrier.[7] By then the sunlight would be sufficiently bright for him to use the attack periscope. He woke Smith and ordered the boat to the bottom of the channel for an hour so the crew could rest and the amphetamines could take effect. Once on the bottom everyone, except the indestructible Reed, fell fast asleep. Lit by soft electric lights, the men slumbered as best they could inside the white-painted interior of the submarine, pressed uncomfortably against wheels, gauges and pipework. They tried to ignore that they were resting inside a giant bomb. The submarine, a black shape beneath the green water, was immobile and silent, sitting upright on the muddy bottom like some large brooding prehistoric animal. The dawn sunlight above had yet to penetrate the gloom 40 feet below the water's surface.

*

Shean's plan for Operation Sabre was simple. He would attempt to snag the Saigon to Singapore telephone cable over the Cap St Jacques sandbank. The shallow water would be perfect for his two divers, Ken Briggs and Jock Bergius – currently resting in the battery compartment – to work safely. If Shean failed to locate the first cable on his initial pass he would come about and sweep seaward into slightly deeper water. The advantage of depth was, as the Cable & Wireless engineer had explained to them aboard

HMS *Bonaventure* when the missions were first discussed, that the cables would be buried shallower in less silt and debris. But the disadvantage was the shortened time the divers would have outside of the submarine before oxygen narcosis became a dangerous factor. Everyone was constantly mindful of the deaths of David Carey and Bruce Enzer in Australia.[8]

Once Shean had located and severed the first cable he would then sweep for the Saigon to Hong Kong cable on the same bearing and cut that too. Shean avoided searching for the cables between the sandbank and the Indochinese coast because two unused cables were also nearby as well as some old bits of cable, with all of them converging in the shallow water offshore. He couldn't have been sure that he had located and cut the right ones; operating further out meant that the cables would be widely spaced and easy to pinpoint on his accurate charts.

Shean's specially designed grapnel ploughed through the gravelly bottom, slowing the *XE-4* to only 2.5 knots.[9] The noise and vibration sounded through the submarine as Shean, Kelly and Coles watched their instruments like hawks.

'Steer oh-eight-five degrees,' ordered Shean, licking his dry lips.

'Aye aye, skipper,' said Ginger Coles. 'Oh-eight-five degrees, sir.' It was 8.12am. Shean's chart showed an obstacle in their path, the wreck of a cable ship sunk in 1935. The wreck was supposed to be visible but Shean could see nothing through the periscope.[10]

*

When Fraser awoke at 7.45am he felt refreshed and rejuvenated. The Benzedrine had done its job.[11] He shook Smith awake and ordered him to put a fresh tin of Protosorb in the fan intake to scrub the stale air.

'Right, it's oh-eight-hundred,' said Fraser a short while later, glancing at the chronometer. 'Stand by to get under way, and I hope lady luck is with us.'[12] The others smiled.

'Ship's head?' asked Fraser.

'Three-two-five degrees, sir,' replied Reed. The sounding machine was switched on and as expected read zero feet as the submarine was still on the bottom.

'Right, let's wipe the sub,' said Fraser, ordering the degaussing equipment switched on in case of underwater indicator loops. Being 'wiped' meant that they were safe from magnetic mines.[13]

'Make your depth ten feet,' continued Fraser.

'Aye aye, skipper,' said Smith, 'depth ten feet.'

'Steer three-two-five degrees,' ordered Fraser.

'Aye, sir, steering three-two-five degrees,' repeated Reed.

'Steady at ten feet,' reported Smith a few moments later.

'Up periscope,' ordered Fraser.[14] Magennis quickly raised the instrument with the press of a button.

Fraser had his face to the viewing lenses before the periscope head even broke the surface, watching as the view slowly resolved itself from swirling green seawater to green jungle-covered coastline and bright blue sky.

'Watch your depth, number one,' said Fraser to Smith. Fraser didn't want the periscope head to extend too far out of the water.

'Steady at ten feet, skip,' replied Smith, his eyes fixed to the depth gauge.

Fraser made a quick sweep either side of the XE-3. No danger. But something was wrong.

'Not a sign of the boom,' he muttered, his eyes still pressed firmly against the periscope lenses. 'I wonder where the devil we are.'[15]

Fraser took four quick bearings on land formations. 'Down periscope,' Fraser ordered, slapping the viewing handles back into place as Magennis retracted the instrument into its brass tube. He laid the bearings on his chart.

'Blast!' he exclaimed, throwing down his pencil. 'We're still three-and-a-half miles from the boom!'

Fraser also realised that as well as being much further away from the defence boom than he had first thought, he was also way behind schedule. About two hours behind, according to his rough calculations. Jack Smart and the *XE-1* should be 90 minutes ahead of the *XE-3*, but Fraser guessed that his friend had probably experienced similar problems and would also be off his schedule.[16] There was nothing for it but to run the submarine at full speed, though he risked using up his remaining battery power. If it came to it, Fraser supposed that he could remain inside the anti-submarine boom after his attack on the *Takao* and find a quiet creek, haul up and recharge his batteries overnight. But it was an enormous risk. His charges would have already gone off and hopefully sunk the *Takao*, and the Japanese would be looking everywhere for the culprits. Fraser made up his mind.

'Nine-seven-oh revolutions,' he ordered Reed.

'Make your depth 40 feet,' he said to Smith.[17] The *XE-3* sank deeper into the channel and suddenly picked up speed, the electric motor powering the little submarine through the water at almost full speed. But the sinking feeling in Fraser's stomach had nothing to do with the decrease in depth. He would get the *XE-3* to the *Takao*, by hook or by crook, but the odds against him and his crew getting out of the Strait again had suddenly shortened appreciably.

*

Fraser was right to assume that Jack Smart and the *XE-1* had been held up by navigation problems and their encounters with surface vessels.[18] But Fraser had underestimated just how much trouble Smart was experiencing. The *XE-1* was supposed to have penetrated the defence boom and started up the Johor Strait to the *Myoko* 90 minutes before the *XE-3*.[19] But repeated close encounters with Malay fishing vessels and the difficulties of accurate navigation at night without lit points of reference had placed Smart over 90 minutes *behind* Fraser.[20]

Smart was getting increasingly frustrated by the delay and worried about whether he could reach the *Myoko* at all. He assumed that the *XE-3*'s part of the mission was going according to plan, meaning that Fraser would drop his charge and place his limpet mines long before the *XE-1* passed the *Takao* on its way to the *Myoko*. By the time the delayed *XE-1* actually laid its own charge, Fraser's might have already detonated and Smart would find himself trapped inside the strait.[21] There was no way that Smart could coordinate his attack with Fraser's – both skippers had to do the best they could to make up the lost time and get in and out of the Strait with as little delay as possible. Like Fraser, Smart also ordered maximum revolutions on the motor, a knot of anxiety forming in his chest.

*

The *XE-4* smashed into the wreck of the cable ship off the Cap St Jacques sandbank at 9.00am.[22] Fortunately, the British submarine was travelling slowly and although there was a loud bang and the sound of scraping metal, no damage was done. Two bone-white faces suddenly appeared around the battery compartment door. Briggs and Bergius had been jerked to life from their slumbers atop the batteries by the crash. Shean roared with laughter at the concern on their strained faces.[23]

The first run had come up empty-handed. Shean swung the submarine to starboard. He would now begin his second run at locating the Saigon to Singapore cable. The *XE-4* moved out into deeper water, with Ben Kelly keeping depth as best he could with the heavy grapnel dragging along behind and Ginger Coles holding the submarine on course with difficulty. It was like trying to steer an underpowered car pulling a plough through deep mud. There was also the added difficulty of coping with depth changes as the grapnel tugged and yawed on its chain.[24]

All five men aboard the *XE-4* were exhausted. It had been

almost 24 hours since they had last slept, apart from a few minutes catnapping at their stations. Shean was feeling the pressure more keenly than his crew. It was his responsibility, and his alone, to locate and cut the two cables. But he was worried. What if he couldn't find them? What if they were buried deeply beneath deposits washed out from the Mekong River? What if? What if? What if? The questions and the doubts shuffled through his head like cards, his exhaustion heightening his stress.

His hands gripping his binocular strap tightly, Shean took a deep breath and let it out slowly to steady himself. His hand moved to his shirt pocket where a small sliver of timber rested, wrapped in a handkerchief. When he touched the wood he felt better, fortified somehow. He had acquired the relic in 1942 when he had first left Portsmouth for Scotland after the diving course at HMS *Dolphin*. He had been apprehensive about what lay ahead, and making his way to Portsmouth railway station he had passed HMS *Victory*, Lord Nelson's first-rate man-of-war, preserved in her dry dock beside the naval base. The Luftwaffe had plastered Portsmouth and a bomb had fallen into the dry dock and exploded beneath the *Victory*. Shean had climbed down beneath the historic ship and discovered that the German bomb had blown a hole in her bottom. Impulsively, Shean had reached up and pulled off a fragment of damaged timber and put it into his pocket.[25] Now this self-same sliver of oak from the most famous ship in the navy acted like a talisman to Shean. He drew strength from it, embodying as it did the 'heart of oak', the spiritual centre of the Royal Navy. He was carrying a piece of history from Britain's greatest naval victory at Trafalgar, 140 years earlier, on his own daring mission against the most recent of the Empire's enemies.

'Heart of oak,' Shean muttered to himself in an almost silent voice. He told himself to stop worrying. Time was not an issue. Even if he didn't make the rendezvous with HMS *Spearhead*, he knew that the mother submarine would not abandon him but would hang around the pick-up point for several days until Lieutenant Roy Youngman was satisfied that Shean and the *XE-4* were not coming.

Things were going well. Although he hadn't snagged a cable on the first run, the submarine was fine, with all systems working perfectly. The Japanese had not yet made an appearance. True, the number of junks up top made it impossible to surface, but for the time being the air inside the submarine was bearable. Shean relaxed a little and consulted his chart with the cables marked on it, accurate to 50 yards.

'Up periscope,' ordered Shean at 10am, pulling down the viewer's handles and pressing his eyes to the instrument. Following X-craft practice, he quickly scanned 180 degrees along each flank of the submarine. Clear. He then took a bearing on the Cap St Jacques Lighthouse and the nearby mountains. Consulting his chart, it was clear that the *XE-4* had completed the second run without success. He had no choice but to take his submarine deeper and set up for a third run. Shean ordered a turn to port and set the new course depth to run in 40 feet of water.[26] Such a depth was already perilously close to the danger zone should they snag the cable this time round and attempt to make the cut. The look in Briggs' and Bergius' eyes was unmistakable when the depth was read out.

*

'Changi on the port quarter,' said Fraser, looking through the periscope. Changi Jail, a grey and forbidding bastion at the eastern tip of Singapore Island, could be clearly seen in the bright sunshine. A tall tower capped by a flagpole stood in its central yard. A flash of colour caught Fraser's eye – a large Japanese flag flapped in the breeze at the top of the tower. It was what the Americans disparagingly referred to as the 'fried egg', the round, red sun centered on a pure white background.

'The Japs are home,' Fraser muttered to his crew. Fraser thought about the Britons held inside the prison. He wished they knew that passing by their place of appalling imprisonment was a British sub-marine, on her way to sink a Japanese cruiser.[27] He imagined that those poor souls must feel abandoned by Britain, left to rot inside the jail, not knowing how close the Allies now were to ultimate victory.

On the *XE-3* motored at periscope depth, nosing into the Johor Strait towards its goal. Every so often the periscope head would dip beneath the flat calm water as the submarine lost buoyancy when it passed through patches of fresh water. Kiwi Smith worked hard to maintain the *XE-3*'s depth and trim.

'Defence boom in sight!' exclaimed Fraser at 9.00am. His crew all stiffened in their seats. Fraser could make out a line of large float-ing buoys that stretched across the channel, and he knew that sus-pended from them was the formidable British-built anti-submarine net. Carefully, he studied the line of buoys, quickly locating the gate section that could be opened and closed to permit the passage of surface ships.

'Ha ha!' laughed Fraser, 'the bloody gate's open! Thank God for that. Saved you one job, anyway, Magennis, hasn't it?'[28] Fraser beamed at Magennis, who grinned back. If it had been closed Magennis would have swum out and cut a hole for the *XE-3* using the hydraulic cutters.[29]

'There's a trawler at the north end,' said Fraser. 'Must be the boom guard vessel. Down periscope.'[30]

After a few minutes Fraser ordered the periscope raised again. The defence vessel jumped sharply back into focus, much closer this time.

'Hell,' exclaimed Fraser, 'there's a couple of Japs leaning over the side; they look as though they're fishing. Down periscope.'[31]

Fraser rubbed his chin reflectively. This could be a problem.

'Up periscope,' he ordered, pressing his tired eyes back to the viewfinder. 'Yes, we're getting nearer now. God, but the sea's calm, flat and oily, and it looks as clear as crystal.' It seemed inconceivable that the Japanese would not notice the large dark shadow of the *XE-3* passing through the shallow water at the open boom gate.

'Ship's head?' demanded Fraser.

'Two hundred and ninety degrees, skipper,' replied Smith.

'Steer two hundred and seventy degrees,' ordered Fraser. 'Slow as you can, Kiwi.' Fraser turned to the chart table and snatched up a slide rule. He needed to calculate how long before they would be through the gate. The answer was eight minutes.

'Let me know when we've been eight minutes on this course, Magennis,'[32] ordered Fraser. The Irishman picked up his stopwatch and set it going with a heavy click. The electric motor hardly made a sound as the 50ft-long black submarine approached the gate just ten feet below the crystal clear waters. The men crouched inside her, their faces sweaty and pensive. This was it. The only other sounds they could hear were the steady 'tick, tick, tick' of Magennis's stopwatch and their heartbeats pounding in their ears like thunder.

CHAPTER FOURTEEN

Dire Straits

'I always considered our operations were those of a humane killer.'

—Sub-Lieutenant Adam Bergius[1]

The minutes dragged agonisingly by. The slight vibration of the hull as the electric motor powered the little *XE-3* forward at barely two-and-a-half knots was the only indication to the crew that they were moving – that, and the occasional sudden change in depth when the submarine passed through another patch of fresh water. Mick Magennis sat bolt upright, the stopwatch clasped in one hand, its rhythmical ticking almost hypnotic. Kiwi Smith sat at the hydroplanes, keeping the submarine level 15 feet below the surface of the clear greenish waters of the Johor Strait. Charlie Reed ran an oily rag over his sweaty face at the steering controls. Tich Fraser knelt in the periscope well, waiting, his khaki shirt stained with sweat and grease.

No one talked; they just waited for the eight minutes to run. With nothing to do but wait, thoughts inevitably turned to home, to wives and loved ones, and to the awful prospect that these few minutes might be their last. If the Japanese had mounted hydrophones on the boom defence tender they would probably be detected. What then? Turn and run for the open sea? Surrender? Fraser's face remained a mask of confident concentration in front of his crew, but inside he was thinking again about his wife and baby and of the chances of imminent detection.

'Eight minutes, sir,' piped up Magennis suddenly, his voice jolting everyone out of their private reveries.

'Right,' sighed Fraser, glad again to be doing something. 'Up periscope.'

Fraser conducted a quick scan of the surface. An expression of relief crossed his face.

'Down periscope.' He turned from the instrument and let out a long breath. 'Gentlemen, we've made it, we're through.'[2]

The relief inside the submarine was almost palpable. But there was no time to celebrate. They had just entered the lair of the beast. *So far, so good*, thought Fraser shakily.

For the next few minutes Fraser monitored the *XE-3*'s progress up the gently curving strait, popping the periscope up and down to take quick navigational fixes. He couldn't leave the instrument up because the water was so flat calm that someone was bound to notice the slight wake the small periscope head made as it cut the surface.

Fraser noticed that there was plenty of activity in the strait – small craft of different sizes and types were buzzing around on the surface, some Japanese Navy and some Malay. That could be a problem.

'Down periscope!' said Fraser urgently after another quick peek. 'There's a launch coming up on our stern.' He had noticed the grey-painted Japanese motor patrol boat immediately, bulling its way through the water towards the British submarine's position at high speed, a red and white Rising Sun Imperial battle ensign fluttering from its tall mast. The crew of the *XE-3* tensed and listened intently. Had the Japanese seen something?

A few seconds later came the unmistakable throb of propellers passing overhead before they faded away ahead into the distance. The *XE-3* continued on her way unmolested.

'Magennis,' said Fraser, turning from the periscope well, 'you'd better get dressed.'

'Right, sir,' said Magennis, moving further back into the engine compartment where the diving equipment was stored. The *XE-3* had just passed the western tip of Pulau Ubin Island. The island blocked off any view of mainland Malaya until it was passed, when the banks of southern Johor came back into focus.[3] The *XE-3* had already been submerged for seven hours and the atmosphere inside the submarine was hot and stuffy and getting worse by the minute. Neither Smith nor Reed had moved from their posts for almost the whole time. Fraser glanced at the periscope tower thermometer. It read an uncomfortable 85 degrees Fahrenheit.[4] He knew that it would get a lot worse before it got better.

*

Max Shean started his third run over the Saigon to Singapore cable just after 10.00am. His first two attempts had resulted in failure. But, once his initial frustration and panic had subsided, Shean had settled down – he would keep ploughing with the grapnel until he found it, no matter how long it took.

The depth was now over 40 feet. The danger for the divers increased considerably every foot of depth that was added.

With a sudden lurch the *XE-4* came to a halt. Shean glanced at the marine chronometer. 10.27. He ordered Ben Kelly to increase revolutions. When the motor was up to full power the *XE-4* suddenly started to move again. Shean ordered the submarine about and went back over the same position. The same thing happened – the *XE-4* was brought to a sudden, jarring halt. Had they snagged the cable?

But something was wrong. During the training exercises in Australia when the flat fish grapnel had caught the cable it had not let it go. Nonetheless, Shean had to be sure.

'Stop the motor,' ordered Shean. The *XE-4* was settled onto the seabed.

'Ken,' said Shean, turning to Sub-Lieutenant Briggs, his fellow countryman. 'Time to suit up, I think.'

'Okay, Max,' replied Briggs. The other diver, Jock Bergius, helped Briggs put on the diving suit. It was hard work in the cramped interior of the submarine. Briggs pulled on the suit's hood and Bergius helped him strap into the DSEA diving lung.

'Good luck,' said Shean, shaking Briggs' hand.

'No worries, skipper,' replied Briggs, grinning.

Then Briggs crawled into the Wet and Dry Compartment. Shean glanced at the depth gauge. It showed 40 feet, which meant a bottom depth of 50.[5]

'Ken, you mustn't stay out for more than fifteen minutes,' said Shean through the W&D's open door. 'Attach yourself to the cutter hose.'

'Will do, boss,' replied Briggs. The door to the compartment was closed and the process of flooding the W&D begun.

For safety, Shean wanted the divers to tie themselves to the hydraulic cutter hose so that if they passed out from oxygen narcosis he could probably save them by surfacing the boat and dragging them inside. The diver could then be revived while the submarine dived away and awaited the reaction of the Japanese. It wasn't the best plan in the midst of enemy territory, but it was the only practical way of saving a diver under the circumstances.

Shean positioned himself at the night periscope, the shorter instrument used for seeing underwater, and watched as the W&D hatch came open. Briggs gingerly clambered out into the half-a-knot current and gave Shean a confident thumbs-up signal. 'Diver out,' announced Shean to the crew. Briggs began to pull himself hand over hand down the grapnel line towards the seabed, disappearing from sight in the gloom. Shean remained at the periscope, his eyes pressed to the viewfinder, waiting. No one spoke. Shean glanced several times at his wristwatch or the chronometer, acutely conscious of the diver's 15-minute limit.

Ken Briggs suddenly reappeared five minutes after leaving the *XE-4*. He pulled himself back onto the submarine's deck and gave

Shean another 'thumbs-up' signal indicating that he was fine. But something must be wrong. Shean hadn't seen him remove the cutters from their storage closet on deck.

'Diver in,' said Shean, as Briggs closed the W&D compartment hatch and flooded down. A few moments later Shean had the internal door to the W&D open. Briggs, soaked and panting for breath, crawled back through.

'Nothing there, Max,' he said. 'It's a dirty great boulder.'

'A boulder?' exclaimed Shean.

'Yeah. A big bugger,' panted Briggs.[6]

Shean was disappointed, but it explained why the grapnel had come away from the obstruction twice. It was back to square one.

*

While Shean's *XE-4* had begun dragging her grapnel across the seabed south of Saigon, and the *XE-3* had penetrated the Johor Channel off Singapore and Jack Smart's *XE-1* was about to, Pat Westmacott and the crew of the *XE-5* were still crawling their way towards Hong Kong. Operation Foil was now 24 hours behind schedule, meaning that not only would the operation to cut the telephone cable in Hong Kong's West Lamma Channel take far longer than planned, the crew would have to spend an additional exhausting day at the very least inside the submarine. 31 July passed slowly for Westmacott and his crew as they silently motored through the sea towards Hong Kong. There was nothing for it but to wait and for Westmacott and his first lieutenant, Beadon Dening, to go over their charts and timings yet again.[7]

*

'Stop the motor,' yelled Max Shean as the *XE-4* swayed violently on the grapnel cable. She had snagged something at 12.05pm. Shean had ordered her full ahead group up, but she hadn't budged like before, and instead she had swung to port. Shean had Kelly take her down to the bottom. The depth beneath the keel was 54 feet, well beyond safety limits for the divers.

Ken Briggs prepared for his second dive of the day. Once more he went through the W&D and Shean watched as he exited the submarine and swam aft at 12.29. A wave of elation swept through Shean when onboard gauges indicated that Briggs was powering up the hydraulic cutters. He must have found something worth investigating.[8]

The wait inside the *XE-4* seemed interminable, but in reality it was only a matter of a few minutes.

'He's back,' exclaimed Shean, as the murky outline of Briggs clambering along the deck came into view in the night periscope. Briggs was carrying something in one hand and breathing hard into his DSEA.

When Shean got the W&D Compartment door open at 12.42, Briggs immediately thrust something heavy, metallic and about a foot long into his hands.[9] It was a length of thick armoured telephone cable, with insulated copper wires in the centre. At either end were colourful ribbons, placed there by the diver before cutting to guide him. They had their evidence.

'There's my paperweight,'[10] panted Briggs, grinning.

'Bloody well done,' said Shean, shaking his hand vigorously. They'd done it. The first cable, Saigon to Singapore, was cut. Now all they needed to find was the northbound cable that ran from Saigon to Hong Kong and the primary mission would be complete.

'Steer oh-seven-five degrees,' ordered Shean, 'half ahead group down.' The *XE-4* turned and began her fourth run of the day. Morale was good, and Jock Bergius, the second diver, waited for his turn.

*

Jack Smart and the *XE-1* were playing catch-up. When the *XE-3* passed the defence boom at 10.30am, *XE-1* was supposed to have already passed through 90 minutes before and be well on her way towards the *Myoko*, moored close to the Singapore–Johor Causeway. Instead, Smart was several miles behind.

He first caught sight of the anti-submarine boom slightly before 12.00. Following the same penetration method as Tich Fraser, he took several quick periscope bearings before passing through the still-open boom gate just after noon without incident. Leaving the gate wide open was a major security breach on the part of the Japanese, but Smart described the gate as a 'ramshackle affair.'[11] Clearly, the Japanese were not maintaining the high standards of the boom's previous owners, or they were arrogant enough to think that the Allies would not attack the naval base. It was even more surprising because the Imperial Japanese Navy had been a pioneer of small attack craft, and had used midget submarines to penetrate Pearl Harbor in 1941 and Sydney Harbour in 1942.

Singapore Naval Base was one of the best facilities in the Japanese Empire. The Japanese had repaired most of the damage inflicted by the British during their ignominious retreat in early 1942. The centrepiece was the King George VI Graving Dock, at 1,000 feet long the largest dry dock in the world. Renamed No. 1 Dry Dock by the Japanese, it had seen extensive use repairing their battleships. There was also the 50,000-ton Admiralty IX Floating Dry Dock, the third-largest in the world. The Royal Navy had attempted to deny this marvel of engineering to the Japanese by scuttling it, but Japanese engineers had managed to return it to service. The British had also blown the gates off the King George VI Dock and wrecked the machinery, but this too was repaired. Complementing these facilities was a huge floating crane and a 5,000-ton floating dry dock from the Netherlands.

The United States Army Air Force had had some success against these targets, flying B-29 Superfortress heavy bombers to the extreme of their range from a base in India. On 5 November 1944, B-29s had managed to put the King George VI Dock out of action for three months. The Admiralty IX Floating Dock had been sunk on 1 February 1945.

The lax Japanese attitude to security at Sembawang saved Jack Smart a lot of time, and motoring just below the surface at fifteen feet he pushed on down the channel between Singapore Island and Pulau Ubin Island as fast as he dared.[12] But his eyes were constantly drawn to the deck head chronometer or to his wristwatch. It felt like time was running through his fingers and he was powerless to slow it down.

*

Mick Magennis struggled to pull on the heavy rubber diving suit inside the cramped confines of the *XE-3*. Sweat poured from his naked upper torso and his face turned red from the effort. His black hair fell in his eyes as he struggled and cursed. Just getting dressed was enough to completely exhaust a man inside the tiny overheated submarine. Unlike in the cable-cutting *XE-4* and *XE-5* there was only one diver instead of two, so there were no free hands to help Magennis dress. Charlie Reed leaned over to try to help him, but in doing so knocked the steering slightly off course, earning a sharp rebuke from Fraser.

'All right, Reed,' snapped the skipper in an irritable voice, 'leave him alone and watch your course.'[13] Fraser was under a lot of pressure, which, combined with the challenging conditions inside the *XE-3*, would have tested anyone's good humour. But Magennis couldn't manage to get dressed alone. He needed help.

'Make your depth 40 feet,' said Fraser.

'Aye aye, skipper, 40 feet,' repeated Smith. Fraser stood away from the periscope and went to help Magennis. After a few more minutes of struggling and sweating, Magennis was finally dressed. All he needed to put on now was his rubberised hood and the DSEA oxygen rebreather. He could manage those by himself when the time came.[14] Fraser returned to the control room and ordered

Smith to take the *XE-3* back up to periscope depth. Magennis stood by to control the periscope motor. It would be a much more uncomfortable journey for Magennis now that he was dressed in the thick diving suit – everyone else was already suffering from the heat even in thin khaki shirts and shorts.

'Ten feet,' called out Smith.

'Up periscope,' said Fraser, pulling down the handles as the eyepiece came level with his face. 'Down periscope,' he ordered a few seconds later after completing a sweep. The *XE-3* was on course and all was well.

Fraser repeated the process over and over again. He would raise the periscope, have a brief look around, and then order it lowered.

When the clock read 12.50pm Fraser felt excitement pulse through his chest. By his calculations the submarine should be close to the last reported position of the *Takao*. The heavy cruiser should soon be visible.

'Up periscope,' he ordered, kneeling in the well and pressing his eyes to the viewfinder. He watched as green bubbles and foam once more resolved into land and clear sky. He began his sweep. The mangrove swamps that marked Singapore Island's northern shore were on his left. He made a mental note – they might prove to be useful hiding places later tonight if the *XE-3*'s batteries were empty. He might lie up in a tidal creek and make a standing charge. It was a last resort but he might not have any choice. He continued his scan, looking back briefly at the way he had come, the wide expanse of the Johor Strait framed on both sides by low-lying green scrub, swamp and jungle, flocks of tropical birds wheeling about above the treetops.

Fraser swung the periscope back to face the ship's head and gasped. The *XE-3* had just negotiated a slight bend in the Strait, her way ahead partly obscured by mangrove swamp. But suddenly a great dark mass of green and grey angular shadows filled the little periscope's lenses, jutting out into the Strait like a huge finger. Fraser could scarcely believe what he was seeing.

'There she is!' cried Fraser, unable to contain his excitement. His three companions all gasped. 'There she bloody well is!' repeated Fraser, grinning wildly. There, as plain as day, dominating the Strait, sat the heavy cruiser *Takao*, looking as massive and as solid as a battleship. 'Well, I'll be damned,' repeated Fraser several times in a low voice, his eyes still pressed firmly against the periscope.

Fraser's eyes busily ran over the *Takao*, taking in as much detail as he could in the short time that was available. Visibility was excellent, the sun high in the sky, and the water clear. The barrack blocks and dockyard cranes were visible behind the *Takao*'s great bulk marking the old British naval base. There were several Japanese vessels moored midstream and as Fraser watched he could make out numerous small craft making their way back and forth between them and both sides of the Strait. A smaller warship that Fraser judged to be a destroyer escort was tied up between large floating buoys mid-channel. This was the 1,720-ton destroyer *Kamikaze*, built in 1922, and one of the last Japanese escort vessels still afloat in southeast Asia. The *Kamikaze* was armed with three 4.7in guns as well as ten 25mm anti-aircraft guns, torpedo tubes and mines. Fraser made a mental note of the destroyer's position – she might be worth attacking, if time permitted, on the way back. Now that would be a record, a heavy cruiser and a destroyer bagged on the same mission.

But Fraser's eyes were soon drawn back to the *Takao*.[15] She had been painted in a green and brown disruptive pattern camouflage scheme that allowed her to blend in well with the shoreline. Her three forward 8in gun turrets were arranged like 'Olympic winners on a rostrum, the centre one above the other two, and all three close together'.[16] The guns of the third turret, 'C' Turret, pointed backwards, something only seen on Japanese warships. Her bridgework was massive, rising up like a giant pagoda, with a thick black-topped funnel raking astern of it. There was a second, smaller smokestack, stuck between the two tripod-like masts. Two more 8in gun turrets were located aft. Secondary armament consisted of eight 5in guns and an astounding 66 25mm autocannon primarily for use against aircraft.

Fraser saw that the *Takao* was still moored in the position last photographed by RAF air reconnaissance, with her bow sticking out into the Johor Strait. From her curved bow two thick anchor cables plunged into the water. On her starboard side was a gangway for crew to access her from cutters. The ship appeared to be quiet. Fraser couldn't see anyone on deck, though there was plenty of activity all around her, with tiny boats puttering to and fro close by.

'Down periscope,' ordered Fraser. He had seen enough for the time being. They would continue their current course towards the target. Fraser felt wired up, his senses heightened, and the knot of anxiety that had been plaguing him on and off since starting the mission had suddenly evaporated. He was all business. He turned briefly to his crew, his eyes suddenly flinty and hard. When he spoke his voice was low and confident.

'Stand by to commence attack.'[17]

The *XE-3* continued motoring towards the *Takao*. Fraser had the periscope raised again.

'Time?' asked Fraser, not moving his eyes from the viewfinder.

'Fourteen-oh-two hours, Tich,' replied Kiwi Smith, glancing at the chronometer.

'Our range is two thousand yards,' said Fraser. Just one more mile to go. The *Takao* was moored 30 degrees on the starboard bow.

'Down periscope. Four hundred and fifty revolutions, steer two-one-eight degrees, stand by to start the attack,' said Fraser, his voice quick and firm.

'Course two-one-eight degrees. All ready to start the attack, skipper,' said Smith.

'Start the attack,' ordered Fraser in a flat voice. Magennis immediately started his stopwatch with a solid click.

'Up periscope,' Fraser ordered once more. 'Bearing right ahead, range two degrees on her funnel ... down periscope.'[18]

Magennis worked fast, calculating the range by turning the degrees into yards on his slide rule.

'Length 1,600 yards, sir,'[19] said Magennis.

The training had now taken over completely. They were all utterly focused on the job at hand. The heat, the stuffy atmosphere, the danger, were forgotten. The men were focused only on completing their sections of the attack run efficiently, just as they had done on countless occasions during the intensive training in Scotland, Trinidad and Australia.

For the next few minutes the *XE-3* kept coming up from her depth of 40 feet to periscope depth so that Fraser could check his position and scan for danger.

'Length 400 yards,' announced Magennis.

'Up periscope, stand by for a last look round,' said Fraser. Grasping the periscope's rubber-covered brass handles he slowly scanned the instrument to port. The *Takao* danced back into focus, huge at this range, completely filling the viewfinder. Fraser could now see figures walking on her superstructure and decks, Japanese sailors in khaki shirts and peaked caps. 'Range eight degrees,' said Fraser, who then swung the periscope to check the starboard quarter.

'Jesus!' Fraser suddenly screamed, 'Flood "Q"! Down periscope! Thirty feet!'[20] Smiling and laughing Japanese faces had suddenly filled Fraser's periscope viewfinder. Less than 40 feet away on the submarine's starboard side was a cutter crammed with Japanese sailors going ashore on leave. It was on a direct collision course with Fraser's periscope. There were only seconds to spare.[21] The dozen Japanese sailors surely couldn't miss the periscope in the crystal clear water or the dark shadow of the British submarine just ten feet below them. The last thing Fraser saw before he jumped back from the periscope was a Japanese sailor's hand trailing in the water.[22] The cutter's bows were on a collision path with the periscope. Fraser winced and looked at the deck head. It was all over – it had to be.

CHAPTER FIFTEEN

The Dirty Bastard

*'The bottom of the target resembled something
like an underwater jungle.'*

—Acting Leading Seaman James Magennis, HMS *XE-3*

'Thirty feet, skipper,' called out Kiwi Smith. Tich Fraser nodded. Above they heard the Japanese cutter's little outboard
engine drone past, its propeller thrashing the water. That had been
close, too damned close, thought Fraser. A second or two longer
and the cutter would have smashed into the *XE-3*'s periscope.
Fraser tried not to think about the consequences had the Japanese
been alerted to the presence of an enemy submarine, or if his vessel
had had its one eye suddenly poked out. A single mistake and the
Japanese would depth-charge them to the surface and either kill the
crew or take them prisoner, and the XE-men all knew from their
briefing that the latter option was really only delaying the former.

Fraser took a deep breath and cleared his throat.

'All right,' he said. 'Magennis, the range is 200 yards. We should
touch bottom in a moment.' As the *XE-3* crept up on the *Takao*
the Johor Strait became shallower, posing an entirely new set of
potentially life-threatening problems.

*

Aboard the *XE-4* Max Shean prepared for his next task – finding
and cutting the northbound cable that ran from Saigon to Hong
Kong.

'Slow ahead,' ordered Shean. 'Steer oh-seven-five degrees.'

'Aye aye, skipper, oh-seven-five degrees,' repeated Sub-Lieutenant Ben Kelly.

'Take us up to periscope depth, Ben,' ordered Shean a few minutes later. He quickly took a bearing before ordering the little submarine down deep. Shean glanced at his watch. 1.13pm.

'Alter course to oh-four-oh degrees,' Shean ordered, the *XE-4* coming onto a bearing designed to take it across the buried cable at right angles.[1]

The submarine continued on its course, the grapnel dragging behind it, the hull vibrating and occasionally lurching from the movement of the heavy object through the bottom sediments. The minutes ticked by. The grapnel ploughed on without any result. Inside *XE-4* the tension was palpable. Shean glanced from his watch to Jock Bergius's face. The second diver was sweating inside his thick suit, waiting for his moment to come.

For thirteen agonisingly slow minutes the *XE-4* ground on just above the surface of the seabed, hauling the peculiar contraption like the master of some truculent dog that was resisting the leash. Suddenly, the submarine came to a dead stop, as if it had been driven into a brick wall. The *XE-4* heeled over to starboard before Kelly reasserted control on the hydroplanes and she settled, hovering just above the seabed with her grapnel cable taut behind her. Shean looked at his watch.

'Thirteen twenty-six hours,' he said. 'Ship's head?'

'One hundred and eighty degrees, sir,' reported Ginger Coles. 'Depth?'

'Depth 51 feet, sir.' Shean grimaced. Fifty-one feet was too damned deep. Bergius would be taking a big risk working for even a few minutes this far down.[2] Shean glanced at the diver, but his eyes, though tired, betrayed no emotion except a keenness to be on his way.

'Take her down to the bottom,' ordered Shean.

A few minutes later and the *XE-4* was settled on the seabed, her motor running on dead slow to keep the grapnel cable taut. A weak tide was running past the bilges, but nothing to worry about.

'Okay, Jock,' said Shean to Bergius. 'Good luck and be aware of the time.'

'Right, skipper.' They shook hands. Bergius clambered into the Wet and Dry Compartment and began the flooding process. Shean assumed his position by the compartment's little window and watched as Bergius gulped air as the chamber filled with cold seawater. He then turned to the night periscope and watched as Bergius opened the hatch and clambered out onto the deck in the murky green water.

'Diver out. Fourteen-oh-seven hours,' said Shean, Ben Kelly making a note. Now it was just a question of waiting.

*

The *XE-3*'s bow struck the bottom of the Johor Strait with a bang, the crew thrown off balance by the impact. Loud scraping noises reverberated from below as the submarine's keel bumped along the uneven bottom.

'Depth?' yelled out Tich Fraser above the din.

'Thirteen feet, skipper,' replied Kiwi Smith, struggling to trim the vessel. Fraser winced – the submarine was only just below the surface, and very vulnerable. Fraser pressed his eyes to the night periscope. The water was crystal clear, which was not good either. He could see the shimmering surface from below. Suddenly, the colour began to drain from the optics as the *XE-3* passed into the great shadow cast by the *Takao*'s huge hull. A new sound merged with the scraping sounds from the keel, a horrid metal-on-metal squealing coming from the starboard side. Before Fraser could work out what was causing the racket the *XE-3* crashed head-on into the *Takao*'s hull with a reverberating thud.[3] The lights flickered several times before the submarine settled back onto an even keel. Fraser ordered the motor stopped. Something was wrong.

He could see nothing through the periscope. But Fraser was experienced enough to realise that the scraping sound had probably come from one of the *Takao*'s huge bow anchor cables that he had noted during the run in. This meant that the *XE-3* was too far forward along the heavy cruiser's keel. Drop the side cargo here and all it would do would be to blow the *Takao*'s bows off, damage that would not be fatal. The two-ton explosive charge and the six limpet mines had to be placed amidships to tear the guts out of the behemoth and sink her where she lay.

'Port 30,' ordered Fraser, 'half ahead group down.' He had decided to veer away from the *Takao*, take a fresh bearing and then make another approach. But the *XE-3* did not move. 'Half ahead group down!' repeated Fraser, the first signs of anxiety creeping into his voice. Nothing. The *XE-3* refused to budge. The water's depth was only fourteen feet.

For eight increasingly fraught minutes Fraser struggled to free his little submarine from beneath the 15,500 tons of Japanese warship that loomed above him like a giant metal cloud.[4]

The four men inside the tiny submarine listened as the *XE-3*'s electric motor whined and complained as Fraser repeatedly shunted the boat forwards and backwards, attempting to wriggle free from whatever invisible trap held them tight.

Then, like a miracle, the *XE-3* was suddenly released, the submarine dragging itself back across the shallow bottom like a wounded animal, shingle grinding against her keel. Fraser ran a damp rag over his sweaty face and mopped out the inside of his cap before replacing it on the back of his head. No one cheered. Lieutenant Potter, 14th Submarine Flotilla's intelligence officer, was amazed when he heard later that the *XE-3* had managed to evade detection in only fourteen feet of water. He later wrote, 'Considering that it was flat calm, it was surprising that the swirls of water were not seen.'[5] Anyone looking over the side of the *Takao* would have seen a considerable disturbance, with white water foaming to the surface as the propeller spun desperately.

The crew of the *XE-3* had just had a narrow escape, but Fraser's next task was to take them back in towards the *Takao* and once more dive underneath her great bulk. Worse was sure to follow. Fraser altered course, steering for a position more on the *Takao*'s beam, aiming for the ship's second funnel.[6] This would mean a longer run over the shallow bank and more chance of being spotted by anyone looking down into the clear water. But Fraser knew that it was worth the risk, as it would place the *XE-3* amidships of the *Takao*, the perfect position to plant the explosives. Slowly, the *XE-3* backed away from the *Takao*, out into deeper water until she was 1,000 yards from her target.

*

Max Shean and his crew watched as the needles for the hydraulic cutter gauges jumped to life. It meant that Jock Bergius was cutting the Saigon to Hong Kong cable. Shean turned back to the night periscope and watched for Bergius's return through the green murk.

Bergius was concerned about oxygen poisoning and was working as fast as he dared. The bottom was reasonably hard with a soft layer on top about eight inches deep.[7] He watched as the bulky hydraulic cutters that he held in his hands did their work. With a steady hiss the blade moved slowly out from its guide towards the cable. Bergius depressed the large trigger on the cutters and the blade sank into the cable as if it wasn't there. There was a crunching sound, followed by a snap and then, nothing.[8] Something wasn't right.

'He's back,' exclaimed Shean to his crew as Bergius was sighted pulling himself along the *XE-4*'s casing dragging the cutter with one hand. He spent a few minutes fiddling with the hydraulic cutter before stowing it, gave Shean a quick 'thumbs-up' signal and then clambered back into the W&D compartment, closing the hatch behind him.

'Diver in,' announced Shean. 'Time?'

'Fourteen fourteen hours, skipper,' replied Ben Kelly. Bergius had been outside the submarine for twelve minutes working on pure oxygen in 51 feet of water. It was close.[9]

Once Shean had the W&D compartment door open, Bergius, his lips slightly blue, pulled himself into the control room, panting for breath. He was shaking his head.

'I cut the cable twice, Max,' said Bergius, water dripping off his suit. 'But the damned cutters are defective. The cable didn't part.'

'Damn it!' exclaimed Shean. 'Are you sure?'

'I am. No doubt about it. The cable's damaged, but it's still intact.'[10] Bergius looked crushed. 'I've already fitted the spare cutters.'[11]

'Well, we'll have to try again,' said Shean.

'I'm rested up, skip,' piped up the lead diver, Ken Briggs. 'I'll go out and have a crack at it, if you like.'

'No, Max, I'll do it,' interrupted Bergius.

'Are you sure you feel up to it, Jock?' asked Shean.

'Aye, skipper, you don't need to worry about me,' replied Bergius fiercely.

Shean smiled. He could afford to wait a little while to give Bergius time to recover from the exertions of his first dive. The cable wasn't going anywhere.

*

Jack Smart thumped the flat of his hand against the *XE-1*'s periscope standard in frustration. He was still one-and-a-half hours behind schedule. And now he faced a very difficult decision. His target, the heavy cruiser *Myoko*, was moored two miles beyond the *Takao*. Smart had to assume that Fraser in the *XE-3* had managed to stay on schedule and had already laid his charge and limpet mines beneath the *Takao* and was on his way back towards the defence boom gate. The side charge and limpets were set to detonate six hours after emplacement. Smart had lost 90 precious minutes during the approach to the boom, 90 minutes that should have been spent racing up the Johor Strait ahead of the *XE-3*.[12] He had two choices. He could continue with his mission and motor on towards the distant *Myoko*, use up more time placing his charge and limpets and then sail the thirteen miles all the way back past the *Takao* towards the distant boom gate. Or he could abandon his mission and go for his secondary target, the *Takao*.

The first option was looking increasingly unattractive. If Fraser was progressing with his mission on schedule, by the time Smart made it to the *Myoko*, set his charges and started back, darkness would have fallen. He assumed that the Japanese closed the defence boom gate at night. Though it was perfectly feasible for Smart to use his diver, Leading Seaman Walter Pomeroy, to cut a hole in the boom gate to escape through, the flotilla divers had not been trained to work in the dark. No artificial illumination would be possible, as the Japanese would see it immediately. Unable to pass through the boom the *XE-1* would, in effect, be trapped in a narrow and shallow channel a few miles long when the *XE-3*'s explosives detonated beneath the *Takao*, scheduled to occur at approximately 9.00pm. It was a safe assumption that the Japanese would begin an immediate search of the area within the boom for enemy infiltrators or saboteurs.

The second option was much more attractive, though perhaps even more risky in some ways. Smart could divert towards the *Takao*, creep in and drop his charge underneath the warship, then exfiltrate back down the Strait and out through the hopefully still open gate *before* Fraser's charges exploded. But Smart knew that there was great danger in approaching an already mined ship. The fuses on the charge and mines were not foolproof and they would already have eaten into a big chunk of their six-hour run by the time the *XE-1* showed up. The mines in particular were a concern as they were fitted with anti-tamper devices that were set off by movement.

Smart discussed these problems with his first lieutenant, Harold Harper.

'Alright, it's decided,' said Smart, grimly confident after a few minutes of animated conversation. 'We'll switch to our secondary target, the *Takao*.'[13] Glancing at his charts Smart realised that he wasn't far away from the big warship. Like Fraser in the *XE-3*, he constantly ordered his submarine to periscope depth to check his bearings and search ahead. He had no way of knowing that Fraser and the *XE-3* had experienced similar delays to the *XE-1* and had not yet mined the *Takao*. But Smart's plan made sense. Better to make sure that the *Takao* was fatally damaged than risk almost certain discovery and destruction if he stuck to his original plan.[14]

Smart told Pomeroy to stand down. He wouldn't be required to dive on the *Takao*. Smart's concern was that using a diver on an already mined ship was asking for trouble.

The counter-mining device was terrifying. Once a diver had placed one of the rectangular-shaped limpet mines onto a ship's hull all he had to do to start the preset timer was to pull a little cotton pin out of a hole in the weapon's front. This started the time clock.[15] The counter-mining device consisted of two needle heads stuck together with a sort of sleeve over them. Once the diver started the clock, the sleeve started to retract until the two needles were left sticking out. If an enemy diver got hold of the mine and pulled it or banged into it the needles would drop apart and the charge would immediately explode.[16] Smart was not going to risk Pomeroy accidentally brushing against one of *XE-3*'s already live limpet mines while he swam around setting his own. A catastrophic chain reaction would not only cause the six already armed limpets, each containing 200lbs of high explosive, to detonate, but the *XE-3*'s two-ton side charge would also go up, along with that of the *XE-1* as well. Smart and his crew would be vaporised in a fraction of a second.

It would be dangerous enough just manoeuvring the *XE*-1 beneath the *Takao* without upsetting the *XE-3*'s limpets. The slightest bump or vibration could cause those delicate pins to part company with the mine. Smart tried to put these thoughts to the back of his mind.

'Up periscope,' he ordered. As he swung the lenses the *Takao* suddenly jumped into focus on the port quarter. She was several miles off, but she was very real.

'Target sighted,' said Smart, his bearded face creasing into a smile. 'Down periscope. Time?'

'Fourteen forty hours, Jack,' said Harper.[17] Altering course, Smart began his slow and methodical approach run towards the *Takao*. He had just bought himself some time, now it was up to him to make sure that it wasn't wasted.

'Prepare to begin attack,' he said in a low but confident voice.

*

One minute after Jack Smart first sighted the *Takao*, Jock Bergius left the *XE-4* on his second dive to sever the Saigon to Hong Kong cable. He swam over to the storage bays on the side of the submarine and retrieved the spare hydraulic cutters. Working fast, he quickly swam down the grapnel cable to the seabed where the flatfish had hauled a large section of the thick telephone cable up out of the mud. Bergius moved over to where he had already made two incisions with the defective cutters and went to work once more. In just a few seconds the cutters had sliced through the cable, Bergius cutting away an entire one-foot section as proof, just as Ken Briggs had done with the Saigon to Singapore cable.[18]

'Diver in,' said Shean, once Bergius was safely inside the W&D compartment with his prize. 'Time?'

'Fourteen fifty-two hours, skipper,' said Kelly. Bergius' second dive had lasted nine minutes. Shean was ecstatic – his principal objective was now fully complete.[19]

*

'Half ahead, group down,' ordered Fraser, his eyes once more glued to the night periscope. It was 3.03pm. The *XE-3* began her second attack run, grinding across the rough bottom like a shark nosing towards its prey in the shallows, her little propeller almost silently cutting through the sparkling water. The *Takao* sat astride a trench in the bottom of the Johor Strait, surrounded by relatively shallow water. Fraser intended to creep into this deeper hole directly beneath the warship's keel to lay his charge.

The *XE-3* slid through the shallow approach water. In one place the depth was only thirteen feet. Fraser prayed that no Japanese sailor was looking over the side of his ship. Once again, the great dark keel of the *Takao* came into view as the *XE-3* passed into her shadow, and at the same time the depth gauge began to register deeper water.

'Fifteen feet, Tich,' said Smith in a concerned voice as he watched the gauge. 'Eighteen feet ... twenty feet.' Smith sounded relieved. Fraser remained at the night periscope. He glanced up briefly through the submarine's small upper viewing window, watching it fade to black as the *XE-3* passed directly beneath the massive Japanese warship.

'Stop the motor,' ordered Fraser. 'Depth?'

'Twenty-two feet, skipper,'[20] replied Smith. The propeller stopped.

'Full astern,' ordered Fraser. As the *XE-3* reversed, tendrils of light started to fill the window and Fraser's night periscope. 'Stop the motor!' ordered Fraser.[21] The *XE-3* was in position. There was a little light for the diver to work in, but they were still well beneath the warship's keel.

Fraser and his crew looked up through the little window at the dim outline of the *Takao* floating just a foot or so above them. The entire underside of the Japanese warship was festooned with marine life – barnacles and thick seaweed that drifted lazily in the current with green and brown tendrils.[22] It was like looking at an upside down coral reef, hardly recognisable as a man-made object except for the way the weed-encrusted bottom tapered away neatly towards stem and stern.

Fraser decided to let each man have a quick look at his prize.

'Christ, what a dirty bastard!'[23] exclaimed Charlie Reed when he took a look. The *Takao* was indeed a 'dirty bastard' – she evidently hadn't been dry-docked and properly cleaned in years. When Mick Magennis saw the state of the warship's bottom he knew that it spelt trouble for him.

'Raise the bow antennae,' ordered Fraser.

Smith reached over and pulled down a lever that raised the two bow antennae. They were designed to allow the submarine to rest against the bottom of the target vessel, leaving a sufficient gap for a diver to open the W&D compartment hatch and exit the boat.[24] Because of the angle of the submarine in relation to the *Takao*, Fraser didn't bother to raise the aft antennae.

Once everything was ready Fraser gave his diver a nod.

'Magennis,' said Fraser, as the Irishman finished strapping on his DSEA apparatus. 'Place all six limpets as quickly as you can, and for God's sake don't make *any* noise.'[25]

'Right, sir,' replied Magennis. Fraser fitted the diver's Perspex window before clapping him on the shoulder.

'Good luck,' said Fraser. Magennis grinned and raised his thumb then clambered awkwardly into the W&D as Fraser closed the door behind him. For a moment Fraser actually felt a little jealous of Magennis, for soon he would be out of the overheated, stuffy boat and swimming in the cool water. But then he thought about what Magennis was about to do, and of the very great dangers that he faced.[26]

Fraser crouched down and watched as Magennis flooded the chamber, the water quickly rising to cover the diver's dark-clad body. Fraser noted that Magennis was breathing steadily – he didn't appear apprehensive in the least. The boy from the Falls Road was about to make history.

*

Although the principal objectives of Operation Sabre had been achieved, Max Shean harboured a nagging worry: although Jock Bergius had cut the northbound Saigon to Hong Kong cable on his second attempt, he was not one hundred percent sure that it was actually the right cable. The area had several disused cables, so Shean decided to double-check his charts. After a further perusal everything appeared to be correct. He decided to trust his navigation. Bergius *had* cut the right cable. But being a methodical and cautious man, Shean decided to cut it again, just to be absolutely sure. He would navigate the *XE-4* into a fresh position over the northbound cable where it was marked on his chart and then detail one of the divers to go out again.

The chart stated that the cable crossed a shallow patch in the position Shean had decided to cut it, but when the *XE-4* man-oeuvered into position it didn't look promising.

'Depth?' asked Shean.

'Sixty feet, skipper,'[27] replied Ben Kelly, screwing his face up as he spoke. Shean sighed. Sixty feet was twice the safe operating depth for divers using the DSEA rebreather apparatus. The previous four dives had lasted between six and twelve minutes each. More than ten minutes at 60 feet would cause the fast onset of oxygen poisoning. And the divers were both tired, meaning that they would have even less resistance than before. It would be asking for trouble. No, Bergius *had* cut the right cable, Shean assured himself. He told himself to stop worrying about it. The operation had gone off like a charm so far, so why risk an accident at this stage? Shean stared into space for a few moments, his mind turning over the situation.

'Let's call it a day, gentlemen,' said Shean confidently.[28] There was a definite lessening of tension inside the boat after he spoke.

But they were not out of the woods just yet. Shean's secondary mission was to enter Saigon harbour and sink Japanese ships, but he was required to first rendezvous with HMS *Spearhead* and receive the latest intelligence summary, whereupon a decision would be made over whether to proceed.[29] The *XE-4* was certainly well prepared for such a mission. Clamped to the outside of the hull were two side cargoes, each containing six 200lb limpet mines.[30]

Shean gave orders for the *XE-4* to shift position further away from the coast of Indochina, away from possible observation by the large numbers of junks plying the waters off Saigon.

The air inside the boat was becoming so bad that Shean realised he needed to ventilate the submarine, and soon. But this presented an entirely new set of challenges, and dangers. As the *XE-4* crept away from the Cap St Jacques sandbank into deeper waters Max Shean's face, his eyes ringed by dark shadows of exhaustion, was set once more deep in thought. The air inside the *XE-4* was as thick as molasses. It was hard to concentrate, even to stay awake. Something had to be done, and done very soon.

CHAPTER SIXTEEN

'Diver out'

'The Takao *held no interest for us, other
than the need to blow her up.'*

—Lieutenant Ian Fraser, HMS *XE-3*

Max Shean had a problem; or, rather, he had two problems, and two possible but problematical solutions. The *XE-4* could not continue submerged indefinitely. The electric motor would eventually use up all the battery power and stop. Together, the two big batteries gave the boat a maximum range of about 80 miles.[1] Secondly, the air inside the submarine, though scrubbed with Protosorb canisters, would eventually grow toxic enough to suffocate and kill the crew.

The solution was obvious – surface the boat. On the surface the XE-craft commander could start his diesel engine, which would simultaneously recharge the electric batteries and the compressed air canisters. He could also air the boat, replenishing the atmosphere and reviving the crew with fresh salty air from outside. But Shean, lying just off Japanese-occupied Saigon, could not safely do either of these things, as there were too many local fishing vessels around. There was also the risk that the XE-craft, though very low in the water, could be caught on enemy radar or that the noisier diesel engine could be picked up by underwater hydrophones mounted on Japanese patrol vessels. One mistake could mean death, and so far Operation Sabre had gone very well indeed. Taking needless and dangerous risks at this stage would be foolhardy in the extreme.

But there was another option. It was risky and very challenging for a tired crew, but was really the only course of action available to Shean. Lying on the submarine's deck was the air induction trunk, which could be raised and lowered from inside the XE-craft. It was a primitive *schnorkel* device that theoretically allowed a submarine to remain submerged but able to run its diesel engine, charging the batteries, airing the boat and allowing for an increased submerged speed useful in confrontations with enemy surface craft.[2]

The trunk could be used when the submarine was sailing at periscope depth, ten feet below the surface. The planesman had to watch the depth gauge very carefully because if the *schnorkel*'s head dipped beneath the waves water would rush into the engine compartment. The engine would continue to burn air, but from the atmosphere inside the submarine, causing the air pressure to fall steadily. The effect on the crew was alarming, with their eardrums popping painfully. Once the *schnorkel* head emerged from the sea, the engine would resume sucking in air from above, causing the air pressure to dramatically rise again. If this happened too often, it caused nausea and pain among the crew.

If the helmsman was not fast enough in shutting the air valve when the *schnorkel* head dipped below the water the submarine could flood and sink like a stone, drowning everyone on board.[3] Shean and the other XE-craft skippers had tried *schnorkeling* during practice sessions in Scotland and Australia, with mixed results, and none of them wanted to do it unless no other option was available. The Admiralty had actually told commanders not to attempt it. For Shean and his crew, however, it was their only chance.

'Stand by to raise the induction trunk,' ordered Shean after bringing the *XE-4* up to periscope depth. The crew exchanged concerned glances. Shean made doubly sure that Ben Kelly and Ginger Coles were completely ready at their positions before he ordered the *schnorkel* to be engaged.

On the ocean's calm surface the small British *schnorkel* left a minimal white wake as it cut through the water.

'Half ahead, group down,' ordered Shean, cautiously running the diesel engine at half speed.[4] After a few minutes the superheated atmosphere inside of the boat began to clear, a blessed relief for the five men crammed inside its fetid interior. Shean made constant sweeps with the attack periscope, checking for dangers and taking bearings off landmarks.

*

Aboard the *XE-3* in the Johor Strait, the time to use the limpet mines had arrived. Tich Fraser watched through the night periscope as the W&D compartment hatch clip slid round. It was 3.30pm. As the hatch came open it was clear that there was not enough room for Mick Magennis to get out, the hatch clanging against the underside of the *Takao*.

Magennis, unfazed by the narrow exit gap, decided instead to make diving history. Working quickly inside the flooded W&D, he took a deep breath and deflated the DSEA bag that was strapped to his chest until it was as flat as possible. Magennis then wriggled through the gap, unable to breathe until he was clear of the hatch. Once outside of the submarine he quickly reinflated the DSEA, dragging heavily on the mouthpiece before giving Fraser a thumbs-up.[5] Fraser was speechless. It was the first time that a diver had ever voluntarily stopped breathing underwater. Fraser shook his head slowly in disbelief, feeling a tremendous surge of pride in his diver.

Magennis could feel the one-knot current running against him as soon as he left the submarine. The water was cool and intensely refreshing after the *XE-3*'s furnace-like interior. The water visibility was extraordinary – he could see far along the *Takao*'s keel towards her bow and stern. But he was also struck by a feeling of loneliness engendered by such a sudden change in environment. One minute he was stuck inside a tiny overheated submarine with three other

221

sweating men, now he was free in a vast expanse of cool water that stretched away beyond the limit of his vision. It was unsettling.

Vision was becoming a problem. A trickle of small bubbles was emerging in a constant stream from Magennis's breathing set and passing in front of his face. It could only mean one thing: a leak. Looking closely, he found the leak in the join between the oxygen cylinder and the reducing valve. The bubbles quickly rose up into the weeds hanging beneath the *Takao*'s dark keel.[6] Perhaps he had damaged the set when he dragged himself through the W&D hatch? This was dangerous. If he moved to the side of the warship the bubbles would rise to the water's surface. This was why commando frogmen used a rebreather, to prevent telltale bubbles being seen on the surface by vigilant enemy lookouts. Magennis could go back inside the submarine and change his DSEA over, but that would take some time to accomplish and he knew that Fraser wanted to get the job over and done with as quickly as possible and be on his way.

As he was operating in shallow water, making it an easier dive than it otherwise might have been, Magennis decided to disregard the leak and get on with his job. Shutting the W&D compartment lid with a solid clang, Magennis swam over the starboard side of the submarine towards the limpet carrier, out of sight of Fraser who was watching through the night periscope. Fraser too had noticed the leak in Magennis's equipment, and it concerned him, but he had no way of communicating with the Ulsterman now that he was outside the *XE-3*. With typical stoicism, Magennis had decided to press on when a lesser man would have returned to rectify the fault.

*

Pat Westmacott aboard *XE-5* glanced at his watch. He still could not shake the feeling of being the last guest to arrive at the party. His submarine was still on its way to Hong Kong. The unfortunate 24-hour delay to Operation Foil forced Westmacott to face an uncomfortable reality. The *XE-5* would shortly begin the 30-mile final approach to the West Lamma Channel. But Westmacott knew that by the time his submarine arrived on station in the vicinity of the submerged telephone cable, he would have to impose another agonising delay. It would be dark, or very nearly so, and his two divers could not work at night. So the *XE-5* would have to remain off the target area, waiting for the dawn. This was very danger- ous, because loitering inside enemy waters unable to get on with their assigned mission could have disastrous results. The longer any of the British XE-craft spent in Japanese waters, the slimmer the chances that they would all remain undetected. And the waters off Hong Kong, like those off Saigon, were busy with native fishing ves- sels and trading junks. This consideration meant that Westmacott would have to keep the *XE-5* submerged for long periods, further adding to his men's exhaustion. All in all, Operation Foil was turn- ing out to be the hardest mission of the lot from the standpoint of human endurance.

The New Zealander sighed in frustration and tried to stretch his 6ft frame inside the narrow confines of the tiny submarine. He announced that operations to begin dragging for the two cables were postponed until first light on 1 August.[7] His crew looked at him with hollow eyes and said nothing.

*

Jack Smart dragged his aching eyes away from the attack periscope for what seemed like the hundredth time in as many minutes and ordered another slight course adjustment. Since deciding to aban- don attacking the *Myoko* in favour of taking out his secondary tar- get, Smart and the *XE-1* had been slowly and carefully approaching the *Takao*, meeting some of the same problems that Tich Fraser and the *XE-3* had experienced. There were a lot of Japanese surface craft about, making it perilous to constantly take bearings off the *Takao* using the periscope, but it had to be done. In spite of this,

Smart felt buoyed up. He should be able to reach and mine the *Takao* leaving plenty of time to exit the boom gate before darkness fell, and should be well away from the scene of the crime when he and Fraser's explosives went up. But he couldn't get out of his mind the fear of approaching an already mined ship. He would have to exercise extreme caution during the run-in. In front of his crew he continued to exude confidence and they reacted well to his feigned insouciance.

'Right, up periscope, please,' Smart ordered once again. 'Range?'

'One thousand seven hundred yards, skipper,' replied Beadon Dening.

'Four hundred and fifty revolutions, if you please, Mr Greenwood,' said Smart to the engine room artificer.

'Aye aye, sir, 450 revolutions.'

The corner of Smart's mouth turned up in a crooked grin as his fork-bearded face continued to press against the periscope viewer. It was the almost vulpine leer of a pirate who had just spotted a particularly juicy target on the horizon.

*

Fraser expected Magennis to take about 30 minutes placing the limpets on to the *Takao*'s bottom. For the time being Fraser had nothing much to do. Charlie Reed and Kiwi Smith were also temporarily unemployed. Fraser kept watch through the night periscope but only caught the occasional glimpse of Magennis moving about.[8]

After all the excitement of creeping up on the *Takao*, and getting stuck, this was rather an anticlimax. None of them inside the *XE-3* could really rest, as they had to be ready in case Magennis came back earlier or some other problem arose, so they were relegated to staring into space at their positions, clock-watching and drinking cold and very satisfying tins of American orange juice out of the Freon container. The juice was a welcome refreshment, helping to stave off dehydration as the *XE-3* sat with her motor switched off on the seabed. Fraser had also been forced to switch off the air conditioning, as they couldn't afford to make any noise. But this meant that the temperature inside the boat, already high, had by now climbed into the high 90s. It was like sitting inside a sauna, each breath hot in the back of the throat. Their shirts were drenched in sweat and beads of perspiration constantly ran down their faces or trickled off their chins, slapping on the metal deck with tiny plops. They panted like exhausted dogs, mouths open. Conversation was practically non-existent.

Every so often the three crewmen inside the *XE-3* heard a dull thump or a metallic clang on the outside of the casing. It was the sound of Magennis removing a limpet mine from the carrier.[9] The noise sounded more serious than it actually was, but at least it meant that Magennis was still alive and well. The men inside the submarine tried not to think about the vast amount of high explosives that Magennis was playing with just a few feet from where they sat. He had emplaced plenty of practice mines during training in Scotland, Trinidad and Australia, but live ones were another matter entirely. Make a mistake with one of those and it would be your last.

*

Mick Magennis was soon struggling. The dense marine growth hanging down from the *Takao*'s bottom danced and swayed in the current like a forest in the wind. Looking at it, Magennis knew that the magnetic mines would not adhere to such a dirty surface. He had no choice but to manually clear patches to expose the *Takao*'s steel hull plates in order to give the weapon's magnet something to stick to.[10] He reached down and pulled out his large diver's knife from its scabbard strapped to his left leg and wearily began hacking and scraping at the dense growth like some bizarrely dressed horticulturalist weeding a vast upside-down garden. His arms soon ached from the effort of cutting and slashing at the weeds. Breathing hard, the trail of bubbles leaking from his defective apparatus soon became a torrent. This meant that he was using up his precious oxygen much faster than normal and that the Protosorb tin inside the breathing bag would gradually become less and less successful at scrubbing the air clean for him to breathe again.

Whenever Magennis cleared a patch of weeds, he then had to scrape off dozens of barnacles and other shellfish that cratered the steel surface beneath. His hands were soon bleeding from numerous cuts and scrapes as he laboured, little crimson tendrils seeping into the water from his fingertips. He tried not to think about sharks.

After approximately twenty minutes of hard labour, Magennis had managed to clear a good-sized patch of the *Takao*'s hull. He was going to clear another patch some distance away and then secure the limpet mines in two groups of three, one group in each patch.

Returning to the *XE-3*, he pulled out the first mine from the starboard carrier. It was a heavy, rectangular thing with carrying handles and most of the XE-men thought that they were badly designed. Hauling this ungainly object into position, he pressed the mine's magnetic plate against the *Takao*'s hull, hearing it connect with a muffled thump. So far so good, he thought. Magennis successfully emplaced three mines into the first patch. But then his eyes widened with alarm as the mines started to slide slowly upwards towards the surface as if under their own power. Magennis immediately swam after them, shepherding them back into position. But just as he prepared to gather the other three limpets from the carrier, the first three mines started to move again. The problem was the mines' design. The magnetic plates that held each mine to the ship's hull were too weak, and the explosive charge inside the mine had positive buoyancy. This combined to make the mines crawl along the hull plates towards the water's surface like large metal crustaceans. Left to the laws of physics, the mines would eventually emerge at the waterline and be clearly visible to any moderately alert Japanese sailor.[11]

Thinking quickly, Magennis came up with a plan. He cleared another patch on the opposite side of the *Takao*'s keel from the first one, and then swam back over to the *XE-3*. He squeezed into the tight gap between the bottom of the *Takao*'s keel and the top of the *XE-3*, noticing that the space seemed to have shrunk slightly, opened the W&D compartment hatch, deflated his breathing lung and clambered inside. Once inside he quickly re-inflated the DSEA, collected a length of coiled rope, gulped a few lungfuls of air, deflated his rebreather, and wriggled through the gap. Once outside he laboriously re-inflated the DSEA using the valve. It was an extraordinary display of diving skill and courage.[12]

Magennis swam over to the first three mines, gathered them back together and then tied them to the rope. He then returned to the submarine and over the next few minutes emplaced three more limpets in the second cleared patch of hull 45 feet away on the opposite side of the ship, attaching the rope to these mines as well. The rope ran underneath the *Takao*'s keel like a harness, preventing the mines from creeping towards the surface.[13] It was a brilliant piece of improvisation and indicative of what Captain Banks's X-craft training programme had tried to instil in its recruits – the ability to think for themselves under pressure without reference to instructions from higher command. Such ability was, and remains today, the hallmark of all properly trained Special Forces personnel.

Magennis was by now completely exhausted. He had been outside the submarine longer than he had anticipated and oxygen poisoning was starting to set in. Ignoring the telltale tingling in his hands and lips, Magennis now had to arm the mines. He carefully pulled the cotton triggers on all six, starting the detonation timers. But he only managed to arm three of the counter-mining devices that prevented enemy divers from interfering with the limpets. In twenty minutes' time the counter-mining protective sleeves would withdraw on these three mines, meaning that any bumps would set off the explosives.

By now, Magennis was dragging poisonous breaths into his lungs, rasping like an exhausted carthorse. He had just made history for the second time, becoming the first diver to mine an enemy ship using limpets. But whether this registered with Magennis in his current state was unlikely. The onset of narcosis was slowing his thought processes, confusing him. All he wanted to do was to get inside the submarine before he passed out.

Gripping the *XE-3*'s hull he climbed slowly up to the W&D compartment hatch. But getting inside was not going to be easy. The gap between the W&D hatch and the bottom of the *Takao*'s keel had shrunk even further as Magennis had worked on placing the mines. The tide was falling rapidly. If everything had gone according to plan, the *XE-3* should have arrived beneath the *Takao* at around 12.00pm, when the tide was at its highest. But Fraser was by now seriously behind schedule. The tide, which had a range of eight feet in the Strait, was ebbing fast. The *XE-3* rested in a 30ft depression beneath the *Takao*'s hull, but with each passing minute the *Takao* slowly closed this distance as the tide went out.

Peering through the night periscope, Fraser, tension steadily increasing inside him, watched Magennis. Fraser was anxious to get away from the *Takao* as quickly as possible – the falling water levels in the Strait were seriously concerning him. Magennis gave him a slow thumbs-up gesture and wearily went through the process of deflating his DSEA apparatus once again so that he could drag himself back inside the W&D. Fraser watched the hatch close tight and the clip rotate 120 degrees and breathed a sigh of relief. 'Diver in,' he announced to the crew, Smith jotting down the time.

'Right, chaps, let's release the side cargoes and get the hell out of here,' announced Fraser as Magennis was in the process of draining down inside the W&D.

'Arm port charge,' ordered Fraser, now all businesslike and coldly calm.

Smith and Reed immediately jumped into action.

'Arming port charge,' replied Kiwi Smith as he reached over and began to unscrew the small wheel that started the side cargo's fuse mechanism. The little wheel spun effortlessly in Smith's hand until it stopped with an audible click.

'Charge armed, Tich,' reported Smith. The port charge, a huge black detachable box-like structure containing two tons of Amatol high explosive, was now live. In effect, the *XE-3* had just become a floating bomb.

'Flood the charges,' ordered Fraser, and Reed immediately began to unscrew a larger wheel. It was 4.05pm.[14]

As Reed unscrewed the wheel, a Kingston valve opened in the bottom of the charge, flooding the port side bomb until it was negatively buoyant and therefore unable to float. The now empty limpet mine carrier, the starboard side cargo or 'charge', was also flooded by Reed's action. The last turn of the wheel would cause both charges to drop clear of the *XE-3* and fall to the seabed below.

The port charge detached perfectly. The crew heard it bump several times down the side of the submarine on its journey to the bottom. But the limpet mine carrier refused to budge. Fraser went immediately to his contingency plan. An additional wheel had been provided to help detach the charge in the event that it got hung up. The operator would turn the wheel out as far as it would go, the idea being to physically push the carrier off the submarine. Smith wound the wheel out to its maximum and they all heard and felt the bottom of the flooded limpet carrier come away, but the top remained stuck fast to the *XE-3*.[15]

The crew now had a very serious problem. The submarine had two tons of dead weight fastened to its starboard side. The boat's trim characteristics would be shot to pieces. It would be like trying to drive a car with both of the tyres on the right-hand side replaced with concrete wheels. If they couldn't remove the limpet carrier they might not be able to get out from under the *Takao*, and if they didn't hurry up the ebbing tide would bring the weight of the warship down on top of them.[16] They would be trapped while six limpet mines containing a total of 1,200lbs of explosives ticked down to destruction above their heads and a two-ton bomb did the same right beside them. If they didn't get away, in less than six hours they would perish along with the *Takao*.

For a few seconds the crew all looked at each other silently. No one said it, but it was beginning to look as though the mission was unravelling before their very eyes.

CHAPTER SEVENTEEN

Trapped

'It is said that an expert makes the difficult look easy.'

—Lieutenant Max Shean, HMS *XE-4*

At 4.00pm, just five minutes before Tich Fraser ordered Kiwi Smith and Charlie Reed to drop the *XE-3*'s side charges beneath the *Takao*, Jack Smart was ready to begin his final run in to attack the exact same heavy cruiser.

Smart knew that he was close now; just ten minutes on half power would bring his submarine alongside the *Takao*'s starboard flank.[1] Then it should be a simple operation to release his side cargo and head for home.

The *XE-1*'s diver, Leading Seaman Walter Pomeroy, gripped his stopwatch and consulted his slide rule. Harold Harper was at the hydroplanes, while ERA Henry Fishleigh monitored the electric motor. Their brows were all furrowed in concentration, beads of sweat running down their faces.

'Nine minutes, sir,' announced Pomeroy.

'Very well,' replied Smart. 'Up periscope.' Every time Pomeroy called out a minute, Smart had him raise the attack periscope so that he could take a quick look around and make any slight course changes.

Smart thought that things looked good topside. The *Takao* sat impassively, looking massive, solid and very menacing in the harsh tropical glare. The number of small Japanese motorboats seemed to have thinned, and after the close calls that the *XE-1* had suffered on the approach, Smart was thankful. He could now concentrate on moving his submarine into a position midway along the *Takao*'s hull ready to release his side cargo.

'Depth?' asked Smart.

'Twenty-five feet, Jack,' replied Harper. The shallowness of the water was a concern, as it had been for Fraser in the *XE-3*. Its clarity also made everyone very nervous as it made effective defensive manoeuvring should they be seen almost impossible. Smart knew from his detailed Admiralty chart that the *XE-1*, like the *XE-3* before her, would shortly strike the shallow bottom of the Johor Strait. The plan was to remain at maximum available depth and slowly crawl across the bottom like a cat approaching its prey until his submarine passed into the *Takao*'s great shadow. Smart licked his dry lips and ordered the periscope lowered once again.

'Stand by to touch bottom,' he said, waiting for the grinding sound that would indicate their close proximity to the target. He switched over to the night periscope for a quick look but they were still too far away from the *Takao* to make anything out.

Smart had no idea that the *XE-3* was close by, having just laid her charges, and was about to depart for home. He assumed that she was long gone. With a sudden shudder the *XE-1* started to drag along the stony seabed, Harper fighting to control the submarine's trim.

'Depth?' Smart demanded.

'Eighteen feet, skip,' replied Harper over the din.

They were close now, very close. Smart issued another flurry of orders, his voice tense and direct in the cramped and hot interior.

For Jack Smart, this moment had been a long time coming. He could take satisfaction from how well his mission had gone so far. Although he hadn't made it to the *Myoko*, he had managed to infiltrate his submarine deep behind Japanese lines without being detected, penetrated one of their main bases, and would shortly attack one of their last remaining major warships. The contrast to his previous X-craft mission could not have been starker. His mind slipped momentarily back two years earlier, to Operation Source, when Smart's submarine *X-8* had been detailed to act alone and attack the German heavy cruiser *Lützow* in Langfjord, Norway while the rest of the X-craft went after the battleships *Tirpitz* and *Scharnhorst*. His attack on the German warship should have gone off like that on the *Takao*, but Smart's role in the Norway attacks had been an epic of endurance rather than a triumph of audacity. He had managed to keep his crew alive for 37 agonising hours after his leaking and damaged submarine had lost its tow and one of its side cargoes had exploded prematurely.[2] He had shown everyone that he was a tough and inspirational leader, but he hadn't been able to demonstrate his ability to close with the enemy and sink him. The *Takao* was an even more impressive target than the *Lützow*; at 15,500 tons, she was over a thousand tons heavier than the German ship. At this moment, deep inside the Johor Strait, Jack Smart knew that he would shortly make his mark on naval history after his false start in 1943 – and it guaranteed to be a spectacular show.

*

'Bloody well done, Magennis,' declared Fraser, as the diver crawled through the open W&D compartment door and back into the *XE-3*'s control room. He looked all in. He lay in a wet pile on the floor panting for air, his mouthpiece hanging in front of his face, the diving visor open. They all knew what he had been through outside and what he had just achieved, in spite of his faulty equipment and the evident onset of oxygen poisoning.[3]

Though Fraser was in awe of Magennis's efforts, he couldn't afford to give a long congratulatory speech; that would have to wait until later when they were all, God willing, safely back aboard the 'mother' submarine HMS *Stygian*. For the time being, more pressing matters concerned the diminutive lieutenant.

The *XE-3* was, literally and metaphorically, in a hole. Fraser needed to exit that hole as fast as possible. As the tide in the Johor Strait ebbed away the Japanese warship sank lower and lower on to the trench in which the *XE-3* rested. Delay his exit for too long and Fraser and his crew would be trapped in the space beneath the *Takao*, unable to move until the tide rose again in several hours' time. The mines were ticking down to destruction and couldn't now be stopped.

The flooded limpet mine carrier was sure to add to their difficulties. With that amount of extra weight hanging off the starboard side, the *XE-3* would be hard to manoeuvre, to say the least. But they would give it a go. If they could just get clear of the *Takao* they could worry about the limpet mine carrier afterwards.

'Group down, half ahead together,' ordered Fraser, 'and let's get the hell out of this hole!'

'Main motor, half ahead, skipper,' replied Kiwi Smith, the propeller engaging with a muffled whir. 'May I start the fan, Tich?'[4]

During the time that they had spent sitting on the seabed beneath the *Takao* Fraser had switched off the motor and the air conditioning to prevent detection by underwater hydrophones. Fraser gave his consent and the little fan started up, providing some relief from the heavy, stifling heat.

Magennis slowly struggled out of his DSEA rebreather and diving hood, partially recovered after his exertions outside. But he still had the look of a man who had been through a very trying experience and had only escaped by the skin of his teeth.

Fraser switched on the sounding machine to monitor the depth. He then returned to his usual position at the night periscope. He would oversee the *XE-3*'s exit from the hole beneath the *Takao*. But it was apparent that something was wrong, very wrong.

*

HMS *XE-4* had been running at *schnorkel* depth for 40 minutes without mishap. It was a testament to the professionalism of Max

Shean's crew that the *schnorkel* head had remained above the waves during their withdrawal to deeper waters for a rest. They had managed to avoid the sudden depressurisation and ear pain caused when the head was submerged by a wave. No one had fallen sick from the experience, and in Shean's book that meant they were using the equipment properly. With the boat open to fresh air, the crew started to feel much better. After hour upon hour stuck inside the sealed submarine, the psychological uplift from being connected once more with the surface was almost as important as the clean, salty air that poured inside the boat. The batteries were being charged and the air pressure cylinders used to blow the ballast tanks filled.

After motoring for three miles Shean ordered a stop. He had a decision to make. In consultation with his first lieutenant, Beadon Dening, they looked at the charts and discussed their options. First and foremost in Shean's mind were his secondary orders – to attack Japanese shipping in the Mekong River. It was for this reason that *XE-4* was loaded down with twelve limpet mines in two side cargoes. But Shean was averse to pushing his luck. His two divers had managed to cut both submerged telephone cables off Saigon without undue trouble. He would return to HMS *Spearhead* and see what the intelligence boys had to say regarding fresh targets in Saigon. Unlike Tich Fraser and Jack Smart, Shean had not been given any specific targets. British Naval Intelligence had little idea of what ships were in Saigon harbour, if any. If Shean were ordered to attack Saigon, it would be a case of sailing into unknown waters and perhaps spending a long time searching for something worthwhile to attack. But Shean was prepared to follow his instructions, whatever they might be.

Shean considered his divers. Ken Briggs and Jock Bergius were both exhausted. Each man had completed two short though physically gruelling dives, both reaching the limit of their endurance working at man-killing depths breathing pure oxygen. He could see that they had both had enough for one day.[5] Shean knew that if he was ordered to attack shipping in the Mekong River, both men would immediately volunteer, regardless of their fatigue. It was in their makeup as XE-men to do so. But Shean also knew that to send these brave men on third and even fourth missions might tip them over into very dangerous ground indeed. He could conceivably lose one or both to oxygen narcosis. Were the potential targets even worth risking either of these men's lives? he wondered. As far as everyone knew, there was no *Tirpitz* or *Takao* moored on the Mekong, perhaps just a few rusty Japanese tramp steamers or oilers.

Shean announced that they would take the boat down to the bottom so that everyone could have a rest. Once it was dark they would leave the area and rendezvous with HMS *Spearhead*.[6] It was a decision that was greeted with great relief by the other members of the crew. Everyone was exhausted.

*

It was beginning to look as though Tich Fraser and the crew of the *XE-3*, unlike their comrades in the *XE-4*, would not be heading home any time soon. Though Fraser had ordered the electric motor engaged at half speed, nothing happened. The *XE-3* refused to budge from beneath the *Takao*. He had set a course of 200 degrees to clear the warship and begin their journey back to the defence boom gate.

'Full ahead!' Fraser barked, listening with mounting panic as the submarine's propeller spun madly but the boat refused to move an inch. The problem wasn't the limpet mine carrier. That would make manoeuvring difficult but would not stop the XE-craft moving completely.

'Stop, full astern, group up,' ordered Fraser.[7] He would try backing out of the hole beneath the *Takao* instead. But again, the *XE-3* didn't move. Fraser glanced at Kiwi Smith. He looked very concerned. Fraser felt more than concerned, he felt virtually hysterical, and he struggled to control his panic in front of his men. He was, after all, their commanding officer, and they were looking to him to get them out of this situation. He tried to take hold of himself and think the problem through.

It was the second time his boat had become stuck beneath the *Takao*, but this time it was obviously a much more serious situation, with live explosives just yards from the sub and a falling tide. Fraser guessed, correctly, that the *Takao*'s massive keel was now resting directly on top of the *XE-3*, pinning her like a mouse beneath an elephant.[8] It was an appalling realisation. He had only a limited number of options to play with, but his training kicked in.

'Stop,' ordered Fraser. 'Full ahead, group down.' Nothing. No major movement.

'Lift the red,' he ordered. This would give the motor maximum power, but even though she vibrated madly from the effort, her propeller spinning at maximum revolutions, the boat still would not budge. Fraser, his mind a riot of emotion, decided to pause for a few seconds.[9]

'Stop the motor,' he ordered, there being no sense in draining the batteries. *What to do?* an urgent voice in his mind repeated over and over.

Fraser weighed his options. If he couldn't free his submarine from beneath the *Takao* the only realistic option was to abandon her. No captain ever abandons his ship unless there is absolutely no alternative, but this was beginning to look like one of those situations. He decided that if this was the only option after he had exhausted all others, they would remain aboard the *XE-3* until half an hour before the charges were set to explode. Then, donning their DSEA breathing gear, they would flood the submarine and swim out towards the shore, approximately 200 yards away. The plan, if it could be called that, was to hide in the mangrove swamps until the British retook Singapore, whenever that might be.

Fraser glanced at the packs containing their survival kit, stored in one corner of the submarine, and inwardly grimaced. He knew with dreadful certainty that they might well make it ashore, but after the charges had gone off and the *Takao* had been destroyed, the Japanese would make every effort to find those responsible. Japanese divers examining the *Takao*'s hulk would discover the remains of the British submarine beneath her and no sign of her crew. It would be obvious that they had swum ashore.

Similar circumstances had befallen the crew of a Japanese Type-A midget submarine that had attacked the British supply port of Diego Suarez in Madagascar on the night of 30 May 1942. Like Fraser and the crew of the *XE-3*, Lieutenant Saburo Akieda and Petty Officer Masami Takemoto had completed their mission, severely damaging the 33,500-ton battleship HMS *Ramillies* and sinking the tanker *British Loyalty*. But as they were trying to escape from the harbour and rendezvous with the 'mother' submarine *I-20* that was lying several miles offshore, Akieda had run his submarine aground on a hidden rock. It was too damaged to complete the journey, and Akieda had had no choice but to abandon ship. He and Takemoto had swum to shore. Each man was armed with a Nambu 8mm pistol and Akieda as an officer also carried a *wakizashi*, a short samurai sword.[10]

They had planned to march overland to Madagascar's northern coast and attempt to signal the *I-20* by lamp and arrange a rescue. In many respects the two Japanese had been in a much better position than Fraser and his crew were now, as their mother submarine had been close inshore, whereas HMS *Stygian* was at least 30 miles from Singapore.[11]

Akieda and Takemoto were hunted by British troops from virtually the moment that they stepped ashore and were cornered on 2 June after 59 hours on the run. In the resulting melee the two Japanese managed to kill one soldier and wound four others before they were in turn both gunned down and killed.[12]

Rear-Admiral James Fife, commander of submarines, US 7th Fleet (*left*) with Captain Fell (*right*) on the bridge of HMS *Bonaventure*, Brunei Bay, July 1945.

The attack and passage crews of *XE-1* and *XE-3* being addressed by
Rear-Admiral Fife on the quarterdeck of HMS *Bonaventure* shortly
before departing Brunei Bay for Singapore, 26 July 1945.

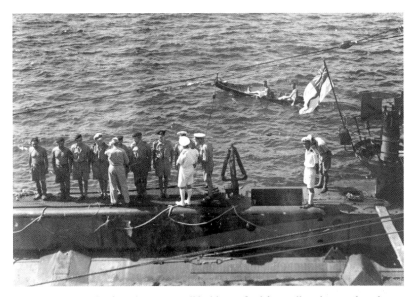

Rear-Admiral Fife and Captain Fell bidding a final farewell to the attack and passage crew of one of the XE-craft involved in Operation Struggle. The crews are assembled on the casing of the towing submarine, Brunei Bay, 26 July 1945.

Tich Fraser's *XE-3* departs for Singapore under tow from HMS *Stygian*, 26 July 1945.

XE-craft interior: the crewman in the foreground mans the steering position while right aft sits the planesman who controls the submarine's depth with the hydroplanes and pump. The engine and main motor are further aft of a white timber bulkhead. On the extreme right is the commander's tiny chart table.

The planesman sits at his position controlling the submarine's depth.

The Japanese heavy cruiser *Myoko*.

Captain Fell (*left*) and Lieutenant-Commander Brown on HMS *Bonaventure*.

VJ Day party aboard HMS *Bonaventure*, Brunei Bay, 2 September 1945. For the XE-men, the war was finally over and they would shortly be heading home.

The VJ Day party one hour later. The men are pictured in high spirits in the *Bonaventure*'s wardroom.

Jimmy Fife salutes the quarterdeck as he departs HMS *Bonaventure* for the final time in early August 1945. During his time with 14th Submarine Flotilla the American admiral had formed close bonds of friendship with many of the 'little guys with a lotta guts'.

An XE-craft surfaced in Brunei Bay shortly after the end of the war. Sadly, almost all of these amazing little submarines would soon be scrapped following the end of hostilities.

The two officers who shaped the midget submariners into one of the conflict's most potent fighting units photographed at Buckingham Palace just after the war: Captain William Fell (*left*), commander of 14th Submarine Flotilla and the man whose persistence brought his men glory; and Captain William Banks (*right*), commander of 12th Submarine Flotilla, who used X-craft to attack the *Tirpitz* in 1943 and laid the foundations for XE-craft operations against the Japanese.

In Fraser's mind, should they abandon the *XE-3* it would come down to a choice of being killed while emptying their Colt .45s at a Japanese patrol, becoming prisoners and enduring torture before being decapitated, or, perhaps the most depressing of all, crunching down on cyanide pills and dying in some muddy, mosquito-blown ditch thousands of miles from home. None of those options held the least appeal to any of the crewmen. A few terse remarks had been quietly made about Operation Struggle being a 'suicide mission' before Fraser and Smart had departed from Brunei, and Admiral Nimitz and other American officers had certainly voiced similar opinions about the XE-craft programme in general. But Fraser was not prepared to accept such a fate. In fact, given their terminal options if they left the *XE-3*, it spurred Fraser into making a final effort to get his boat free from beneath the *Takao*.

For the next few minutes Fraser ordered water ballast pumped aft and then forward, repeating the process over and over again, rocking the little submarine while also running the motor forwards and in reverse. He even partially blew the number 2 ballast tank – anything to try to shake the *XE-3* loose.[13] The frantic movement was designed to nudge a hole in the seabed so that the submarine could make a little space and crawl out from under the *Takao*.[14]

Suddenly, as if by a miracle, the *XE-3* started to move. But the movement, though life-saving, was soon far from easy to control.

*

The *XE-1*'s bow connected with the starboard side of the *Takao* around the same time that the *XE-3* was limping away from the warship on her port side. The two submarines had attacked widely separated points along the *Takao*'s massive hull, and Jack Smart could see no evidence of his comrades' busy mining activities.

The *XE-1* vibrated from the impact and several pieces of equipment fell from the racks and chart table with a clatter. But the submarine was not damaged.

'Stop!' yelled Smart. The last thing he had wanted to do was hit the *Takao* but it had been next to impossible to avoid contact as the little submarine ground its way slowly across the shallow seabed, control spasmodic and visibility limited due to the night periscope's small optics.

'Time?' demanded Smart.

'Sixteen ten hours, sir,' replied Pomeroy.[15]

Smart had intended to slip into the long trench beneath the *Takao* and drop his side cargo, but it soon became clear that the Japanese warship had sunk very low with the ebbing tide, making such a manoeuvre nearly impossible without getting trapped.[16]

He adjusted his depth and the *XE-1* slipped into the shadow of the *Takao*'s overhanging hull. Smart was on edge. He had no way of knowing if he was approaching a mined section of the ship. If everything had gone according to schedule, Fraser would have laid his charges hours ago. Of course, Smart had no way of knowing that the *XE-3* had laid its charges only in the last hour and was at that very moment just a few hundred feet away from the *XE-1* on the warship's port side. But as far as Smart was concerned the *Takao*'s hull was littered with British limpets, each with its counter-mining pins fully exposed, while a two-ton saddle charge lay somewhere beneath the ship, ready to go up at any minute. He would have to be extremely careful when manoeuvring the *XE-1* near to the *Takao*'s keel, lest he accidentally brush one of the *XE-3*'s limpets.

'Right chaps,' said Smart, his eyes red-rimmed with exhaustion, 'prepare to flood the charges.'

*

'Ship's head swinging to starboard, sir,' shouted Reed. 'I can't control her.'[17]

As the *XE-3* passed out from under the *Takao*'s shadow, harsh sunlight flooded into the submarine through the little inspection window in her top, the crewmen all squinting in the sudden glare. The submarine crawled across the bottom of the strait like a wounded animal, its head dragging constantly down and to the right.[18]

'It's the damned limpet carrier,' yelled Fraser as the submarine gave another sickening lurch to starboard and crunched into the seabed. The limpet mine carrier on the starboard side had only partially released when the port explosive charge had dropped off and now it was completely flooded with seawater. Weighing close on two tons it was dragging the *XE-3* in a nose-down circle back towards the *Takao*, the very last place that Fraser wanted to go. They were in only fifteen feet of water, perfectly visible to anyone passing overhead in a boat or taking any notice from the *Takao*'s tall superstructure, a large dark shadow moving erratically on the seabed.[19] It seemed almost certain that the *XE-3* must be spotted and attacked.

Fraser ordered the motor stopped. The submarine came to a juddering halt and settled on the bottom of the strait. Fraser judged that the *XE-3* was only about twenty feet away from the *Takao*'s port side.[20] This was dangerously close. But the *XE-3* could go no further. If Fraser continued trying to push the boat it would simply drive straight back into the side of the warship. There was no way the submarine could be navigated back down the strait and out through the anti-submarine boom to safety. The jammed limpet mine carrier would have to be removed before they could continue.[21]

The question was, who was going to go out there and remove it?

Frogman VC

*'Magennis displayed very great courage and devotion
to duty and complete disregard for his own safety.'*

—Official Citation, 1945

'**A**rm the port charge,' ordered Jack Smart.

'Aye aye, skipper, arming the port charge,' repeated Sub-Lieutenant Harper. He immediately began unscrewing the small wall-mounted wheel that controlled the bomb's internal timing mechanism. Ten turns was all it took to prime the two tons of Amatol high explosives mounted in the *XE-1's* side cargo.

'Charge armed and ready,' reported Harper.

'Very good, number one,' replied Smart, wiping a slick sheen of sweat from his brow with the back of his hand. The submarine was gloomy inside, the *XE-1* sitting in the shadows slightly under the overhang of the *Takao's* massive keel. Very little light penetrated the boat through the small porthole in the control room roof.

Smart needed to get as close as possible to the Japanese ship to make sure that his bomb did the maximum damage. He had settled the *XE-1* in a good position under one of the huge gun turrets. If the bomb managed to set off one of the *Takao's* magazines where hundreds of 278lb shells were stored for the 8in guns the ship would be completely destroyed. Either way, Smart believed that his bomb would cause serious structural damage to the warship. Amatol packs a mighty punch, being a highly explosive blend of TNT and ammonium nitrate. The damage that side cargoes had inflicted on the mighty *Tirpitz* in 1943, a vessel three times heavier than the *Takao* and considerably better armoured, had been very impressive. Smart's comrades in *X-6* and *X-7* had laid four of these two-ton charges under the German battleship. Their detonation had torn shell plating, ruptured fuel oil tanks, hammered a huge indentation in the bottom of the ship and buckled the bulkheads in the double-bottom, causing extensive internal flooding.[1]

Once Smart had added his side cargo to that already deposited by Fraser, together with Fraser's six limpet mines, the *Takao* would be sitting on 10,000lbs of British high explosives. That was an explosive power equivalent to twelve of the conventional torpedoes carried aboard the large Royal Navy hunter-killer submarines operating in the Pacific.

Due to time considerations and the risks inherent in working on an already mined ship, Smart had earlier decided that diver Walter Pomeroy would not be required to add the *XE-1*'s limpet mines to the *Takao*'s hull. Pomeroy might yet get a chance to prove his skills on the journey back, as there was no guarantee that the boom gate would still be open. Both Fraser and Smart thought that they got through the gate during the journey in purely by luck.

Now, though, was the moment that Smart and his crew had been awaiting for so many long, stressful and uncomfortable hours: the chance to attack a ship and then slink quietly away. Everyone aboard the *XE-1* could feel the tension as they ran through the bomb release drills that they had practised so many times during training.

'Flood and release port and starboard charges,' ordered Smart.

'Aye aye, sir, flooding and releasing port and starboard charges,' repeated Henry Fishleigh, who immediately started to unwind the larger wall-mounted wheel that began to push the big saddle charges off the sides of the submarine. At the conclusion of the final turn of the wheel there was a loud click followed by several muffled bangs, thumps and groans from both sides of the boat.

They all listened as the port charge, the bomb, fell away, its flooded bulk banging against the side of the *XE-1* before it landed on the seabed and settled, kicking up a cloud of sediment. The starboard limpet carrier, with its six unused and unprimed mines, also fell away smoothly from the submarine.[2]

'Side cargoes clear, Jack,' said Harper, his face betraying his enormous sense of relief.

'Well done, chaps,' said a grinning Smart. Everyone smiled back at the young lieutenant, and the tension inside the submarine decreased markedly. There was a feeling that the worst of the mission was now behind them. Smart started issuing orders to the helm. Now there just remained the tricky business of retracing their steps back down the strait and getting out through the anti-submarine boom. None of them could afford to relax until they were safely attached once more to HMS *Spark*, and that wasn't going to happen for a very long time yet.

*

The *XE-3* was out of control. Although she was off the seabed, her bow was down five degrees in seventeen feet of water. Any attempt to move resulted in the submarine continuing an uncontrollable turn to starboard, back towards the *Takao*.[3]

Tich Fraser looked at Mick Magennis. The diver, his wet dark hair plastered to his scalp, was still dressed in his suit, though he had removed his DSEA apparatus and held his hood in one hand. It was clear that physically Magennis was exhausted after the ordeal of placing the limpet mines on the *Takao*'s filthy and encrusted bottom. His face was unnaturally pale and sickly-looking, the lack of colour highlighting the dark exhaustion smudges beneath his eyes. Fraser didn't think he could order the Ulsterman back out to release the jammed limpet mine carrier in his present state.

Fraser's eyes flicked around the boiling hot boat, looking at his crew. They fell on Charlie Reed. No, Reed had little experience of diving apart from the basic course that every man in the unit had completed as part of his submarine training. His eyes moved on to his number one, Kiwi Smith. The New Zealander was keen but frankly not much good underwater either. What had befallen Bruce Enzer and particularly his best friend David Carey in Australia was never far from Fraser's mind. The enquiry that had followed their loss at sea had concluded that the deaths were most probably due to the fact that, as both men were not full-time divers, their bodies had not built up a sufficient underwater endurance when using the DSEA apparatus and that they had both succumbed quickly to oxygen narcosis.

There was nothing for it, thought Fraser – he would have to do it himself. He had, after all, dived a lot in Scotland and Australia and was a natural. But though he was certainly a better option than Reed or Smith, Fraser too lacked the endurance that was built up with constant dives. And, if he went, he would be breaking a naval regulation that Captain Fell had been very keen to enforce. The commanding officers of XE-craft were expressly forbidden from leaving their boats under any circumstances. That was how Fraser had been trained and that was the rule, pure and simple. But under the current circumstances Fraser knew that he had to bend that particular rule or the mission would be over and their lives in mortal danger regardless of whatever decision he took after they abandoned the submarine. Fraser had great faith in Smith as second-in-command, and he knew that if anything should happen to him outside the boat, as long as he managed to free the limpet carrier, Kiwi would get the *XE-3* out of the strait and make the rendezvous with HMS *Stygian*. Fraser decided that he had to make the dive to save his men and his boat. He was their leader; he should take the risk.

'Come out of the way, Magennis,' said Fraser roughly. 'I'll go out and release it myself.'

Magennis's eyes looked hurt.

'Hand me the spare set from the battery compartment,' continued Fraser, asking for the second DSEA apparatus.

Magennis held up the flat of one hand and spoke.

'I'll be all right in a minute, sir,' he said. 'Just let me get my wind.'[4]

Fraser was in awe. Magennis's sense of duty was overwhelming. He could have sat this one out in the submarine and no one would have thought any less of him. He had already gone beyond the call of duty with the very difficult dives beneath the *Takao*. He was physically shattered but from somewhere deep inside he managed to drag out a few more ounces of tenacity and courage. But above all that, Magennis was the only dedicated diver on board the *XE-3*, and he would perform that task come what may; even, it seemed, to the point of his own destruction.

Fraser didn't say anything, just solemnly nodded. He felt an immense surge of pride not just in Magennis, but also in Smith and Reed as well. They were like a well-oiled machine.

For the next five minutes they all sat quietly at their stations, not speaking. Although the fan was running it was still like a furnace inside the submarine, the air heavy and starting to turn noxious. The danger that Fraser and his crew were in was immense. The *XE-3* was stopped dead in crystal-clear water that was only seventeen feet deep and they were just twenty feet away from the *Takao*. If a Japanese sailor looked over the side at the wrong moment there was a better than average chance that he would see the 50ft-long shadow of the British submarine. Until the limpet mine carrier was levered off the *XE-3* there was absolutely no way that Fraser could try to avoid any Japanese search for his craft or run to deeper water. Their fate was in the lap of the gods, and they all knew it.

When five minutes had slowly passed, Magennis, with Fraser's help, wearily donned his diving hood and DSEA apparatus once more. Magennis still looked exhausted but his mind was made up, his jaw set.

Few words were spoken as Magennis clambered back into the W&D compartment, slumping in the seat, eyes glazed. Reed and Smith sat at their stations, monitoring the dials and gauges while Fraser returned once again to the night periscope to watch Magennis exit the boat.

The pumps started and the chamber flooded. Magennis's equipment was still leaking. He hadn't swapped his rig with the spare set. Of more concern to Fraser was the large number of bubbles that were released when the W&D hatch was opened. As Fraser watched through the night periscope they wobbled slowly up, expanding and contracting as they went, forming on the water's surface a short distance above. They were more than enough to betray the submarine's presence.[5]

Why the *XE-3* wasn't spotted during its many problematical manoeuvres in the attack on the *Takao* remains a mystery. Probably it was because the *Takao* was moored, and unlike in a vessel at sea, a warship in harbour would have a reduced crew, with only general maintenance and training being conducted. Many Japanese would have been on shore leave. The gun crews that manned the main batteries and numerous anti-aircraft weapons probably made up the majority of those aboard, along with a reduced engineering department working below decks to maintain power.

There was also a psychological element at play. The Japanese, as Fraser later noted, evidently felt secure in the Johor Strait, and so may have been less vigilant in watching for enemy infiltrators.[6] Unlike Lieutenant-Colonel Ivan Lyon's Force Z attack on merchant ships in Keppel Harbour in 1944, located on the open seaward side of Singapore Island, the old British naval base at Sembawang was tucked away down a long and easily defended narrow strip of water.

But perhaps the biggest factor was luck. Fraser and Smart had both been lucky so far. But there were plenty of Japanese patrol launches about, so even though two British midget submarines had successfully penetrated the defences, they could not afford to relax their guards for even a second. The perilous situation being faced by Fraser demonstrated just how high the stakes were in the game of cat-and-mouse that the XE-men were playing with the Japanese.

Fraser watched as the exhausted Magennis dragged himself out of the open hatch carrying a huge spanner in one hand. He paused to give Fraser a signal that he was okay, even though the leak in his equipment continued to plague him. He then swam over to the limpet mine carrier and started work.

The three crewmen inside the *XE-3* waited with bated breath. They had already been stationary and highly exposed in enemy waters for five minutes while Magennis had attempted to recover his composure before the dive. Now they were forced to endure an agonising seven-minute wait while Magennis worked to free the mine carrier.[7] The only sound inside the boat was the steady click of the marine chronometer. Every so often Magennis's spanner would clang against the submarine's outer hull, causing those inside to jump at the sudden loud noise.[8] They were all as nervy as cats. 'What the fuck is that fool doing?' exclaimed a tense Fraser after one particularly loud crash from outside.[9] He had specifically told Magennis that he must be as quiet as possible, the fear of Japanese hydrophones still firmly in Fraser's mind.

Fraser was starting to lose his cool. The perilous nature of the situation would have tried the patience and forbearance of any man, and the burden of command sat heavily on young shoulders. Exhausted and impatient to be moving again, he found himself suddenly overtaken by an impotent anger against those who had placed him and his men in such an intolerable situation. He swore about Captain Fell, Lieutenant Potter and the other officers that had planned the mission, and railed inwardly at the Admiralty and perhaps mostly at himself for having been so foolish as to have volunteered in the first place. He cursed himself for not going out there in person to release the limpet carrier instead of sending Magennis, who, thought Fraser, in his current exhausted state was making enough noise to wake the entire Imperial Japanese Navy.[10]

*

The only sound that could be heard aboard the *XE-4*, sitting on the seabed south of Saigon, was the gentle snoring of several members of her crew. Max Shean had crept three miles south from where his two divers had severed the Saigon telephone cables, airing the boat and recharging the batteries as he went. Shean had taken the *XE-4* down to the bottom and ordered the crew to rest.[11]

The air conditioning fan whirred quietly while the crew tried to get what rest they could inside the boat's cramped and uncomfortable interior. Shean remained by the periscope standard, dozing in his chair, while Ben Kelly slept in the control room's single bunk. ERA Coles remained at his post, eyes half open, apparently as immovable as Charlie Reed on the *XE-3*. The two exhausted divers, Briggs and Bergius, lay on boards over the battery compartment snoring fitfully.

Shean's plan was to wait for darkness, surface and then head for his rendezvous with HMS *Spearhead*. He would employ the same technique that all of the XE-craft had used when approaching their targets – running on the surface with the commander on deck with binoculars, communicating with the crew by shouting down the partially raised air induction trunk. This would mean that the boat was well ventilated and comfortable and Shean would be able to find the *Spearhead*.

Shean's head lolled forward until his forehead was touching the periscope standard. He had never felt so tired, so washed out, in his life. He closed his eyes and concentrated on listening to the patient click of the chronometer. He quickly dozed off again, the heat enervating.

*

Outside the *XE-3*, Magennis barely registered the time. His only battle was against the limpet mine carrier and just staying conscious. Once out of the W&D, he swam over to the carrier and sat astride it like a jockey. The water was a little muddy towards the bottom, churned up by the recent movement of the submarine across it.

Magennis looked closely through his face visor at the carrier – he could see that the lifting clips had not fallen away as they had been designed to. Using the large spanner, he slowly undid one of the clips; the effort was almost too much, but eventually it fell away. The two-ton carrier, already released at the bottom from inside the submarine, was now held on to the *XE-3* only by a single remaining lifting clip.[12]

Magennis was again breathing hard, and his equipment was venting a steady stream of bubbles from the faulty reducing valve that slightly obscured his vision. These bubbles were collecting on the surface like foam, and could be easily seen by anyone who looked.[13]

It was hard physical labour, even underwater. The spanner was heavy and awkward, and Magennis's hands, already badly cut from scraping off barnacles from the *Takao*'s keel, were sore and bleeding. His position astride the limpet carrier was ungainly and uncomfortable.[14] He worked on the second lifting clip, slowly turning its giant screws. It was difficult to concentrate, his mind wanted to wander, and he knew that he was being slowly poisoned with each new breath that he dragged through the DSEA. The spanner head kept slipping off the screws, and he was forced to slowly reposition the tool several times before continuing. Suddenly, the clip fell off and the heavy carrier, with Magennis still straddling it, dropped off the side of the submarine with a lurch and fell towards the seabed.

The instant the limpet mine carrier was released, the *XE-3*, suddenly two tons lighter, began to drift off on the current. Magennis's eyes grew wide in his visor as his ride home started to pull away from him, out of his reach, as he tumbled towards the seabed atop the sinking carrier.[15]

*

Jack Smart and the *XE-1* were already on their way home while Mick Magennis was struggling to release the flooded limpet carrier. With both side cargoes successfully released, Smart did not linger near the *Takao*. He set an immediate course back down the strait towards the boom gate. Still assuming that Fraser had mined the *Takao* several hours earlier, Smart was determined to be outside the gate when the *XE-3*'s charges went up. He assumed that Fraser was probably already close to the boom and would shortly be heading out into the open sea to make his rendezvous with his mother submarine.

Smart knew that it would be a long, slow and cautious journey back down the strait. But he had some advantages. He had bought himself some time by switching targets from the distant *Myoko*. The mining of the *Takao* had gone without any problems, and his diver was still fresh and ready to tackle the boom net if the gate was closed when they arrived. As long as he arrived at the boom before darkness fell everything should be okay.

'Time?' asked Smart.

'Sixteen fifteen hours, skipper,' replied Harold Harper.

'Excellent. Half ahead group down,' said Smart, and the *XE-1* began to move away from the *Takao* on its carefully worked-out course.[16]

*

Magennis dropped the heavy spanner as he tumbled off the moving limpet mine carrier. The spanner plummeted down and embedded itself upright in the mud. Within seconds the *XE-3* had moved several yards away from him, drifting on the current. The shock of suddenly being thrown off his submarine was swiftly replaced by a fear of being left behind. He struck out madly for the *XE-3*, his fatigue suddenly forgotten, hands stretching out to try to reach her, fins kicking wildly in the water, his breathing panicked and fast. Time seemed to slow down, Magennis's entire being concentrated on just reaching the submarine's hull before the gap widened any further.

Suddenly he felt metal beneath his fingertips, and kicking even harder, both hands came to rest on the *XE-3*'s cold, hard surface. Magennis lay for a few seconds on the drifting submarine's hull, hugging the metal until he felt strong enough to head back to the W&D compartment.

When he arrived at the hatch he gave Fraser, watching through the night periscope, a slow and distracted thumbs-up before he hauled the hatch open and clambered down inside. Wearily, he closed the lid. He sat in the flooded chamber, his breathing heavy and laboured. Just raising his aching arms to engage the pumps to drain the chamber was an immense effort. Summoning up his last reserves of determination, Magennis began to drain down.[17]

Once the W&D was empty he rested his head against its hard metal interior and closed his eyes, one hand absently dragging the DSEA mouthpiece from his lips and pulling off his visor. He just wanted darkness to envelop him. But he fought the feeling – he couldn't allow himself to drift into unconsciousness. The air inside the chamber revived him a little and soon Fraser had the door to the control room open and was helping to drag him out.

*

With the flooded limpet carrier detached, the relief was palpable inside the submarine. Fraser, recovered from his fury, was suddenly all business again. When he got the barely conscious Magennis into the control room he clapped him roughly on the back. 'You're a gem, Mick,'[18] he said with feeling, 'a bloody gem!' Magennis muttered something unintelligible and propped himself in a corner where he sipped water from a tin cup and began to slowly return to the land of the living.

'Starboard twenty, steer oh-nine-oh degrees,' Fraser ordered, his voice decisive and quick.

'Aye aye, skipper,' said a grinning Kiwi Smith, 'steering oh-nine-oh degrees.'

'Half ahead group down,' said Fraser to Reed, who engaged the electric motor.

'Aye aye, sir,' replied Reed as the whine of the propeller started up.

'Twelve hundred revolutions,' ordered Fraser. The submarine's head swung about and under power she started to move forward.

'Okay,' said Fraser, smiling gently. 'Home, James, and don't spare the horses.'[19]

Magennis raised his head and seemed to perk up slightly at the good news. 'You heard the man. Let's get the *fuck* out of here,'[20] he said, the tiniest ghost of a smile crossing his blue lips.

CHAPTER NINETEEN

Home Run

'The hazards of the sea are enough. So are its glories.'
—Lieutenant Ian Fraser, HMS *XE-3*

Eleven miles to freedom, that was all the two British submarines needed to travel in order to exit the Johor Strait into the open sea. It didn't sound like much, but those eleven miles would take the *XE-1* and *XE-3* about three hours to cautiously negotiate, and a lot could yet go wrong. Though the navigation was straightforward, hidden dangers existed in the mile-wide channel; dangers that threatened to sink the whole British enterprise when the players were almost at the finish line. Lieutenants Smart and Fraser would relax once they had conned their boats through the anti-submarine boom, but until that time both remained as keyed-up and nervy as racehorses. Exhaustion added to their woes – the hours spent sealed inside the overheated and unventilated submarines while they hunched over instruments and dials had taken their toll, and their eyes were strained and tired.

Smart and Fraser both expected that the Japanese would close the boom gate at sunset, and the two submarines would arrive around that time. It seemed inconceivable that the Japanese would leave the gate wide open during the hours of darkness.[1] It wouldn't make sense.

Looking at their watches and charts, the two skippers calculated that they would arrive at the gate when it was still light, but any problems that either boat encountered on the way down the strait could put them over time. If darkness fell *before* they reached the boom, it was effectively mission over. They could try to find a quiet creek and hide for the night but the Japanese would be looking for them and they didn't have too big an area to search.

Fraser and Smart pushed all thoughts of hiding among the mangroves to the backs of their minds. The divers, Walter Pomeroy and Mick Magennis, were their best chance. As long as there was still some light the divers were expected to leave their submarines and cut holes in the net so that the XE-craft could slip through the boom.

For Leading Seaman Pomeroy the prospect of action was exciting. Smart had not used him to mine the *Takao*, and though he helped out with navigational duties he had been feeling like a spare wheel for some hours. He was relatively fresh and very capable, and Jack Smart knew that he could rely on him if the time came.

Fraser, however, was worried about Mick Magennis. Though he would have over three hours to recover from his exertions against the *Takao* and the errant limpet mine carrier before the *XE-3* reached the boom, Magennis had physically pushed the envelope. He was shattered, and remaining cooped up inside the submarine for several more hours would not help him to recover his strength. Sending him out on one final mission to cut a hole in the boom could be enough to push him over the edge. It was all too easy for a man, even one as experienced as Magennis, to fall victim to 'Oxygen Pete'. It had already begun to happen twice before during the attack and their complicated exit from the vicinity of the *Takao*. A punch-drunk diver was the last thing that Fraser needed, especially for a job as delicate and dangerous as cutting a hole in the guarded anti-submarine boom right under the noses of the Japanese. Make a mistake there and the whole mission would be compromised in an instant, and hell would most assuredly follow.

Inside the *XE-3* the electric motor was running quietly, though the air conditioning fan remained switched off to cut down on noise. They were headed in the right direction at a steady speed. But there was still plenty that could go wrong.

*

'Christ!' shouted Fraser, 'she going to broach!' Everything had been normal just a few seconds before the crisis erupted, the *XE-3* quietly motoring along at about 30 feet below the surface. They were 1.1 miles from the *Takao* when they drove into a 'freshwater pot', a patch of desalinated water in the midst of the seawater-filled strait.

Freshwater streams and rivers cut through the surrounding mangrove swamps and fed into the saltwater Johor Strait, and the water in the vicinity of the *Takao* changed its consistency as the tide fell. It had become very 'fresh' as the seawater levels had fallen, an extremely hazardous situation.[2]

The submarine immediately became uncontrollable and rose fast for the surface, suddenly extremely buoyant. Kiwi Smith fought to try to regain control of her, but nothing seemed to stop the *XE-3*'s rapid rise. For the men inside of her, the realisation that their submarine was about to appear on the surface in the midst of one of the enemy's busiest and most sensitive harbours terrified them out of their wits.

The *XE-3* broached the strait like a whale coming up for air. First her black bow pushed out of the water, followed by the boat's upper deck, spray blasting into the air as greenish water sloshed over her bilges, concentric rings of white disturbed water marking her position like a giant rifle target.

'We'll soon know if we've been spotted!'[3] yelled a distraught Smith, who wrestled with the hydroplane controls like a man possessed. The submarine had never been so exposed. Her black hull sat on the clear, glassy surface of the strait in plain view of any Japanese who cared to look from ship or shore.

'Dive, dive, dive!' shouted Fraser frantically, slamming his hand repeatedly against the periscope standard as he yelled, issuing orders to blow the two main ballast tanks in an effort to get the submarine back below the water as fast as possible. The sounds of the compressed air being forced from the ballast tanks was loud, clouds of spray pluming noisily over the submarine's hull before she slid below the surface leaving just a patch of disturbed water to mark her position. The *XE-3* was only at the surface for six seconds, but for Fraser and his crew those six seconds felt like an eternity[4]. They felt naked and worked in a lather of sickly panic to get the *XE-3* back into the depths. She was still moving forward on her electric motor, and Fraser's swift action combined with her passing out of the freshwater pot into saltier waters soon restored the boat to her safe depth.[5]

Inside the *XE-3* Fraser was almost having palpitations, and the rest of the crew didn't feel much better. It was the suddenness of the crisis that was the most worrying. They wiped nervous sweat from their faces and swore and cursed. For several minutes the crew all listened, waiting for the sound of approaching propellers from above to signal that their unplanned manoeuvre had been spotted and the Japanese had sent a patrol launch to investigate, perhaps a launch with grey, barrel-shaped depth charges stowed on her fantail. But there was nothing. No sound, just the *XE-3*'s propeller whirring gently.

They had lost effective depth control over the submarine, and Fraser knew that he had to expect more episodes like this to occur during the remaining miles to the boom gate. He knew that the crises when they came would begin without warning and leave the crew struggling to react and reestablish control. Fraser had to try and minimise the chances of their surfacing again. He may have got away with it this once – time would tell. But Fraser knew that his boat wouldn't last long if it started behaving like a giant metal porpoise, popping up on the surface every few miles. Eventually they would surely be seen and destroyed. For Fraser and his cohorts it felt as though Mother Nature herself was conspiring against them, trying to keep them from reaching the boom gate before darkness fell, holding them in the strait against their will.

*

'By my calculations, the boom is 2,000 yards away,' said Jack Smart. Just one more mile and they would be out of the strait and on their way home. 'Everything clear,' he added as he took a quick scan of the way ahead with the attack periscope.

Jack Smart had had a few scares himself as *XE-1* headed away from the *Takao*, the freshwater pots also causing him some momentary problems, but he managed to avoid completely losing control of his submarine. Unlike the *XE-3*, the *XE-1* had remained resolutely submerged, though more by luck than by design.

As the *XE-1* edged further towards the mouth of the Johor Strait the water became saltier and much more stable until normal conditions returned. The tide was coming back in and the sun was going down, the sky taking on a reddish-orange glow as dusk approached.

'Take us back down to 40 feet, number one,' Smart ordered Harold Harper.

The *XE-1* submerged deeper into the channel. She was running almost silently on her electric motor. Smart turned to Walter Pomeroy.

'You'd better get ready,' he said. Pomeroy nodded and fetched his hood and DSEA set, checking it carefully. He had mixed feelings about what he might have to do, though at the same time he wanted an opportunity to practise for real what he had learned in training. Cutting through an anti-submarine net was a slow and physically demanding process, particularly so under combat conditions where any mistake could lead to disaster. About the last place any XE-craft skipper wanted to be was stopped beside a heavily defended anti-submarine boom, particularly one that was hanging in such shallow water as that in the Johor Strait.

Pomeroy knew that he would have to work as fast as possible. Smart would place the bows of the submarine against the net. The motor would continue running at 'dead slow', holding the *XE-1* in the net. Pomeroy would then exit the submarine and collect a pair of hydraulic cutters from their storage box. Working as fast as he dared, and fighting against the current, which at this time of day and location would probably be running at at least a knot, perhaps more, Pomeroy could begin to slice through the thick steel mesh that made up the old British boom. Smart would monitor him using the night periscope.

Pomeroy reckoned that it would take him about fifteen minutes to cut a hole. The *XE-1* would then pass through and Pomeroy would swim after her, stow the cutters and re-enter the W&D before the submarine resumed her passage. At least that was how it had been done in training in Scotland – doing it for real was going to be quite different. Even in the safety of Scotland several divers, including Mick Magennis, had half-poisoned themselves working hard at depth, trying to make the cuts as fast as possible. If 'Oxygen Pete' seized a diver there was no way he could rush to the surface where a safety boat would be waiting to retrieve him. The only thing waiting up top in the Johor Strait would be the muzzle of an Arisaka rifle and a 6.5mm bullet courtesy of Emperor Hirohito.

During the trip through the open boom earlier that morning Smart had reported that the Japanese had placed a defence vessel beside the gate. This boat might be equipped with hydrophones that could detect the noises made by the submarine's motor and the all-important hydraulic cutters. And like Fraser in the *XE-3*, Smart had also noticed several Japanese sailors fishing or simply looking down at the clear water as he passed through. That time both submarines had passed through the open gate quickly, but stopping against the boom for twenty or so minutes while the divers worked was courting disaster. A 50ft-long submarine wouldn't be hard to spot in clear, shallow water.

The light would soon begin to fade from the sky. If Pomeroy failed in his mission the *XE-1* would have to retrace her steps some way back up the strait and Smart would have to find a quiet mangrove creek where they could lie up during the hours of darkness before attempting to get through the boom at first light on 1 August. This would mean that the *XE-1* would be within the strait when the *Takao* blew up in a few hours' time. It was a safe assumption that the Japanese would definitely close the boom gate after such an attack, and perhaps also station further vessels at the entrance to the strait if they suspected midget submarines were responsible. As Captain Fell later commented, with admirable understatement, if they had been caught inside the boom after the *Takao* went up, it would 'have been most unpleasant, and probably fatal'.[6]

Smart was certainly worried about such a fate, not only because of the danger to his own life and that of his crew, but because capture would mean 'blowing the gaff'. It would jeopardise all future XE-craft operations against the Japanese. The Japanese would immediately improve their anti-submarine defences throughout their remaining territory and the chance of further XE-craft missions being successful would be seriously threatened.

Pomeroy finished dressing, the suit constricting and uncomfortable. After wearing a shirt and shorts for so many hours, the diving suit was extremely hot. Sweat streamed from his red face. Putting the set and the face visor to one side for the moment, Pomeroy returned to assisting Smart with the navigation.

*

'I'm losing her again!' shouted Kiwi Smith as the *XE-3* started once more for the surface of the strait, completely out of control.

'I can't fucking hold her!' Smith wrestled with the hydroplane controls to no avail, his face a rictus of fear and frustration.

Fraser instantly ordered more ballast blown, trying to control the boat's trim by whatever means he could think of. Suddenly, a low buzzing sound started up outside the submarine, growing louder by the second. All eyes turned upwards towards the pressure hull, even though they could see nothing.

'Christ, it's a fucking motor boat,' cried Fraser. By the sound of it, it was coming directly towards them. They were still stuck in the freshwater pot, the submarine wanting to surface. Smith and Charlie Reed continued to wrestle with the controls and the ballast tanks as the whine of the Japanese patrol craft grew louder and louder, starting out as the faint buzzing of a wasp until it grew to the deafening racket of a bandsaw.

'Depth?' yelled Fraser over the din, which filled the inside of the submarine, making the hull thrum and vibrate.

'Eight feet,' yelled back Smith. Fraser's face was ashen. They were practically at the surface.

Closer and closer came the motor boat, its engine noise growing in intensity. Fraser was convinced that the Japanese must have detected them. If the boat came any closer she was going to run them down.[7]

'Depth?' screamed Fraser, the sound of the motor boat's engine vibrating through his head.

'Five feet and still rising, Tich!' screamed back Smith.

'Brace for impact!' yelled Fraser, before stuffing his fingers in his ears against the unholy racket.[8] The rest of the crew did the same, at the same time squeezing their eyes shut as they waited for the sickening crunch of the patrol boat's bow as it smashed into the XE-3's barely submerged hull.[9]

*

'That's it – Lamma Bloody Island,' said Pat Westmacott, turning his head away from the periscope. 'Finally,' he added in a weary and irritable voice.

The XE-5 had carefully worked its way the last 30 miles to Hong Kong.

'Well, boys, we can't do anything today, it's too late,' said Westmacott to his crew. The delay caused by breaking the towline to HMS *Selene* had completely ruined Westmacott's chances of arriving in the West Lamma Channel in time on 31 July to start hunting for the two cables that he had been sent to sever. There was nothing for it but to rest and wait for dawn to break on 1 August.

*

'Depth!' screamed Tich Fraser one last time as the sound of the Japanese patrol boat's big engines filled the *XE-3*'s interior. The submarine had only been a few feet beneath the surface when Fraser had given the warning to stand by for a collision. Kiwi Smith mouthed something to Fraser in reply but he didn't hear, the New Zealander's voice drowned out by the roar of the Japanese engines. Fraser closed his eyes and jammed his fingers back in his ears. Was this it, he thought? Was this how it would be?

But no devastating crash occurred. The patrol boat passed directly over the heads of the four praying sailors crouched inside the submarine with barely a foot of clearance before it started to pull away from them, the dreadful sound easing rapidly down. At the same time, the *XE-3* passed out of the freshwater pot and started to sink, the crew quickly regaining control of her. Fraser thought it was a miracle that the patrol boat hadn't hit them. The crew's luck had continued to hold. It was another close call to add to the growing catalogue of calamities that had defined their mission thus far. Fraser set a course for the boom gate once again, his heart thumping in his chest, slightly light-headed from the excitement and the cloying atmosphere inside the boat.

*

'Stand by, chaps, the gate's coming up,' said Jack Smart, as he looked through the attack periscope. The rest of the crew stiffened in their seats, ready for action. The trickiest part of the exfiltration down the strait was now upon the *XE-1* and her pensive crew. Smart could see the defence vessel, still in its original position, and the line of large buoys stretching right across the mouth of the strait from which the huge anti-submarine net was strung. The light was fading and he really had to concentrate to see any detail.

'Wait a minute,' said Smart slowly, pressing his face harder against the viewfinder.

'By George, the gate's still open,' he exclaimed, his face beaming. 'Down periscope!'

A few minutes later and Smart and his submarine were correctly positioned to begin an approach towards the open boom gate. He had the submarine as deep as he dared and running slow ahead. Walter Pomeroy, now rather relieved that his services had not been required after all, sat sweating inside his redundant diving suit with a stopwatch and a slide rule in front of him. Once more the countdown began, each minute slowly dragging by as the *XE-1* came closer and closer to the wide-open gap. The risk of detection was huge. Jack Smart waited by the periscope, his cap tipped back on his head. Harold Harper and Henry Fishleigh watched their dials and gauges intently, two statues rigid in their seats, hands on the control levers, awaiting orders.

When Pomeroy suddenly announced that the run was complete Smart immediately ordered him to raise the periscope.

'Chaps, we've made it, we're through!' shouted Smart. The other crewmen laughed or swore in equal measure, a wave of relief sweeping through the boat like a fresh breeze.

'Time?' demanded Smart.

'Nineteen fifteen hours, Jack,' replied Harper. They had made it much earlier than any of them had anticipated.[10]

*

Full control had by now been asserted over the *XE-3*, the submarine reaching the end of the Johor Strait where the water salinity increased. There were no more surprises from nature or the Japanese. The *XE-3* approached the boom gate just over three hours after leaving the *Takao*. Fraser, like Smart, was both surprised and relieved to find the gate still open. HMS *XE-3* slipped through unnoticed at 7.49pm.

The relief was as great as that aboard the *XE-1*. Fraser paused for a moment to reflect on what he and his crew had achieved. He also thought about his friend Jack Smart, and wondered how things were going for him.[11] He had no idea that the *XE-1* had passed through the gate over half an hour before him.

'Right, Magennis,' said Fraser, 'let's get you out of that suit.'

Fraser helped Magennis to strip off the thick diving suit. The diver had been wearing blue overalls underneath and these were wringing wet with sweat. Magennis shook them off and put on a fresh khaki shirt and shorts.

'Start the fan,' ordered Fraser, and Smith switched on the ventilation, easing the uncomfortable atmosphere inside the boat a little. But the heat didn't seem to bother the men any more. 'The job was done. That was what mattered,'[12] said Fraser afterwards.

The crew settled down to getting the boat to her rendezvous with HMS *Stygian*. With the pressure mostly now off, Fraser relaxed and for the first time in many hours he was able to actually converse with his men instead of just issuing orders and commands.

'What will you do when you get back, number one?' he said to Smith.

Smith smiled wearily and rubbed his stubbly chin. 'Sleep for three days,'[13] he replied. His face was deathly pale. The stress and tension were starting to leave them all. Smith's shoulders sagged with exhaustion.

'I think I'll get the jar of rum from under my bunk and swig the lot,'[14] said Fraser, wincing slightly in pain as his spoke. His knees were starting to bother him after kneeling for so many hours. But the thought of a drink cheered him up. Beneath his bunk aboard

HMS *Bonaventure*, hidden in a cupboard, was a gallon stone jar. Before the *XE-3* had departed on the mission, Fraser had had the forethought to draw the entire rum ration for his crew and stash it.

'Just put me on a ship and send me home,' piped up Charlie Reed, as stolid and reliable as ever, still at his station, eyes fixed to his gauges.

'I'll help you with the rum, sir,'[15] said Magennis, a mischievous grin forming across his face. He'd more than earned a drink on this trip.

Every so often Fraser had the periscope raised and he swept for danger and corrected his course. As the light continued to dim to dusk, Fraser could make out low hills, jungle, swamp and the occasional farmer's field begin to fade from sight as the *XE-3* headed for the open sea. Somewhere out beyond Singapore lay the *Stygian* and that bed in her seamen's mess.

CHAPTER TWENTY

Fire in the Night

'One man inspired us all on that mission:
Lt. Fraser. He was cool, real cool.'

—Acting Leading Seaman James Magennis, HMS *XE-3*

'Prepare to surface,' ordered Lieutenant Fraser at 8.00pm. He had given up trying to see anything through the attack periscope. The light was fading fast. Fifteen minutes later Fraser changed his mind and, ever cautious, decided to attempt to have one last look around, just for the sake of his peace of mind. The periscope was run up but unsurprisingly Fraser could see very little and he abandoned the attempt soon after.

'Take her down to 30 feet, number one,' said Fraser to Kiwi Smith.

'Aye aye, skip, making my depth 30 feet,' replied Smith. Fraser had decided to wait for darkness before surfacing the *XE-3*. The electric motor was running at full power, propelling them further and further from Singapore and danger and towards their agreed rendezvous point with HMS *Stygian*.

'I'll check the batteries,' said Mick Magennis. After a few moments, he reported that the battery density was 1,195, far higher than any of them expected. Fraser was relieved – he had plenty of reserve if he needed it.[1]

'Stand by to surface,' ordered Fraser at 9.00pm. The main vents were closed and everyone waited tensely at their stations.

'Surface on number 2 main ballast only,' said Fraser to Charlie

Reed. Fraser wanted to make a gentle and quiet ascent to the dark surface.

Gathering his binoculars, Fraser clambered into the W&D compartment and reached up and took hold of the hatch clip.

'Surface the boat,' he ordered.

'Aye aye, skipper, surfacing the boat,' replied Smith.

'Twenty feet to fifteen feet from number 1 open the induction,'[2] said Fraser to Reed. Reed slammed the lever down, water pouring into the submarine as the air forced its way out. The boat was at the surface. Fraser took off the clip from the W&D compartment hatch. Suddenly, the hatch was torn from Fraser's fingers as a violent rush of pressurised air shot out of the *XE-3*, the hatch clanging open loudly. Fraser was bucked hard against the compartment's coving and almost blown out of the submarine by the force of the explosion. Pressure had built up steadily inside the sealed submarine for fourteen and a half hours as the crew had constantly vented air from the diving tanks and oxygen cylinders. They had no way of checking the pressure because the small aircraft barometer in the control room was broken. When Fraser released the W&D hatch it was like lifting the ring-pull on a shaken can of soda water.

A second after the hatch had blown open the interior of the submarine filled with an ethereal fog as the colder outside air mingled with the submarine's oppressive interior.[3] It was like the opening of a cold tomb in some Victorian graveyard, eerie and strange.

Fraser, after recovering from the shock of the explosive depressurisation, gingerly raised his head out of the W&D compartment's hatch. The moment his eyes adjusted to the darkness he spied trouble.

*

Aboard the *XE-1*, a similar scene played out to that aboard the *XE-3*, with Jack Smart and his crew shaken by the turbulence when the hatch was opened. Smart had surfaced the boat, thankful for the fresh air. He could feel some of the stress of the past two days beginning to leave his body. He remained on deck armed with his trusty binoculars, communicating with his crew down the raised air induction trunk. The search had now begun for HMS *Spark*, his ride home.

*

The moment Tich Fraser had his head out of the open W&D compartment hatch he saw the dark outline of a large boat right on top of him. His stomach flipped and he ducked involuntarily before raising his head again as a junk's high stern passed just a few feet from the submarine, the only sounds the creaking of her rigging and the slap of water against her blunt bow as she moved slowly through the sea.[4] Fortunately, Fraser didn't see anyone aboard her. He glanced at the sky: it was clear and moonless. He didn't order a crash dive, as the ghostly junk didn't appear to be a threat.

Fraser ducked his head below the hatch parapet and spoke briefly to Kiwi Smith.

'Steer one-eight-oh degrees,' Fraser said quietly. Smith repeated the order and the *XE-3* turned away from the junk.[5] Fraser wasn't going to take any chances at this stage of the mission. It was better that they slink away while everything was peaceful.

Once the submarine was out of earshot of the junk, Fraser ordered the diesel engine engaged so that they could move more quickly towards their rendezvous with the *Stygian*.[6]

'Raise the induction,' ordered Fraser, closing the W&D compartment hatch. He re-entered the control room and opened the main hatch, scrambling up onto the deck. Fraser knew that he was exhausted, and it would be tempting fate for him to simply sit on the edge of the main hatch with his feet dangling inside while he kept a lookout. He would probably fall asleep as the fresh, salty air worked its magic. Instead he closed the main hatch, took up a suitably uncomfortable position leaning over the partially raised induction trunk, and raised his binoculars to his eyes.[7]

In addition to his binoculars, Fraser also carried an ingenious new device that would in theory allow him to communicate directly with the *Stygian* long before he saw her. The Motorola SCR-536 'Handie-Talkie' (HT) was a relatively new invention that had seen extensive service during the Normandy invasion. A radio transceiver with a range of several miles over water, it was a derivation of the more famous 'Walkie-Talkie', though unlike its larger cousin the HT was hand-held rather than back-mounted. It looked like an oversized and boxy green telephone receiver. Fraser pulled out the HT's long aerial. He depressed a long rubber switch and began to call the *Stygian*, using the agreed code words. He would repeat this process every few minutes for the rest of the night until he had established contact with the *Stygian*'s skipper, Guy Clarabut.[8]

*

Aboard the *XE-4* and *XE-5* nothing was happening. Max Shean's boat was sitting on the bottom some miles off the Mekong River, the crew trying to rest. He planned to surface the *XE-4* about 9.30pm when it would be fully dark and he could begin a standing charge of the batteries before attempting to make his rendezvous with HMS *Spearhead*.[9] Once the *XE-4* had found the *Spearhead*, Shean intended to have a short conference with her captain, Lieutenant-Commander Youngman, as it was expected that he would have some updated aerial intelligence concerning Japanese shipping in Saigon. If the RAF or the Americans had identified worthwhile targets there was every chance that Captain Fell would order the *XE-4* to head back in towards the Indochinese coast. It was not a thought that Shean relished.

*

Pat Westmacott and his crew aboard the *XE-5* were also not going anywhere. They were in position off Hong Kong's West Lamma Channel but would have to wait out the night of 31 July/1 August until dawn broke and they could start dragging for the telephone cables. The *XE-5* was on the bottom, the men resting, enduring a seemingly interminable wait for the sun.[10] It was galling because they knew that if the other missions had gone according to plan, their boats would already be on the way back by now.

*

Tich Fraser thought for a moment that his eyes were playing tricks. He stared hard through the binoculars, adjusting the focus. It was dark, but he could just make out a small craft lying very low in the water some distance away on the starboard bow. His eyes strained to make out any details. After a few minutes Fraser decided that it could be the *XE-1*.

Fraser ordered a course change, and slowly the *XE-3* motored closer to the unidentified craft, Fraser still hopeful that it was Jack Smart and his crew. But as the submarine closed the distance, Fraser could see that it was nothing more than yet another small native fishing boat.[11] He hastily ordered a course change and moved away before his submarine was seen. Wherever Jack Smart was, he wasn't near here.

*

Smart was continuing his vigil topside, scanning the gloom with his binoculars and occasionally using the HT that he had been issued to try to contact HMS *Spark*. He saw nothing and he heard nothing, just the hum of his own engine and the slap of water against the casing. He would keep at it for however long it took. Getting home was now his only objective.

*

Mick Magennis took out a box of matches and lit his cigarette. He dragged the smoke deeply into his lungs and exhaled with a long, satisfied sigh. Charlie Reed took a proffered cigarette and held a lit match to the end. Soon the *XE-3* was filled with the smell of tobacco smoke as the two crewmen puffed away cheerfully. They had been denied this pleasure for a day and a half.

Not long afterwards Kiwi Smith asked Fraser, still in position atop the *XE-3*'s casing, if Magennis and Reed could get a little fresh air. Both men were feeling sick. After so long without a smoke, the cigarettes had made them feel light-headed and upset their stomachs. Fraser opened the main hatch and allowed each of the men to climb out onto the casing for a few moments, swinging their arms and walking about a bit until their equilibrium was restored. Kiwi Smith also took a brief turn on the deck.[12]

*

Lieutenant Guy Clarabut stood over the chart table in HMS *Stygian*'s control room. The submarine's interior was lit with red night lamps. Up top, on the conning tower, lookouts constantly scanned the surrounding water searching for the *XE-3*.

'Sir,' said a naval rating at Clarabut's elbow, 'the wireless operator reports that we've just picked up a transmission. It's the *XE-3*, sir.'

Clarabut smiled and made his way down the narrow corridor to the wireless office. The operator handed him a set of headphones. 'He's transmitting now, sir,' he added, fiddling with a large dial on the front of the wireless equipment.

Clarabut listened. The voice was indistinct and full of static, the signal strength weak, but it was unmistakably Tich Fraser's voice slowly repeating his call sign and giving some basic navigational information.

Clarabut was both happy and relieved. Fraser had made it. When he had bid farewell to his friend the night before, Clarabut had been unsure of his chances. It had seemed a tall order to infiltrate the Johor Strait and get back out again. But Clarabut had believed in Fraser and now he knew that Fraser had accomplished an extraordinary feat of seamanship. He ordered the operator to reply and continue monitoring the frequency. He also ordered that a message be sent to Captain Fell aboard the *Bonaventure* in Brunei Bay informing him that the *XE-3* was making for its rendezvous.

*

Fraser never heard the reply from the *Stygian*. He continued to send his message every few minutes in between making visual sweeps with his binoculars, but he had no idea if anyone was listening at the other end. The HT signal was weak. The *Stygian* could only pick up Fraser's signal because it was equipped with a powerful receiver. So Fraser continued with his lonely vigil, passing the occasional word with one of his crewmen each time a head appeared at the hatch, but otherwise alone with his thoughts and fears.

*

Jack Smart was facing the same problem as Fraser – the HT didn't seem to be receiving anything from the *Spark*. Smart wasn't unduly worried at this stage. He knew that he still had several miles to travel before he reached the agreed rendezvous area, but it was nonetheless frustrating to keep sending the same message over and over and hear only the low hum of static each time he released the talk button. He decided not to worry; at least, not yet. He would just follow the agreed procedure and hope for the best.

*

'Stop engine,' ordered Fraser from his position on top of the casing.

'Stop engine, aye aye, skipper,' replied Smith from inside the submarine.

The gentle throb of the diesel died and was replaced by the sounds of waves slapping against the submarine's hull.

'It's almost time, chaps,' said Fraser through the open main hatch. 'Come up onto the casing.'

As Smith, Reed and Magennis clambered up the short ladder onto the deck Fraser glanced at his watch. 9.25pm. It wouldn't be long now. The other three crewmen stretched and gulped in the clean air. They balanced themselves by gripping the induction trunk or each other. Fraser took out a small hand-held marine compass and consulted its luminous face.

'It will come from over there,' he said, pointing with one arm in the direction of the Singapore Naval Base several miles away in the darkness. He raised his binoculars and swept the surrounding ocean. All clear. He could afford this little indulgence after so much hardship and danger. The crew deserved to see it.

*

Aboard the *XE-1* Smart, Harper, Fishleigh and Pomeroy also stood atop their submarine's casing. All eyes were fixed on the dark horizon in the direction of Singapore. They waited with bated breath, not knowing what they might see, but just as determined as Fraser and his crew to witness the results of their illicit handiwork. They were not to be disappointed.

*

Lieutenant Clarabut had moved on to the *Stygian*'s conning tower and was scanning the darkness for the *XE-3* alongside the lookouts. Aboard HMS *Spark*, Lieutenant-Commander Youngman did the same. Both officers knew the approximate time that the two XE-crafts' explosive charges were set to detonate, and they wanted to witness the show. They also knew that Captain Fell was standing by for news of the attacks and of his little submarines.

*

Fraser and Smart's crew checked their watches repeatedly as the minutes slowly passed. At 9.30pm all eyes strained into the gloom. Surely it must happen now? But there was nothing. The minutes ticked on. The first stirrings of worry began to descend upon them. Had something gone wrong with the charges or the limpet mines? Had they come all this way for nothing? Had the mission ended in failure?

'Crikey!' exclaimed Fraser at 9.33 as a huge far-away flash lit up the sky, followed by another, even larger detonation, an orange and yellow glow illuminating the distant land.[13] The second explosion lasted a few seconds longer, and soon a great fire could be observed that burned brightly against the horizon. Then the sound hit them. First a crack followed by another much louder bang and then a long rumbling roar, the death rattle of a great and terrible beast.

*

'Signal from the *Stygian*, sir,' said the wireless clerk as he handed the note to Captain Fell, who had been hovering anxiously near the *Bonaventure*'s radio room for hours.

Fell took the handwritten note scribbled hastily on a signal pad and ran his eyes feverishly over the pencilled words. Then he turned to Commander Graham, his deputy, and grinned fiercely.

'Follow me, Derek,' said Fell, heading off to find Admiral Fife.

'A message from the *Stygian*, Jimmy,' said Fell when he had located the American, barely able to control his excitement.

'Read it to me, Tiny,' asked Fife.

'What a bonfire, consider cruiser well distributed over the countryside,'[14] said Fell, reading Lieutenant Clarabut's message. Fell and Fife shook hands, both grinning from ear to ear. The 'little guys with a lotta guts' had got through. Hardly had the congratulations begun when confirmation arrived from another source.

'Beg pardon, sir,' said the yeoman of signals, interrupting the two senior officers. 'A message has just arrived from the *Spark*, sir.'

Fell took the message from his outstretched hand and read it aloud.

'Huge explosions from direction of Johor Strait followed by more explosions and fires.'[15] Fell was ecstatic. Thirty-six hours of impatient waiting was over. His men had done it – just as he had promised Fife they would. Now his only worry was whether the two submarines had managed to get out of the strait.

*

The crews of the *XE-1* and *XE-3* stood transfixed by the pyrotechnic display, mouths open and eyes wide until they started to cheer and embrace one other, laughing, shaking hands and clapping each other on the back in sheer, unabashed joy.[16] They had done it – eight exhausted men in two tiny submarines had done the impossible. It had taken them 43 hours, including over sixteen and a half beneath the water. The Japanese behemoth was no more, her guts torn from her body, her fuel oil spreading around her sinking hull like dark arterial blood.[17] They had done it, and they had managed to escape from right under the enemy's nose without a single casualty. Compared with the *Tirpitz* operation it was a triumph, practically a textbook raid.

*

When the British explosives had detonated beneath the *Takao* at 9.33pm, the great ship had lifted, the entire weight of the vessel, her crew and all of her stores and ammunition being flung upwards before settling back into the water with a groan. The British charges had been designed in such a way that a detonation close by would cause any other charges to also explode. The effect was that of one enormous bomb beneath the *Takao*.

The force of the explosion sent a powerful shock wave through the interior of the ship, smashing decks and surging through bulkheads and down passageways. Those Japanese sailors inside the ship were violently lifted off their feet and thrown down against unyielding steel or wood surfaces, cracking skulls and breaking limbs.

Flames, smoke and debris burst up on either side of the ship, pluming high into the air before shrapnel started to fall like steel rain over a wide area, Japanese sailors running for cover under the sudden maelstrom. The flashes lit up the entire naval base and the jungle beyond. A wave several feet high surged out from the wrecked ship, threatening to capsize the small craft that were plying the strait, an artificial tsunami. Windows across the naval base imploded as the shock wave swept over the buildings and workshops, while Japanese sailors flung themselves to the ground or ran for their lives. Smaller secondary explosions shook the *Takao*, as burning tendrils of fuel oil spread out across the Strait from her ruptured tanks in orange pools and rivulets. An air raid siren began to wail mournfully while Japanese damage-control parties raced to try to contain the fires, desperately unravelling hoses, their officers yelling orders in all directions.

The *Takao* settled slowly into the strait as water flooded into her belly, her bow and stern coming to rest on the shallow bottom where she would remain, no longer able to float on the tide.[18] If not for the shallow water of the strait, she would have submerged entirely. Beneath the waterline, unseen by those ashore, a gaping hole 60 feet long had been punched into her starboard flank by the *XE-1* and *XE-3*'s explosives, flooding the engine room and dozens of compartments. The damage had spread higher throughout the ship. Electrical power was gone, meaning that she could not fire her boilers and move. The lights had shorted, and some of the gun turrets had been lifted from their bearings, leaving them out of commission with their delicate range finders wrecked.[19] The *Takao*'s days as a fighting ship were well and truly over. She was no longer a threat to anyone, least of all to Lord Mountbatten's Operation Zipper.

*

Epilogue

*'I have the greatest admiration for the forthright
sheer guts of you and your personnel.'*

—Vice-Admiral Lockwood to Captain Fell, 19 August 1945

Nobby Clarke struggled in the thick, armpit-deep white mud beneath the silty waters off Lamma Island, Hong Kong.[1] It was like trying to work half-buried in setting concrete. Clarke was soon breathing hard as he struggled to manoeuvre the heavy hydraulic cutters into position before making a cut on whatever was snagging the grapnel. At this rate, Clarke would soon be at the limit of his breathable air, and walking the fine line between consciousness and oxygen narcosis. Nearby, Pat Westmacott crouched inside the *XE-5*, his eyes clamped to the night periscope, watching and waiting for Clarke to return safely to the submarine. Westmacott's mission plan had gone to hell in a handbasket. He was seriously behind schedule. It was now 1 August 1945 and the crew of the *XE-5* had been on the operation for nearly 40 hours. It had taken Westmacott four-and-a-half hours of dragging from first light on 1 August before the submarine finally snagged something and Nobby Clarke had been sent out to investigate.[2] Each man was at the limit of his endurance and patience since arriving too late on 31 July. Westmacott knew that if things didn't start going his way soon he would have to scrub the mission. He also knew that the other three XE-craft must have completed their missions long before, and if they had survived would be already attached to their mother submarines and on their way back to HMS *Bonaventure* and safety.

*

Indeed, by and large all was well with the other three boats. The *XE-3* had successfully rendezvoused with HMS *Stygian* an hour after the charges beneath the *Takao* had gone off. Jack Smart and the *XE-1* couldn't find HMS *Spark* on 31 July. Instead, the crew was forced to spend the day on the seabed until darkness fell. They were eventually located on the evening of 1 August, exhausted but cheerful.

Max Shean's *XE-4* had met HMS *Spearhead* at midnight on 1 August. After a quick conference with Commander Youngman, Shean was informed that only Japanese flying boats were present in Saigon harbour. Shean offered to go back and deal with them. He mooted the idea of using divers' knives to puncture the floats on the aircraft. This was not considered worth the risk, and the *XE-4* began her journey back to Brunei Bay.[3]

Operation Sabre had been virtually a textbook mission and Shean was very pleased to hear that the Japanese reaction to his severing of the cables was an immediate blizzard of enemy wireless traffic, which was promptly deciphered by the Americans.[4]

*

But for Pat Westmacott and the crew of the *XE-5* the mission continued. While he was still able, Westmacott determined that he would continue with the mission. To return empty-handed would be almost too much to bear, for all of them. They had been through too much to simply give up. The cable was the last remaining line of communication between Singapore and Japan.[5] It was a measure of their determination and dedication that no man aboard the *XE-5* made any complaint about the mission, which was rapidly assuming the form of a test of endurance such as none of them had ever experienced or even contemplated before.

Nobby Clarke batted another huge jellyfish away from his visor as he struggled, a great Portuguese man-o'-war stinging him across the hand as he did so. He was in agony, constantly harassed by jellyfish and virtually immobile in the thick mud. He could barely see anything and instead groped his way along the snag with one hand, then attempted to manoeuvre the heavy cutters into position to make the cut. Clarke depressed the hydraulic cutter's trigger and a sickening blast of intense pain lanced up his arm. He screamed into the DSEA mouthpiece, dropping the cutters as a dark red cloud pumped into the water all around him. Clarke raised his left hand up towards his visor in horror. His thumb was nearly cut through.[6] In the gloomy and muddy conditions he had cut the snag just where his hand was holding it. He was lucky not to have sliced his entire thumb off. Panicking, Clarke struggled back towards the *XE-5*, holding his wounded hand close to his chest as blood continued to cloud in the water all around him. Somehow, he made it back to the Wet & Dry Compartment and pumped out the water. Westmacott had the little door open in an instant. The other crewmen initially recoiled in horror at Clarke's injury, as blood dripped onto the submarine's deck from his mangled hand, before they all joined in the effort to stem the bleeding and get the wound taken care of. Clarke lay motionless on the deck looking as pale as a corpse, moaning in pain until Westmacott managed to get some morphine into him.

Westmacott now faced a further dilemma. Although the working conditions outside of the boat were atrocious, his submarine's grapnel, vital for locating the Japanese telephone cable, was still snagged. With one diver out of action and in need of proper medical attention, Westmacott turned to his second diver, Sub-Lieutenant Jarvis.

'Dennis, go out and cut the grapnel free and stow it and the cutters,' ordered Westmacott. Jarvis didn't hesitate. He was already suited up, and, fitting his DSEA, he was soon flooding the W&D. Within a few minutes Jarvis had managed to free the grapnel and Westmacott could decide on a course of action.

Once Jarvis had returned, Westmacott addressed the crew.

'Clarke needs a vet,' he said, using the accustomed parlance for a medic. 'We'll rendezvous with the *Selene* as planned and offload him. Then we'll return to this area and complete the mission.' Westmacott wasn't asking for opinions, and the other crewmen knew that to return once they had taken care of Clarke was expected. They still had a job to do, even with one man down. It meant that the remaining diver, Jarvis, would have to work twice as hard.

The badly injured Nobby Clarke was transferred to HMS *Selene* where he received emergency medical treatment,[7] and Pat Westmacott and the *XE-5* were back on station off Lamma Island by the early hours of 2 August.

The *XE-5* resumed her search for the Hong Kong to Singapore telephone cable. Jarvis worked alone, repeatedly going outside the submarine to deal with snags and, eventually, after seventeen runs over the supposed cable location, a difficult cut into what was believed to be the target. But because of the atrocious conditions off Lamma Island, with the exhausted Jarvis forced like Clarke to work in armpit-deep white mud in near zero visibility, Jarvis was unable to report to Westmacott that he had successfully severed the cable. He believed that he had managed to damage it, but was unable to say that he had put it out of action for sure. At midday on 3 August 1945 Pat Westmacott, in view of the fact that Jarvis was completely worn out and sending him out any more was tantamount to a death sentence, reluctantly called off the operation. By now there was only about two hours of oxygen left inside of the *XE-5* after three days deeply submerged and Westmacott needed to take his submarine further out to sea and surface somewhere less crowded with junks and patrol boats. With a heavy heart and a feeling of deep frustration, Westmacott set a course back towards HMS *Selene* and home. In total, Westmacott and his crew had spent 84 hours on station under the noses of the Japanese, which was an incredible achievement in itself.[8]

*

Over the next few days the heroes returned home. First back was *XE-4*, arriving alongside HMS *Bonaventure* in Brunei Bay on 3 August. Tich Fraser and *XE-3* arrived on 5 August, followed by Smart's *XE-1* the following day. Pat Westmacott and *XE-5* were last back, arriving alongside the depot ship HMS *Maidstone* in Subic Bay on 6 August.

The same day that the subdued crew of the *XE-5* stepped aboard the *Maidstone* a silver Boeing B-29 Superfortress named Enola Gay appeared in the skies above the city of Hiroshima.

Nine days later, on the morning of 15 August 1945, Captain Fell received the following signal from headquarters: 'Cease hostilities against Japan.'[9] It was all over.

'The relief that there would be no more missions, no more war, no more parting from Melba and our child completely over-whelmed every other feeling,' wrote Tich Fraser. 'Suddenly life itself was friendly and jubilant; and the sun shone for all of us, for we had survived.'[10]

*

During the first weeks of the great peace, while recovering in Australia, Tich Fraser and Mick Magennis learned that they would both receive Britain's supreme award for gallantry, the Victoria Cross.

After the war ...

William Banks

After leaving 12th Submarine Flotilla in late 1944, Willie Banks was appointed Captain Landing Craft Mediterranean, serving through to July 1945. In January 1946 Banks was made commanding officer of the New Zealand cruiser HMNZS *Achilles*. He then moved to HMS *Osprey*, in charge of anti-submarine warfare training at Devonport. Banks's last appointment was as naval advisor to the government of Ceylon before he retired in 1952. Banks died in 1986 aged 86.

Adam 'Jock' Bergius

Awarded the Distinguished Service Cross for his diving during Operation Sabre, Bergius left the navy and married. According to Max Shean, Bergius 'raised a thoroughly Scottish family of five'. He was a director of the famous whisky blenders William Teacher & Son, and a keen yachtsman. Bergius is one of the last surviving participants in XE-craft operations against the Japanese and currently lives in Scotland.

Ken Briggs

Briggs was awarded the Distinguished Service Cross, married and returned to Australia. He worked in Perth for the British United Shoe Machinery Company, and currently lives in retirement in Rochedale, Queensland.

William Britnell

Willie Britnell was awarded a Mention in Despatches for his service as a passage crew skipper. He married an HMS *Varbel* Wren and moved to Canada, where he worked in brewing.

Guy Clarabut

Awarded the Distinguished Service Cross for operations in the Far East, Clarabut left the navy in 1955 and joined his family firm, Crescent Shipping. He was also a director of Hays Wharf, a Deputy Lieutenant of Kent and Commodore of Medway Yacht Club. Clarabut died in 2002 aged 82.

Vernon 'Ginger' Coles

Awarded a Mention in Despatches for Operation Sabre, Coles remained in submarines for several years after the war. Leaving the navy in 1958, he joined the civil service and worked in Malaysia where he was in charge of removing sensitive radar equipment from RAF Penang Hill. Coles was later appointed engineer in charge of the American base at RAF Greenham Common before moving to Newbury where he worked for the dredging company Van Oord UK. A vocal and popular supporter of veterans' affairs, Coles was president of the Royal Berkshire Submarines Association and the HMS *Faulknor* Association. He also appeared on several television programmes about wartime midget submarine operations. Ginger Coles sadly passed away during the writing of this book in May 2014, aged 94.

Beadon Dening

Awarded the Distinguished Service Cross for his part in Operation Foil, Dening went up to Oxford after leaving the navy. He then joined the Colonial Service, with postings far from the sea in Sudan in 1948–55. Dening was an Administrative Officer in Uganda, 1955–65, and Local Government Advisor in Swaziland, 1966–69. He married in 1972 and died at the age of 75 in 1999.

William 'Tiny' Fell

Fell stayed with HMS *Bonaventure* until 1947, bringing the vessel back from the Far East. He was made a Commander of the Order of the British Empire the same year for his inspired leadership of 14th Submarine Flotilla in its actions against the Japanese. Fell then joined the Admiralty's Boom Defence and Salvage Department, organising the clearing of wartime wrecks from the British and Mediterranean coasts until he retired in 1948. Fell continued to work for the Admiralty as a civilian, supervising salvage operations until 1960, including clearing Port Said following the Suez Crisis. He was appointed a Companion of the Order of St Michael and St George in 1957. Fell wrote two books about his wartime experiences: *The Sea Surrenders* (1960) and *The Sea Our Shield* (1966). Tiny Fell died in New Zealand in 1981 aged 84.

James 'Jimmy' Fife

Fife commanded Submarine Force, Atlantic Fleet between 1947 and 1950, and then was Deputy Chief of Naval Operations. His last appointment was as US Naval Commander-in-Chief Mediterranean, ironically serving under a Royal Navy HQ commanded by Lord Mountbatten. After retiring from the US Navy in 1955, Fife was director of Mystic Seaport Museum in Stonington, Connecticut. After his death in 1975 at the age of 78, Fife bequeathed his estate in Stonington to the US Navy, who turned it into a recreational centre. Fife's memory was further memorialised with Fife Hall at the Naval Submarine Base New London and the USS *Fife*, a destroyer that was in service from 1980 to 2003.

Ian 'Tich' Fraser

In addition to the award of the Victoria Cross, Ian Fraser was honoured by the United States for Operation Struggle, being made an Officer of the Legion of Merit. In 1947 Fraser left full-time naval service but he remained with the Royal Naval Reserve until

December 1965, retiring as a lieutenant commander and holder of the Decoration for Officers of the Royal Naval Reserve with Bar.

In 1953 he and his brother Brian managed to get hold of some surplus frogman gear and formed their own company, Universal Divers Ltd, helping to pioneer civilian diving. He published his autobiography in 1958.

In 1980, Fraser was made a Younger Brother of Trinity House and in 1993 an honorary freeman of the Metropolitan Borough of Wirral. He remained married to Melba for the rest of his life, his family growing to include six children, thirteen grandchildren and seven great-grandchildren before he died in 2008 aged 87. Tich Fraser's VC can today be seen on display at the Imperial War Museum, London.

Bernard 'Ben' Kelly

Awarded a Mention in Despatches for Operation Sabre, Kelly moved to Scotland after the war. He never married and lived in Edinburgh until his death in the early 1990s.

James 'Mick' Magennis

Mick Magennis was the only Victoria Cross winner of the Second World War from Northern Ireland. This made him something of a celebrity on his return to Belfast from the Far East: he and his new wife Edna were presented with £3,600 by the grateful local citizenry. The city fathers were, however, not grateful enough to offer Magennis the freedom of the city, probably because he was a working-class Catholic. Unable to handle the fame his VC brought him, Magennis had soon spent all the donated money and left the navy in 1949. Shortly afterwards he even sold his VC, though it was later returned to him free of charge. In 1955, he left Northern Ireland with his wife and four children and moved to Yorkshire where he worked as an electrician until he retired. Mick Magennis died of lung cancer just hours before the Royal Navy Philatelic

Office's issue on 11 February 1986 of a first day cover honouring his bravery during Operation Struggle. Magennis was 66 years old. Since his death Magennis has been honoured with a memorial in the grounds of Belfast City Hall in 1999 and a blue plaque in the city's Great Victoria Street in 2005. His VC is displayed at the Imperial War Museum, London.

Max Shean

For successfully severing the Japanese underwater cables off Saigon, Max Shean was awarded the Bar to his Distinguished Service Order. The United States also honoured him with the Bronze Star Medal, another indication of how important the operation was to the Americans. Shean was discharged in September 1945 and returned to university. He then worked as an engineer with the City of Perth Electricity and Gas Department, then the State Electricity Commission, until he retired as manager in 1978. Shean had also returned to military service when he rejoined the Royal Australian Naval Reserve; he retired as a lieutenant commander in 1956.

Shortly after his retirement from the State Electricity Commission in 1978, Shean sailed his yacht *Bluebell* from Australia to Britain to compete in the Parmelia Race that was part of the Western Australia 150th anniversary celebrations: from Plymouth via Cape Town to Fremantle. Shean won the open division race. While in Scotland he met Willie Banks. Tiny Fell, then living in Wellington, New Zealand, ordered Shean to report each stage of the voyage to him. After his victory Shean received a reply from Fell. It read, simply, 'You splendid man!' Shean went on to publish his memoirs in 1992 and died in 2009 aged 90.

Jack Smart

Awarded the Distinguished Service Order by the British and the Legion of Merit by the Americans, Smart moved to Canada in 1954, becoming a stockbroker in Vancouver and later Victoria. His

Canadian friends dubbed him 'The English Gentleman' because of his quiet and retiring manner and reticence about discussing his wartime exploits. He married twice and was an active supporter of the arts. Jack Smart died in Canada in 2008 aged 91.

William 'Kiwi' Smith

Awarded the Distinguished Service Order for Operation Struggle, Smith was promoted to Lieutenant in December 1945. Six months later he transferred to the Royal New Zealand Navy where he commanded a succession of ships. By 1959 he was a commander and skipper of HMNZS *Shackleton* and hydrographer of the navy. Appointed an Officer of the Order of the British Empire in 1968, in 2006 'Kiwi' opened the Commander William Smith Building named in his honour at Devonport Naval Base, Auckland. The building houses the RNZN diving team and school. Smith, 91, lives in Wellington.

H.P. 'Pat' Westmacott

Westmacott was awarded the Bar to his Distinguished Service Cross for Operation Foil. He was commanding officer of the submarines HMS *Sceptre* (1946–47) and *Spirit* (1947) before several appointments at the submarine training base HMS *Dolphin*. In 1955 he was promoted to commander. Westmacott ended his naval career in 1966 as Naval and Air Attaché Lisbon. He died in January 1995 aged 73.

IJN *Takao*

On 21 September 1945 Captain Takeo Ishisaka formally surrendered the *Takao* to British forces in Singapore. The Japanese made rudimentary repairs to the vessel in the weeks following the successful attacks by the *XE-1* and *XE-3*. Her main guns remained inoperable. Towed out to the Straits of Malacca by two British tugs, the *Takao* was sunk by gunfire by the cruiser HMS *Newfoundland* off Port Swettenham (now Port Klang), Malaya on 27 October 1946. Her wreck remains there to this day.

IJN *Myoko*

The *Myoko* never was attacked by the British, a final operation planned by Captain Fell being cancelled due to the atomic bombings of Japan. Captain Hokao Kagayama surrendered his ship to the Royal Navy on 21 September 1945. She was scuttled by naval gunfire off Port Swettenham (now Port Klang) on 8 July 1946. The wreck is still there today.

Some of the others

Nobby Clarke recovered from his hand wound and was awarded the Distinguished Service Cross for his bravery during Operation Sabre. **Henry Fishleigh** received the Distinguished Service Medal and passed away in December 1996. **Harold Harper** was awarded the Distinguished Service Cross, as was **Dennis Jarvis**. In 1945 the *XE-1*'s passage skipper **Edgar Munday** was made a Member of the Order of the British Empire for 'skill, efficiency and outstanding devotion to duty'. **Frank Ogden**, *XE-3*'s passage skipper, also received the MBE. **Walter Pomeroy** received the Distinguished Service Medal and died in April 1991. The indefatigable **Charles Reed** was awarded one of the highest awards for non-commissioned personnel, receiving the Conspicuous Gallantry Medal for Operation Struggle.

Maps

Page 292: Map of Southeast Asia, showing the region where Operations Struggle, Foil and Sabre were carried out.

Page 293: Map of Singapore and the Johor Strait (Selat Johor) showing the positions of the *Takao* and *Myoko*.

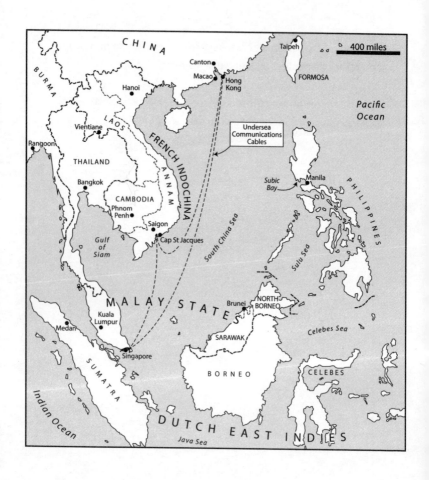

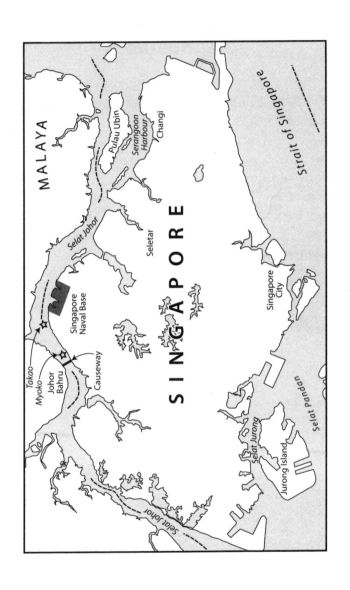

Appendix

List of 1945 place names used in the text, and their modern-day equivalents

Amoy	Xiamen
Batavia	Jakarta
Saigon	Ho Chi Minh City
French Indochina	Vietnam, Cambodia and Laos
Malaya	Malaysia
Netherlands (or Dutch) East Indies	Indonesia
Port Swettenham	Port Klang

Notes

Prologue

1. Peter Thomson & Robert Macklin, *Kill the Tiger: Operation Rimau and the Battle for Southeast Asia* (Dunshaughlin: Maverick House, 2007), p. 239
2. Ibid, p. 239
3. *Operation Jaywick: 60th Anniversary*, Australian Department of Veterans Affairs, 2003
4. *Success and failure in the port of Singapore – Z Special Unit and the Jaywick and Rimau Raids*, www.anzacday.org.au, accessed 12 December 2013
5. Peter Thomson & Robert Macklin, *Kill the Tiger: Operation Rimau and the Battle for Southeast Asia* (Dunshaughlin: Maverick House, 2007), p. 241
6. 'In Memoriam: Major Reginald 'Otto' Ingleton', Old Rendcombian Society Newsletter, May 1998
7. Peter Thomson & Robert Macklin, *Kill the Tiger: Operation Rimau and the Battle for Southeast Asia* (Dunshaughlin: Maverick House, 2007), pp. 240–2
8. Ibid, p. 242

Chapter 1

1. Interview with Ian Edward Fraser, 1987, 9822, Reel 2, Imperial War Museum, London
2. Ibid.
3. Ian Fraser, *Frogman VC* (London: Odhams Beacon Books, 1958), p. 178
4. Interview with Ian Edward Fraser, 1987, 9822, Reel 2, Imperial War Museum, London
5. Ian Fraser, *Frogman VC* (London: Odhams Beacon Books, 1958), p. 99
6. Ibid, p. 119

7. Ibid, p. 119
8. George Fleming, *Magennis VC: The Story of Northern Ireland's only winner of the Victoria Cross* (Dublin: History Ireland Limited, 1998), p. 125
9. Max Shean, *Corvette and Submarine* (Privately published, 1992), p. 122
10. Ibid.
11. 'Training crews to man X-craft and Chariots', ADM1/25845, The National Archives (Public Record Office), Kew
12. Patrick Bishop, *Target Tirpitz: X-Craft, Agents and Dambusters – The Epic Quest to Destroy Hitler's Mightiest Warship* (London: Harper Press, 2012), p. 216
13. Ibid: 216
14. Max Shean, *Corvette and Submarine* (Privately published, 1992), p. 123
15. 'Training crews to man X-craft and Chariots', ADM1/25845, The National Archives (Public Record Office), Kew
16. Patrick Bishop, *Target Tirpitz: X-Craft, Agents and Dambusters – The Epic Quest to Destroy Hitler's Mightiest Warship* (London: Harper Press, 2012), p. 155
17. Ibid, p. 213
18. Audio Interview with Vernon Coles, undated, provided to the author by his daughter Jane Gilbert
19. Max Shean, *Corvette and Submarine* (Privately published, 1992), p. 123
20. Ibid, p. 124
21. Ibid, p. 123
22. Interview with Anthony William Clarke Eldridge, 1989, 11259, Reel 4, Imperial War Museum, London
23. George Fleming, *Magennis VC: The Story of Northern Ireland's only winner of the Victoria Cross* (Dublin: History Ireland Limited, 1998), p. 143

Chapter 2

1. C.E.T. Warren and James Benson, *Above Us The Waves: The Story of Midget Submarines & Human Torpedoes* (Barnsley: Pen & Sword Books, 2006), p. 109
2. Ibid, p. 110

3. Max Shean, *Corvette and Submarine* (Privately published, 1992), p. 126

4. Interview with Ian Edward Fraser, 1987, 9822, Reel 2, Imperial War Museum, London

5. William Fell to the author, 29 April 2014

6. 'British "X" Class Submarines in the 2nd World War', ADM1/21999, The National Archives (Public Record Office), Kew

7. 'The Attack on the German Battleship "Tirpitz" by "X" Craft in Northern Norway – September, 1943', ADM1/21999, The National Archives (Public Record Office), Kew

8. 'British "X" Class Submarines in the 2nd World War', ADM1/21999, The National Archives (Public Record Office), Kew

9. C.E.T. Warren and James Benson, *Above Us The Waves: The Story of Midget Submarines & Human Torpedoes* (Barnsley: Pen & Sword Books, 2006), p. 115

10. 'X-Craft Diver 1943 – Part 1', Roland Hindmarsh, BBC People's War, 24 March 2005, Article ID: A3827342

11. Ibid.

12. 'Training crews to man X-craft and Chariots', ADM1/25845, The National Archives (Public Record Office), Kew

13. Audio Interview with Vernon Coles, undated, provided to the author by his daughter Jane Gilbert

14. 'Training crews to man X-craft and Chariots', ADM1/25845, The National Archives (Public Record Office), Kew

15. Max Shean, *Corvette and Submarine* (Privately published, 1992), p. 134

16. Speech by Adam Bergius, DSC, to West of Scotland Branch, The Submariner's Association, K13 Dinner, January 2013

17. Max Shean, *Corvette and Submarine* (Privately published, 1992), p. 135

18. Biographical Outline, 'Private Papers of Lieutenant-Commander John Beaufoy-Brown, DSC, RN', GB 0099, King's College London

19. 'Naval Stations: HMS Bonaventure parent ship to X-craft', ADM1/18654, The National Archives (Public Record Office), Kew

20. 'X-Craft Diver 1943 – Part 3', Roland Hindmarsh, BBC People's War, 24 March 2005, Article ID: A3827414

21. Max Shean, *Corvette and Submarine* (Privately published, 1992), p. 136

22. 'Lt Cdr Max Shean DSO* RANR retd. Wednesday, 22nd March 1995. X-craft service in the British Royal Navy. A paper prepared by Lt Cdr Max Shean to accompany his talk at the International Submarine Convention, Fremantle'

23. Ibid.

24. C.E.T. Warren and James Benson, *Above Us The Waves: The Story of Midget Submarines & Human Torpedoes* (Barnsley: Pen & Sword Books, 2006), p. 20

25. 'Lt Cdr Max Shean DSO* RANR retd. Wednesday, 22nd March 1995. X-craft service in the British Royal Navy. A paper prepared by Lt Cdr Max Shean to accompany his talk at the International Submarine Convention, Fremantle'

26. Interview with Maxwell Henry Shean, 2005, 28642, Reel 6, Imperial War Museum, London

27. 'X-Craft Diver 1943 – Part 2', Roland Hindmarsh, BBC People's War, 24 March 2005, Article ID: A3827388

28. Ibid.

29. Max Shean, *Corvette and Submarine* (Privately published, 1992), p. 137

30. Ibid: 137

31. Interview with Maxwell Henry Shean, 2005, 28642, Reel 6, Imperial War Museum, London

Chapter 3

1. Ian Fraser, *Frogman VC* (London: Odhams Beacon Books, 1958), p. 126

2. Mark Felton, *The Fujita Plan: Japanese Attacks on the United States and Australia During the Second World War* (Barnsley: Pen & Sword Books, 2006), pp. 24–6

3. Ian Fraser, *Frogman VC* (London: Odhams Beacon Books, 1958), pp. 125–6

4. Interview with Ian Edward Fraser, 1987, 9822, Reel 2, Imperial War Museum, London

5. 'X-Craft Diver 1943 – Part 3', Roland Hindmarsh, BBC People's War, 24 March 2005, Article ID: A3827414

6. Ian Fraser, *Frogman VC* (London: Odhams Beacon Books, 1958), p. 124

7. Max Shean, *Corvette and Submarine* (Privately published, 1992), p. 128

8. Ian Fraser, *Frogman VC* (London: Odhams Beacon Books, 1958), pp. 124–5

9. Ibid, p. 125

10. Ibid, p. 125

11. Ian McGeoch, *Mountbatten of Burma: Captain of War Guardian of Peace* (London: J.H. Haynes & Co. Ltd, 2009), p. 119

12. Ibid, p. 119

13. 'X-Craft Diver 1943 – Part 3', Roland Hindmarsh, BBC People's War, 24 March 2005, Article ID: A3827414

14. 'Operations in the Far East, 12 May 1944', Fell 03 008, Churchill Archives Centre, Churchill College, Cambridge

15. Ibid.

16. Speech by Adam Bergius, DSC, to West of Scotland Branch, The Submariner's Association, K13 Dinner, January 2013

17. Audio Interview with Vernon Coles, undated, provided to the author by his daughter Jane Gilbert

18. George Fleming, *Magennis VC: The Story of Northern Ireland's only winner of the Victoria Cross* (Dublin: History Ireland Limited, 1998), p. 126

Chapter 4

1. Max Shean, *Corvette and Submarine* (Privately published, 1992), p. 235

2. Ibid, pp. 235–6

3. Interview with Maxwell Henry Shean, 2005, 28642, Reel 10, Imperial War Museum, London

4. 'Fourteenth Submarine Flotilla – Second Monthly Letter – January 1945, 3 February 1945', Fell 03 008, Churchill Archives Centre, Churchill College, Cambridge

5. Ibid.

6. Ibid.

7. Ian Fraser, *Frogman VC* (London: Odhams Beacon Books, 1958), p. 128

8. Max Shean, *Corvette and Submarine* (Privately published, 1992), p. 232

9. Patrick Bishop, *Target Tirpitz: X-Craft, Agents and Dambusters – The Epic Quest to Destroy Hitler's Mightiest Warship* (London: Harper Press, 2012), p. 216

10. C.E.T. Warren & James Benson, *Above Us The Waves: The Story of Midget Submarines & Human Torpedoes* (Barnsley: Pen & Sword Books, 2006), pp. 229–30

11. 'British "X" Craft Operations in the Second World War', ADM1/21999, The National Archives (Public Record Office), Kew

12. Patrick Bishop, *Target Tirpitz: X-Craft, Agents and Dambusters – The Epic Quest to Destroy Hitler's Mightiest Warship* (London: Harper Press, 2012), p. 218

13. Ian Fraser, *Frogman VC* (London: Odhams Beacon Books, 1958), p. 128

14. Ibid, p. 126

15. Ian McGeoch, *Mountbatten of Burma: Captain of War, Guardian of Peace* (London: J.H. Haynes & Co. Ltd, 2009), p. 122

16. Max Shean, *Corvette and Submarine* (Privately published, 1992), p. 136

17. Ian Fraser, *Frogman VC* (London: Odhams Beacon Books, 1958), p. 130

18. Adam Bergius to the author, 2 June 2014

19. C.E.T. Warren and James Benson, *Above Us The Waves: The Story of Midget Submarines & Human Torpedoe*s (Barnsley: Pen & Sword Books, 2006), p. 122

20. Max Shean, *Corvette and Submarine* (Privately published, 1992), pp. 153–4

21. 'X-Craft Diver 1943 – Part 5', Roland Hindmarsh, BBC People's War, 26 March 2005, Article ID: A3832346

22. 'X-Craft Diver 1943 – Part 7', Roland Hindmarsh, BBC People's War, 7 April 2005, A3870281

23. George Fleming, *Magennis VC: The Story of Northern Ireland's only winner of the Victoria Cross* (Dublin: History Ireland Limited, 1998), p. 144

24. Ibid, p. 144

25. Ibid, pp. 126–7

26. C.E.T. Warren and James Benson, *Above Us The Waves: The Story of Midget Submarines & Human Torpedoes* (Barnsley: Pen & Sword Books, 2006), p. 215

27. Interview with Ken Clements, 33391, Reel 2, Imperial War Museum, London

28. C.E.T. Warren and James Benson, *Above Us The Waves: The Story of Midget Submarines & Human Torpedoes* (Barnsley: Pen & Sword Books, 2006), pp. 16–17

29. William Fell to the author, 29 April 2014

30. Ibid.

31. C.E.T. Warren and James Benson, *Above Us The Waves: The Story of Midget Submarines & Human Torpedoes* (Barnsley: Pen & Sword Books, 2006), p. 17

32. Ibid, p. 17

33. David Jones and Peter Nunan, *US Subs Down Under: Brisbane, 1942–1945* (Annapolis: Naval Institute Press, 2005), p. 239

34. Max Shean, *Corvette and Submarine* (Privately published, 1992), p. 236

Chapter 5

1. George Fleming, *Magennis VC: The Story of Northern Ireland's only winner of the Victoria Cross* (Dublin: History Ireland Limited, 1998), p. 146

2. Ibid, p. 146

3. 'Fourteenth Submarine Flotilla – Second Monthly Letter – January 1945, 3 February 1945', Fell 03 008, Churchill Archives Centre, Churchill College, Cambridge

4. Speech by Adam Bergius, DSC, to West of Scotland Branch, The Submariner's Association, K13 Dinner, January 2013

5. Adam Bergius to the author, private letter, 14 April 2014

6. William Fell, *The Sea Our Shield: The Story of the Human Torpedo and the Midget Submarine in World War II* (London: Corgi, 1970), p. 209

7. Ibid, p. 210

8. Ibid, p. 211

9. Ibid, p. 211

10. Ian Fraser, *Frogman VC* (London: Odhams Beacon Books, 1958), p. 131

11. Speech by Adam Bergius, DSC, to West of Scotland Branch, The Submariner's Association, K13 Dinner, January 2013

12. William Fell, *The Sea Our Shield: The Story of the Human Torpedo and the Midget Submarine in World War II* (London: Corgi, 1970), pp. 211–12

13. 'Fourteenth Submarine Flotilla – Fourth Monthly General Letter – March 1945, 6 April 1945', Fell 03 008, Churchill Archives Centre, Churchill College, Cambridge

14. Ian Fraser, *Frogman VC* (London: Odhams Beacon Books, 1958), p. 131

15. C.E.T. Warren and James Benson, *Above Us The Waves: The Story of Midget Submarines & Human Torpedoes* (Barnsley: Pen & Sword Books, 2006), p. 215

16. 'Fourteenth Submarine Flotilla – Fourth Monthly General Letter – March 1945, 6 April 1945', Fell 03 008, Churchill Archives Centre, Churchill College, Cambridge

17. Ibid.

18. Ian Fraser, *Frogman VC* (London: Odhams Beacon Books, 1958), p. 132

19. 'Fourteenth Submarine Flotilla – Fourth Monthly General Letter – March 1945, 6 April 1945', Fell 03 008, Churchill Archives Centre, Churchill College, Cambridge

20. Ibid.

21. George Fleming, *Magennis VC: The Story of Northern Ireland's only winner of the Victoria Cross* (Dublin: History Ireland Limited, 1998), p. 146

22. William Fell, *The Sea Our Shield: The Story of the Human Torpedo and the Midget Submarine in World War II* (London: Corgi, 1970), p. 212

23. 'Fourteenth Submarine Flotilla – Fourth Monthly General Letter – March 1945, 6 April 1945', Fell 03 008, Churchill Archives Centre, Churchill College, Cambridge

24. Ian Fraser, *Frogman VC* (London: Odhams Beacon Books, 1958), p. 132

25. 'Fourteenth Submarine Flotilla – Fourth Monthly General

Letter – March 1945, 6 April 1945', Fell 03 008, Churchill Archives Centre, Churchill College, Cambridge

26. Ian Fraser, *Frogman VC* (London: Odhams Beacon Books, 1958), p. 132

27. Max Shean, *Corvette and Submarine* (Privately published, 1992), p. 237

28. William Fell, *The Sea Our Shield: The Story of the Human Torpedo and the Midget Submarine in World War II* (London: Corgi, 1970), p. 213

29. Max Shean, *Corvette and Submarine* (Privately published, 1992), p. 237

30. George Fleming, *Magennis VC: The Story of Northern Ireland's only winner of the Victoria Cross* (Dublin: History Ireland Limited, 1998), p. 146

31. Ibid, p. 146

32. David Jones and Peter Nunan, *US Subs Down Under: Brisbane, 1942–1945* (Annapolis: Naval Institute Press, 2005), p. 239

33. Speech by Adam Bergius, DSC, to West of Scotland Branch, The Submariner's Association, K13 Dinner, January 2013

34. David Jones and Peter Nunan, *US Subs Down Under: Brisbane, 1942–1945* (Annapolis: Naval Institute Press, 2005), p. 239

35. Speech by Adam Bergius, DSC, to West of Scotland Branch, The Submariner's Association, K13 Dinner, January 2013

36. Max Shean, *Corvette and Submarine* (Privately published, 1992), p. 237

37. Ibid, pp. 237–8

38. 'Fourteenth Submarine Flotilla – Fifth Monthly General Letter – April and May 1945, 18 June 1945', Fell 03 008, Churchill Archives Centre, Churchill College, Cambridge

39. Adam Bergius to the author, private letter, 14 April 2014

40. *Undersea Warfare Magazine*, Spring 2011, Issue No. 44

41. Ibid.

42. Ibid.

43. Max Shean, *Corvette and Submarine* (Privately published, 1992), p. 239

Chapter 6

1. William Fell, *The Sea Our Shield: The Story of the Human

Torpedo and the Midget Submarine in World War II (London: Corgi, 1970), p. 216

2. Ian McGeoch, *Mountbatten of Burma: Captain of War, Guardian of Peace* (London: J.H. Haynes & Co. Ltd, 2009), p. 122

3. George Fleming, *Magennis VC: The Story of Northern Ireland's only winner of the Victoria Cross* (Dublin: History Ireland Limited, 1998), p. 146

4. 'Fourteenth Submarine Flotilla – Fifth Monthly General Letter – April and May 1945, 18 June 1945', Fell 03 008, Churchill Archives Centre, Churchill College, Cambridge

5. Richard Hough, *Mountbatten: Hero of Our Time* (London: Book Club Associates, 1981), p. 197

6. William Fell, *The Sea Our Shield: The Story of the Human Torpedo and the Midget Submarine in World War II* (London: Corgi, 1970), p. 215

7. 'Office of Commander-in-Chief, British Pacific Fleet, Route Order, 14 May 1945', Fell 03 006, Churchill Archives Centre, Churchill College, Cambridge

8. William Fell, *The Sea Our Shield: The Story of the Human Torpedo and the Midget Submarine in World War II* (London: Corgi, 1970), p. 215

9. Ibid, p. 216

10. C.E.T. Warren and James Benson, *Above Us The Waves: The Story of Midget Submarines & Human Torpedoes* (Barnsley: Pen & Sword Books, 2006), p. 217

11. William Fell, *The Sea Our Shield: The Story of the Human Torpedo and the Midget Submarine in World War II* (London: Corgi, 1970), p. 216

12. Ibid, p. 217

13. Ibid, p. 217

14. Ibid, p. 217

15. Ibid, p. 218

16. David Jones and Peter Nunan, *US Subs Down Under: Brisbane, 1942–1945* (Annapolis: Naval Institute Press, 2005), p. 239

17. Ibid, p. 217

18. 'X Craft Operations in the Pacific Theatre, January 1945', Fell 03 006, Churchill Archives Centre, Churchill College, Cambridge

19. 'Fourteenth Submarine Flotilla – Fifth Monthly General Letter

– April and May 1945, 18 June 1945', Fell 03 008, Churchill Archives Centre, Churchill College, Cambridge

20. 'X Craft Operations in the Pacific Theatre, January 1945', Fell 03 006, Churchill Archives Centre, Churchill College, Cambridge

21. 'Fourteenth Submarine Flotilla – Fifth Monthly General Letter – April and May 1945, 18 June 1945', Fell 03 008, Churchill Archives Centre, Churchill College, Cambridge

22. David Jones and Peter Nunan, *US Subs Down Under: Brisbane, 1942–1945* (Annapolis: Naval Institute Press, 2005), p. 239

23. Audio Interview with Vernon Coles, undated, provided to the author by his daughter Jane Gilbert

24. Jon Lewis, *The Mammoth Book of SAS and Special Forces* (Robinson Publishing, 2004), Kindle edition

Chapter 7

1. Ian Fraser, *Frogman VC* (London: Odhams Beacon Books, 1958), p. 135

2. William Fell, *The Sea Our Shield: The Story of the Human Torpedo and the Midget Submarine in World War II* (London: Corgi, 1970), p. 219

3. Ibid, p. 219

4. Ibid, p. 219

5. Ibid, pp. 219–20

6. Ian Fraser, *Frogman VC* (London: Odhams Beacon Books, 1958), p. 133

7. George Fleming, *Magennis VC: The Story of Northern Ireland's only winner of the Victoria Cross* (Dublin: History Ireland Limited, 1998), p. 146

8. Speech by Adam Bergius, DSC, to West of Scotland Branch, The Submariner's Association, K13 Dinner, January 2013

9. George Fleming, *Magennis VC: The Story of Northern Ireland's only winner of the Victoria Cross* (Dublin: History Ireland Limited, 1998), p. 146

10. William Fell, *The Sea Our Shield: The Story of the Human Torpedo and the Midget Submarine in World War II* (London: Corgi, 1970), p. 220

11. Ibid, p. 221

12. Adam Bergius to the author, 2 June 2014

13. William Fell, *The Sea Our Shield: The Story of the Human Torpedo and the Midget Submarine in World War II* (London: Corgi, 1970), p. 221

14. Ibid, p. 221

15. David Jones and Peter Nunan, *US Subs Down Under: Brisbane, 1942–1945* (Annapolis: Naval Institute Press, 2005), p. 240

16. Ibid, p. 243

17. 'Fourteenth Submarine Flotilla – Fifth Monthly General Letter – April and May 1945, 18 June 1945', Fell 03 008, Churchill Archives Centre, Churchill College, Cambridge

18. 'Lt Cdr Max Shean DSO* RANR retd. Wednesday, 22nd March 1995. X-craft service in the British Royal Navy. A paper prepared by Lt Cdr Max Shean to accompany his talk at the International Submarine Convention, Fremantle'

19. Ibid.

20. Ibid.

21. Max Shean, *Corvette and Submarine* (Privately published, 1992), p. 139

22. 'Lt Cdr Max Shean DSO* RANR retd. Wednesday, 22nd March 1995. X-craft service in the British Royal Navy. A paper prepared by Lt Cdr Max Shean to accompany his talk at the International Submarine Convention, Fremantle'

23. 'Fourteenth Submarine Flotilla – Fifth Monthly General Letter – April and May 1945, 18 June 1945', Fell 03 008, Churchill Archives Centre, Churchill College, Cambridge

24. Max Shean, *Corvette and Submarine* (Privately published, 1992), p. 240

25. Ibid, p. 240

26. William Fell, *The Sea Our Shield: The Story of the Human Torpedo and the Midget Submarine in World War II* (London: Corgi, 1970), p. 220

27. 'Fourteenth Submarine Flotilla – Fifth Monthly General Letter – April and May 1945, 18 June 1945', Fell 03 008, Churchill Archives Centre, Churchill College, Cambridge

28. Richard Hough, *Mountbatten: Hero of Our Time* (London: Book Club Association, 1981), p. 197

29. Philip Ziegler, *Mountbatten: A Biography* (London: Alfred A. Knopf, 1985), p. 298

30. Ian Fraser, *Frogman VC* (London: Odhams Beacon Books, 1958), p. 134
31. George Fleming, *Magennis VC: The Story of Northern Ireland's only winner of the Victoria Cross* (Dublin: History Ireland Limited, 1998), p. 148
32. Ian Fraser, *Frogman VC* (London: Odhams Beacon Books, 1958), p. 135
33. Ibid, p. 136

Chapter 8

1. Ibid, p. 136
2. Ibid, p. 136
3. George Fleming, *Magennis VC: The Story of Northern Ireland's only winner of the Victoria Cross* (Dublin: History Ireland Limited, 1998), p. 148
4. Max Shean, *Corvette and Submarine* (Privately published, 1992), p. 240
5. George Fleming, *Magennis VC: The Story of Northern Ireland's only winner of the Victoria Cross* (Dublin: History Ireland Limited, 1998), p. 148
6. Ian Fraser, *Frogman VC* (London: Odhams Beacon Books, 1958), p. 137
7. 'Fourteenth Submarine Flotilla – Sixth Monthly General Letter – June 1945, 5 July 1945', Fell 03 006, Churchill Archives Centre, Churchill College, Cambridge
8. Ibid.
9. William Fell, *The Sea Our Shield: The Story of the Human Torpedo and the Midget Submarine in World War II* (London: Corgi, 1970), p. 223
10. 'Fourteenth Submarine Flotilla – Sixth Monthly General Letter – June 1945, 5 July 1945', Fell 03 006, Churchill Archives Centre, Churchill College, Cambridge
11. C.E.T. Warren and James Benson, *Above Us The Waves: The Story of Midget Submarines & Human Torpedoes* (Barnsley: Pen & Sword Books, 2006), p. 216
12. William Fell, *The Sea Our Shield: The Story of the Human Torpedo and the Midget Submarine in World War II* (London: Corgi, 1970), p. 224

13. Ibid, p. 224

14. Ibid, p. 224

15. Ian Fraser, *Frogman VC* (London: Odhams Beacon Books, 1958), p. 138

16. William Fell, *The Sea Our Shield: The Story of the Human Torpedo and the Midget Submarine in World War II* (London: Corgi, 1970), p. 226

17. 'Fourteenth Submarine Flotilla – Seventh Monthly General Letter – July 1945, 1 August 1945', Fell 03 006, Churchill Archives Centre, Churchill College, Cambridge

18. William Fell, *The Sea Our Shield: The Story of the Human Torpedo and the Midget Submarine in World War II* (London: Corgi, 1970), p. 226

19. Ian Fraser, *Frogman VC* (London: Odhams Beacon Books, 1958), p. 138

20. Ibid, pp. 141–2

21. 'Fourteenth Submarine Flotilla – Seventh Monthly General Letter – July 1945, 1 August 1945', Fell 03 006, Churchill Archives Centre, Churchill College, Cambridge

22. Ibid, p. 151

23. Interview with Ian Edward Fraser, 1987, 9822, Imperial War Museum, London

24. 'Staff Officer (Intelligence) to Chief of Intelligence Staff, British Pacific Fleet, 11 August 1945', Fell 03 008, Churchill Archives Centre, Churchill College, Cambridge

25. William Fell, *The Sea Our Shield: The Story of the Human Torpedo and the Midget Submarine in World War II* (London: Corgi, 1970), p. 227

Chapter 9

1. Ian Fraser, *Frogman VC* (London: Odhams Beacon Books, 1958), p. 156

2. Ibid, p. 156

3. 'Fourteenth Submarine Flotilla – Seventh Monthly General Letter – July 1945, 1 August 1945', Fell 03 006, Churchill Archives Centre, Churchill College, Cambridge

4. Ibid.

5. William Fell, *The Sea Our Shield: The Story of the Human

Torpedo and the Midget Submarine in World War II (London: Corgi, 1970), p. 227

6. Max Shean, *Corvette and Submarine* (Privately published, 1992), p. 241
7. 'Fourteenth Submarine Flotilla – Seventh Monthly General Letter – July 1945, 1 August 1945', Fell 03 006, Churchill Archives Centre, Churchill College, Cambridge
8. Ibid.
9. Max Shean, *Corvette and Submarine* (Privately published, 1992), p. 241
10. William Fell, *The Sea Our Shield: The Story of the Human Torpedo and the Midget Submarine in World War II* (London: Corgi, 1970), p. 228
11. Ibid, p. 229
12. 'Fourteenth Submarine Flotilla – Fifth Monthly General Letter –July 1945, 1 August 1945', Fell 03 008, Churchill Archives Centre, Churchill College, Cambridge
13. Max Shean, *Corvette and Submarine* (Privately published, 1992), p. 241
14. 'Fourteenth Submarine Flotilla – Fifth Monthly General Letter –July 1945, 1 August 1945', Fell 03 008, Churchill Archives Centre, Churchill College, Cambridge
15. Ibid.
16. Ibid.
17. Ibid.
18. Interview with Anthony William Clarke Eldridge, 1989, 11259, Reel 4, Imperial War Museum, London
19. Ibid.

Chapter 10

1. 'Attack on Japanese Cruiser Takao by XE3 and XE1', ADM1/21999, The National Archives (Public Record Office), Kew
2. Guy Clarabut obituary, *The Telegraph*, 21 May 2008
3. 'Fourteenth Submarine Flotilla – Fifth Monthly General Letter –August 1945, 18 September, 1945', Fell 03 008, Churchill Archives Centre, Churchill College, Cambridge
4. William Fell, *The Sea Our Shield: The Story of the Human*

Torpedo and the Midget Submarine in World War II (London: Corgi, 1970), p. 232

5. C.E.T. Warren and James Benson, *Above Us The Waves: The Story of Midget Submarines & Human Torpedoes* (Barnsley: Pen & Sword Books, 2006), p. 220

6. William Fell, *The Sea Our Shield: The Story of the Human Torpedo and the Midget Submarine in World War II* (London: Corgi, 1970), p. 232

7. C.E.T. Warren and James Benson, *Above Us The Waves: The Story of Midget Submarines & Human Torpedoes* (Barnsley: Pen & Sword Books, 2006), p. 220

8. Adam Bergius to the author, 2 June 2014

9. Leon V. Sigal, *Fighting to a Finish: the Politics of War Termination in the United States and Japan* (New York: Cornell University Press, 1988), p. 7

10. David Jones and Peter Nunan, *US Subs Down Under* (Annapolis: Naval Institute Press, 2005), p. 249

11. Ian Fraser, *Frogman VC* (London: Odhams Beacon Books, 1958), p. 140

12. C.E.T. Warren and James Benson, *Above Us The Waves: The Story of Midget Submarines & Human Torpedoes* (Barnsley: Pen & Sword Books, 2006), p. 122

13. Max Shean, *Corvette and Submarine* (Privately published, 1992), p. 242

14. Interview with Ian Edward Fraser, 1987, 9822, Imperial War Museum, London

15. Ralph Shaw, *Sin City* (London: Warner Books, 1997), p. 207

16. Stella Dong, *Shanghai: The Rise and Fall of a Decadent City* (New York: Perennial, 2001), pp. 272–3

17. Box 252, Exhibit 1462, Allied Translation and Interpreter Section South West Pacific Area, Document No. 552, Research Report No. 65 (Suppl. No. 1), 29 March 1945, MacMillan Brown Library, University of Canterbury, Christchurch, New Zealand.

18. Mark Felton, *Japan's Gestapo: Murder, Mayhem and Torture in Wartime Asia* (Barnsley: Pen & Sword Books, 2009), p. 30

Chapter 11

1. 'Lt Cdr Max Shean DSO* RANR retd. Wednesday, 22nd March

1995. X-craft service in the British Royal Navy. A paper prepared by Lt Cdr Max Shean to accompany his talk at the International Submarine Convention, Fremantle'

2. Ian Fraser, *Frogman VC* (London: Odhams Beacon Books, 1958), p. 143
3. Ibid, p. 145
4. Ibid, p. 145
5. Ibid, p. 147
6. C.E.T. Warren and James Benson, *Above Us The Waves: The Story of Midget Submarines & Human Torpedoes* (Barnsley: Pen & Sword Books, 2006), p. 229
7. Max Shean, *Corvette and Submarine* (Privately published, 1992), p. 243
8. Ian Fraser, *Frogman VC* (London: Odhams Beacon Books, 1958), p. 149
9. George Fleming, *Magennis VC: The Story of Northern Ireland's only winner of the Victoria Cross* (Dublin: History Ireland Limited, 1998), p. 151
10. Ian Fraser, *Frogman VC* (London: Odhams Beacon Books, 1958), p. 150
11. 'Staff Officer (Intelligence) to Captain S/M 14, 11 August 1945', FELL 03 008, Churchill Archives Centre, Churchill College, Cambridge
12. Ian Fraser, *Frogman VC* (London: Odhams Beacon Books, 1958), p. 152
13. 'Lt Cdr Max Shean DSO* RANR retd. Wednesday, 22nd March 1995. X-craft service in the British Royal Navy. A paper prepared by Lt Cdr Max Shean to accompany his talk at the International Submarine Convention, Fremantle'
14. Ian Fraser, *Frogman VC* (London: Odhams Beacon Books, 1958), p. 154
15. 'Staff Officer (Intelligence) to Captain S/M 14, 11 August 1945', FELL 03 008, Churchill Archives Centre, Churchill College, Cambridge
16. Ian Fraser, *Frogman VC* (London: Odhams Beacon Books, 1958), p. 155
17. 'Lt Cdr Max Shean DSO* RANR retd. Wednesday, 22nd March 1995. X-craft service in the British Royal Navy. A paper prepared

by Lt Cdr Max Shean to accompany his talk at the International Submarine Convention, Fremantle'

18. C.E.T. Warren and James Benson, *Above Us The Waves: The Story of Midget Submarines & Human Torpedoes* (Barnsley: Pen & Sword Books, 2006), p. 229

19. 'Lt Cdr Max Shean DSO* RANR retd. Wednesday, 22nd March 1995. X-craft service in the British Royal Navy. A paper prepared by Lt Cdr Max Shean to accompany his talk at the International Submarine Convention, Fremantle'

Chapter 12

1. 'Attack on Japanese Cruiser Takao by XE3 and XE1', ADM1/21999, The National Archives (Public Record Office), Kew

2. Ian Fraser, *Frogman VC* (London: Odhams Beacon Books, 1958), p. 159

3. William Fell, *The Sea Our Shield: The Story of the Human Torpedo and the Midget Submarine in World War II* (London: Corgi, 1970), p. 169

4. Ibid, p. 237

5. Ibid, p. 237

6. 'X Craft Operations in the Pacific Theatre by William Fell', FELL 03 006, Churchill Archives Centre, Churchill College, Cambridge

7. William Fell, *The Sea Our Shield: The Story of the Human Torpedo and the Midget Submarine in World War II* (London: Corgi, 1970), p. 237

8. Ian Fraser, *Frogman VC* (London: Odhams Beacon Books, 1958), p. 155

9. George Fleming, *Magennis VC: The Story of Northern Ireland's only winner of the Victoria Cross* (Dublin: History Ireland Limited, 1998), p. 151

10. Ian Fraser, *Frogman VC* (London: Odhams Beacon Books, 1958), p. 157

11. 'Staff Officer (Intelligence) to Captain S/M 14, 11 August 1945', FELL 03 008, Churchill Archives Centre, Churchill College, Cambridge

12. 'Attack on Japanese Cruiser Takao by XE3 and XE1', ADM1/21999, The National Archives (Public Record Office), Kew

13. David Jones and Peter Nunan, *US Subs Down Under* (Annapolis: Naval Institute Press, 2005), p. 244

14. 'Submarine Mine Defense of Hong Kong', Coast Defense Study Group Newsletter, February 2009

15. Ibid.

16. Ian Fraser, *Frogman VC* (London: Odhams Beacon Books, 1958), pp. 158–9

17. Max Shean, *Corvette and Submarine* (Privately published, 1992), p. 245

18. 'Lt Cdr Max Shean DSO* RANR retd. Wednesday, 22nd March 1995. X-craft service in the British Royal Navy. A paper prepared by Lt Cdr Max Shean to accompany his talk at the International Submarine Convention, Fremantle'

19. Interview with Ian Edward Fraser, 1987, 9822, Imperial War Museum, London

20. Ibid.

21. Ian Fraser, *Frogman VC* (London: Odhams Beacon Books, 1958), p. 161

22. Ibid, p. 162

23. 'Attack on Japanese Cruiser Takao by XE3 and XE1', ADM1/21999, The National Archives (Public Record Office), Kew

24. Interview with Ian Edward Fraser, 1987, 9822, Imperial War Museum, London

25. Ian Fraser, *Frogman VC* (London: Odhams Beacon Books, 1958), p. 163

Chapter 13

1. 'Attack on Japanese Cruiser Takao by XE3 and XE1', ADM1/21999, The National Archives (Public Record Office), Kew

2. Ian Fraser, *Frogman VC* (London: Odhams Beacon Books, 1958), p. 163

3. 'Lt Cdr Max Shean DSO* RANR retd. Wednesday, 22nd March 1995. X-craft service in the British Royal Navy. A paper prepared by Lt Cdr Max Shean to accompany his talk at the International Submarine Convention, Fremantle'

4. Max Shean, *Corvette and Submarine* (Privately published, 1992), p. 248

5. William Fell, *The Sea Our Shield: The Story of the Human Torpedo and the Midget Submarine in World War II* (London: Corgi, 1970), p. 236

6. 'Lt Cdr Max Shean DSO* RANR retd. Wednesday, 22nd March 1995. X-craft service in the British Royal Navy. A paper prepared by Lt Cdr Max Shean to accompany his talk at the International Submarine Convention, Fremantle'

7. 'Attack on Japanese Cruiser Takao by XE3 and XE1', ADM1/21999, The National Archives (Public Record Office), Kew

8. 'Lt Cdr Max Shean DSO* RANR retd. Wednesday, 22nd March 1995. X-craft service in the British Royal Navy. A paper prepared by Lt Cdr Max Shean to accompany his talk at the International Submarine Convention, Fremantle'

9. Max Shean, *Corvette and Submarine* (Privately published, 1992), p. 246

10. Ibid, p. 247

11. Ian Fraser, *Frogman VC* (London: Odhams Beacon Books, 1958), p. 165

12. Ibid, p. 165

13. C.E.T. Warren and James Benson, *Above Us The Waves: The Story of Midget Submarines & Human Torpedoes* (Barnsley: Pen & Sword Books, 2006), p. 247

14. Ian Fraser, *Frogman VC* (London: Odhams Beacon Books, 1958), p. 166

15. Ibid, p. 166

16. 'Fourteenth Submarine Flotilla, Eighth Monthly General Letter – August 1945, 18 September 1945', FELL 03 008, Churchill Archives Centre, Churchill College, Cambridge

17. Ian Fraser, *Frogman VC* (London: Odhams Beacon Books, 1958), p. 166

18. 'Staff Officer (Intelligence) to Captain S/M 14, 11 August 1945', FELL 03 008, Churchill Archives Centre, Churchill College, Cambridge

19. 'Fourteenth Submarine Flotilla, Eighth Monthly General Letter – August 1945, 18 September 1945', FELL 03 008, Churchill Archives Centre, Churchill College, Cambridge

20. 'Attack on Japanese Cruiser Takao by XE3 and XE1',

ADM1/21999, The National Archives (Public Record Office), Kew

21. Ibid.

22. 'Lt Cdr Max Shean DSO* RANR retd. Wednesday, 22nd March 1995. X-craft service in the British Royal Navy. A paper prepared by Lt Cdr Max Shean to accompany his talk at the International Submarine Convention, Fremantle'

23. C.E.T. Warren and James Benson, *Above Us The Waves: The Story of Midget Submarines & Human Torpedoes* (Barnsley: Pen & Sword Books, 2006), p. 230

24. Audio Interview with Vernon Coles, undated, provided to the author by his daughter Jane Gilbert

25. Max Shean, *Corvette and Submarine* (Privately published, 1992), pp. 124–5

26. Audio Interview with Vernon Coles, undated, provided to the author by his daughter Jane Gilbert

27. Ian Fraser, *Frogman VC* (London: Odhams Beacon Books, 1958), p. 167

28. Interview with Ian Fraser, Reel 2, 9822, Imperial War Museum, London

29. 'Attack on Japanese Cruiser Takao by XE3 and XE1', ADM1/21999, The National Archives (Public Record Office), Kew

30. Interview with Ian Fraser, Reel 2, 9822, Imperial War Museum, London

31. Ian Fraser, *Frogman VC* (London: Odhams Beacon Books, 1958), p. 168

32. Ibid, p. 168

Chapter 14

1. Adam Bergius to the author, 14 April 2014

2. Interview with Ian Fraser, Reel 2, 9822, Imperial War Museum, London

3. George Fleming, *Magennis VC: The Story of Northern Ireland's only winner of the Victoria Cross* (Dublin: History Ireland Limited, 1998), p. 153

4. Ian Fraser, *Frogman VC* (London: Odhams Beacon Books, 1958), p. 170

5. Max Shean, *Corvette and Submarine* (Privately published, 1992), p. 248

6. Audio Interview with Vernon Coles, undated, provided to the author by his daughter Jane Gilbert

7. 'Fourteenth Submarine Flotilla, Eighth Monthly General Letter – August 1945, 18 September 1945', FELL 03 008, Churchill Archives Centre, Churchill College, Cambridge

8. Audio Interview with Vernon Coles, undated, provided to the author by his daughter Jane Gilbert

9. Ibid.

10. C.E.T. Warren and James Benson, *Above Us The Waves: The Story of Midget Submarines & Human Torpedoes* (Barnsley: Pen & Sword Books, 2006), p. 231

11. 'Attack on Japanese Cruiser Takao by XE3 and XE1', ADM1/21999, The National Archives (Public Record Office), Kew

12. Ibid.

13. Ian Fraser, *Frogman VC* (London: Odhams Beacon Books, 1958), p. 171

14. Ibid, p. 171

15. 'Attack on Japanese Cruiser Takao by XE3 and XE1', ADM1/21999, The National Archives (Public Record Office), Kew

16. Ian Fraser, *Frogman VC* (London: Odhams Beacon Books, 1958), p. 175

17. Ibid, p. 175

18. Ibid, p. 176

19. George Fleming, *Magennis VC: The Story of Northern Ireland's only winner of the Victoria Cross* (Dublin: History Ireland Limited, 1998), p. 154

20. Interview with Ian Fraser, Reel 2, 9822, Imperial War Museum, London

21. 'Attack on Japanese Cruiser Takao by XE3 and XE1', ADM1/21999, The National Archives (Public Record Office), Kew

22. David Jones and Peter Nunan, *US Subs Down Under* (Annapolis: Naval Institute Press, 2005), p. 247

Chapter 15

1. Max Shean, *Corvette and Submarine* (Privately published, 1992), p. 248
2. Adam Bergius to the author, 2 June 2014
3. Ian Fraser, *Frogman VC* (London: Odhams Beacon Books, 1958), p. 178
4. 'Staff Officer (Intelligence) to Captain S/M 14, 11 August 1945', FELL 03 008, Churchill Archives Centre, Churchill College, Cambridge
5. Ibid.
6. Ibid.
7. Adam Bergius to the author, 2 June 2014
8. Patrick Bishop, *Target Tirpitz: X-Craft, Agents and Dambusters – The Epic Quest to Destroy Hitler's Mightiest Warship* (London: Harper Press, 2012), p. 228
9. Max Shean, *Corvette and Submarine* (Privately published, 1992), p. 248
10. Ibid, p. 248
11. Adam Bergius to the author, 2 June 2014
12. 'Staff Officer (Intelligence) to Captain S/M 14, 11 August 1945', FELL 03 008, Churchill Archives Centre, Churchill College, Cambridge
13. 'Attack on Japanese Cruiser Takao by XE3 and XE1', ADM1/21999, The National Archives (Public Record Office), Kew
14. 'Staff Officer (Intelligence) to Captain S/M 14, 11 August 1945', FELL 03 008, Churchill Archives Centre, Churchill College, Cambridge
15. Interview with Ian Fraser, Reel 2, 9822, Imperial War Museum, London
16. Ibid.
17. 'Attack on Japanese Cruiser Takao by XE3 and XE1', ADM1/21999, The National Archives (Public Record Office), Kew
18. Adam Bergius to the author, 2 June 2014
19. Audio Interview with Vernon Coles, undated, provided to the author by his daughter Jane Gilbert

20. 'Staff Officer (Intelligence) to Captain S/M 14, 11 August 1945', FELL 03 008, Churchill Archives Centre, Churchill College, Cambridge

21. Ian Fraser, *Frogman VC* (London: Odhams Beacon Books, 1958), p. 179

22. Interview with Ian Fraser, Reel 2, 9822, Imperial War Museum, London

23. Ibid.

24. 'Lt Cdr Max Shean DSO* RANR retd. Wednesday, 22nd March 1995. X-craft service in the British Royal Navy. A paper prepared by Lt Cdr Max Shean to accompany his talk at the International Submarine Convention, Fremantle'

25. Ian Fraser, *Frogman VC* (London: Odhams Beacon Books, 1958), p. 180

26. Ibid, p. 180

27. Max Shean, *Corvette and Submarine* (Privately published, 1992), p. 249

28. Ibid, p. 249

29. Audio Interview with Vernon Coles, undated, provided to the author by his daughter Jane Gilbert

30. 'Lt Cdr Max Shean DSO* RANR retd. Wednesday, 22nd March 1995. X-craft service in the British Royal Navy. A paper prepared by Lt Cdr Max Shean to accompany his talk at the International Submarine Convention, Fremantle'

Chapter 16

1. Ibid.

2. Ibid.

3. Ibid.

4. Max Shean, *Corvette and Submarine* (Privately published, 1992), p. 250

5. C.E.T. Warren and James Benson, *Above Us The Waves: The Story of Midget Submarines & Human Torpedoes* (Barnsley: Pen & Sword Books, 2006), p. 229

6. Ian Fraser, *Frogman VC* (London: Odhams Beacon Books, 1958), pp. 181–2

7. 'Attack on Japanese Cruiser Takao by XE3 and XE1', ADM1/21999, The National Archives (Public Record Office), Kew

8. Ian Fraser, *Frogman VC* (London: Odhams Beacon Books, 1958), p. 182

9. Ibid, p. 182

10. 'Attack on Japanese Cruiser Takao by XE3 and XE1', ADM1/21999, The National Archives (Public Record Office), Kew

11. 'Staff Officer (Intelligence) to Captain S/M 14, 11 August 1945', FELL 03 008, Churchill Archives Centre, Churchill College, Cambridge

12. 'Attack on Japanese Cruiser Takao by XE3 and XE1', ADM1/21999, The National Archives (Public Record Office), Kew

13. George Fleming, *Magennis VC: The Story of Northern Ireland's only winner of the Victoria Cross* (Dublin: History Ireland Limited, 1998), p. 156

14. 'Staff Officer (Intelligence) to Captain S/M 14, 11 August 1945', FELL 03 008, Churchill Archives Centre, Churchill College, Cambridge

15. Ian Fraser, *Frogman VC* (London: Odhams Beacon Books, 1958), p. 183

16. Ibid, p. 183

Chapter 17

1. 'Staff Officer (Intelligence) to Captain S/M 14, 11 August 1945', FELL 03 008, Churchill Archives Centre, Churchill College, Cambridge

2. 'British "X" Class Submarines in the Second World War', ADM1/21999, The National Archives (Public Record Office), Kew

3. 'Attack on Japanese Cruiser Takao by XE3 and XE1', ADM1/21999, The National Archives (Public Record Office), Kew

4. Ian Fraser, *Frogman VC* (London: Odhams Beacon Books, 1958), p. 185

5. Max Shean, *Corvette and Submarine* (Privately published, 1992), p. 250

6. Ibid, p. 250

7. Ian Fraser, *Frogman VC* (London: Odhams Beacon Books, 1958), p. 185

8. 'Attack on Japanese Cruiser Takao by XE3 and XE1', ADM1/21999, The National Archives (Public Record Office), Kew

9. Interview with Ian Fraser, Reel 2, 9822, Imperial War Museum, London

10. Mark Felton, *The Fujita Plan: Japanese Attacks on the United States and Australia during the Second World War* (Barnsley: Pen & Sword Books, 2007), pp. 124–5

11. 'Staff Officer (Intelligence) to Captain S/M 14, 11 August 1945', FELL 03 008, Churchill Archives Centre, Churchill College, Cambridge

12. Mark Felton, *The Fujita Plan: Japanese Attacks on the United States and Australia during the Second World War* (Barnsley: Pen & Sword Books, 2007), p. 125

13. Ian Fraser, *Frogman VC* (London: Odhams Beacon Books, 1958), p. 186

14. Ibid, p. 186

15. 'Attack on Japanese Cruiser Takao by XE3 and XE1', ADM1/21999, The National Archives (Public Record Office), Kew

16. Ibid.

17. Ian Fraser, *Frogman VC* (London: Odhams Beacon Books, 1958), p. 186

18. George Fleming, *Magennis VC: The Story of Northern Ireland's only winner of the Victoria Cross* (Dublin: History Ireland Limited, 1998), p. 158

19. 'Staff Officer (Intelligence) to Captain S/M 14, 11 August 1945', FELL 03 008, Churchill Archives Centre, Churchill College, Cambridge

20. Ibid.

21. 'Attack on Japanese Cruiser Takao by XE3 and XE1', ADM1/21999, The National Archives (Public Record Office), Kew

Chapter 18

1. 'British "X" Class Submarines in the Second World War', ADM1/21999, The National Archives (Public Record Office), Kew

2. 'Attack on Japanese Cruiser Takao by XE3 and XE1', ADM1/21999, The National Archives (Public Record Office), Kew

3. George Fleming, *Magennis VC: The Story of Northern Ireland's only winner of the Victoria Cross* (Dublin: History Ireland Limited, 1998), p. 158

4. Ian Fraser, *Frogman VC* (London: Odhams Beacon Books, 1958), p. 187

5. Ibid, p. 187

6. Interview with Ian Fraser, Reel 2, 9822, Imperial War Museum, London

7. 'Attack on Japanese Cruiser Takao by XE3 and XE1', ADM1/21999, The National Archives (Public Record Office), Kew

8. Ian Fraser, *Frogman VC* (London: Odhams Beacon Books, 1958), p. 188

9. Ibid, p. 188

10. Ibid, p. 188

11. Audio Interview with Vernon Coles, undated, provided to the author by his daughter Jane Gilbert

12. George Fleming, *Magennis VC: The Story of Northern Ireland's only winner of the Victoria Cross* (Dublin: History Ireland Limited, 1998), p. 159

13. Interview with Ian Fraser, Reel 2, 9822, Imperial War Museum, London

14. 'Staff Officer (Intelligence) to Captain S/M 14, 11 August 1945', FELL 03 008, Churchill Archives Centre, Churchill College, Cambridge

15. George Fleming, *Magennis VC: The Story of Northern Ireland's only winner of the Victoria Cross* (Dublin: History Ireland Limited, 1998), p. 159

16. 'Attack on Japanese Cruiser Takao by XE3 and XE1', ADM1/21999, The National Archives (Public Record Office), Kew

17. Interview with Ian Fraser, Reel 2, 9822, Imperial War Museum, London

18. George Fleming, *Magennis VC: The Story of Northern Ireland's only winner of the Victoria Cross* (Dublin: History Ireland Limited, 1998), p. 159

19. Ian Fraser, *Frogman VC* (London: Odhams Beacon Books, 1958), p. 189
20. George Fleming, *Magennis VC: The Story of Northern Ireland's only winner of the Victoria Cross* (Dublin: History Ireland Limited, 1998), p. 159

Chapter 19

1. Interview with Ian Fraser, Reel 2, 9822, Imperial War Museum, London
2. Ian Fraser, *Frogman VC* (London: Odhams Beacon Books, 1958), p. 189
3. George Fleming, *Magennis VC: The Story of Northern Ireland's only winner of the Victoria Cross* (Dublin: History Ireland Limited, 1998), p. 159
4. Ian Fraser, *Frogman VC* (London: Odhams Beacon Books, 1958), p. 189
5. 'Staff Officer (Intelligence) to Captain S/M 14, 11 August 1945', FELL 03 008, Churchill Archives Centre, Churchill College, Cambridge
6. 'Fourteenth Submarine Flotilla, Eighth Monthly General Letter – August 1945, 18 September 1945', FELL 03 008, Churchill Archives Centre, Churchill College, Cambridge
7. 'Staff Officer (Intelligence) to Captain S/M 14, 11 August 1945', FELL 03 008, Churchill Archives Centre, Churchill College, Cambridge
8. 'Attack on Japanese Cruiser Takao by XE3 and XE1', ADM1/21999, The National Archives (Public Record Office), Kew
9. Ian Fraser, *Frogman VC* (London: Odhams Beacon Books, 1958), p. 189
10. 'Attack on Japanese Cruiser Takao by XE3 and XE1', ADM1/21999, The National Archives (Public Record Office), Kew
11. Interview with Ian Fraser, Reel 2, 9822, Imperial War Museum, London
12. Ian Fraser, *Frogman VC* (London: Odhams Beacon Books, 1958), p. 190
13. Ibid, p. 191
14. George Fleming, *Magennis VC: The Story of Northern Ireland's*

only winner of the Victoria Cross (Dublin: History Ireland Limited, 1998), p. 160

15. Ian Fraser, *Frogman VC* (London: Odhams Beacon Books, 1958), p. 191

Chapter 20

1. Ibid, p. 193
2. Ibid, p. 193
3. Interview with Ian Fraser, Reel 2, 9822, Imperial War Museum, London
4. Ian Fraser, *Frogman VC* (London: Odhams Beacon Books, 1958), p. 194
5. Ibid, p. 194
6. Interview with Ian Fraser, Reel 2, 9822, Imperial War Museum, London
7. Ibid.
8. Ibid.
9. Max Shean, *Corvette and Submarine* (Privately published, 1992), p. 250
10. 'Fourteenth Submarine Flotilla – Fifth Monthly General Letter – August 1945, 18 September 1945', Fell 03 008, Churchill Archives Centre, Churchill College, Cambridge
11. Ian Fraser, *Frogman VC* (London: Odhams Beacon Books, 1958), p. 194
12. Interview with Ian Fraser, Reel 2, 9822, Imperial War Museum, London
13. 'Staff Officer (Intelligence) to Captain S/M 14, 11 August 1945', FELL 03 008, Churchill Archives Centre, Churchill College, Cambridge
14. William Fell, *The Sea Our Shield: The Story of the Human Torpedo and the Midget Submarine in World War II* (London: Corgi, 1970), p. 242
15. Ibid, p. 234
16. Interview with Ian Fraser, Reel 2, 9822, Imperial War Museum, London
17. 'Fourteenth Submarine Flotilla – Fifth Monthly General Letter – August 1945, 18 September 1945', Fell 03 008, Churchill Archives Centre, Churchill College, Cambridge

18. Interview with Ian Fraser, Reel 2, 9822, Imperial War Museum, London

19. 'British "X" Craft Submarines in the 2nd World War', ADM1/21999, The National Archives (Public Record Office), Kew

20. George Fleming, *Magennis VC: The Story of Northern Ireland's only winner of the Victoria Cross* (Dublin: History Ireland Limited, 1998), p. 160

Epilogue

1. 'Fourteenth Submarine Flotilla, Eighth Monthly General Letter – August 1945, 18 September 1945', FELL 03 008, Churchill Archives Centre, Churchill College, Cambridge

2. 'Staff Officer (Intelligence) to Captain S/M 14, 11 August 1945', FELL 03 008, Churchill Archives Centre, Churchill College, Cambridge

3. Audio Interview with Vernon Coles, undated, provided to the author by his daughter Jane Gilbert

4. William Fell, *The Sea Our Shield: The Story of the Human Torpedo and the Midget Submarine in World War II* (London: Corgi, 1970), p. 237

5. 'Fourteenth Submarine Flotilla, Eighth Monthly General Letter – August 1945, 18 September 1945', FELL 03 008, Churchill Archives Centre, Churchill College, Cambridge

6. Ibid.

7. 'Staff Officer (Intelligence) to Captain S/M 14, 11 August 1945', FELL 03 008, Churchill Archives Centre, Churchill College, Cambridge

8. 'Fourteenth Submarine Flotilla, Eighth Monthly General Letter – August 1945, 18 September 1945', FELL 03 008, Churchill Archives Centre, Churchill College, Cambridge

9. William Fell, *The Sea Our Shield: The Story of the Human Torpedo and the Midget Submarine in World War II* (London: Corgi, 1970), p. 246

10. Ian Fraser, *Frogman VC* (London: Odhams Beacon Books, 1958), p. 203

Index